New Directions in Budget Theory

SUNY Series in Public Administration
Peter Colby, Editor

NEW
DIRECTIONS
IN
BUDGET
THEORY

Irene S. Rubin, *Editor*

State University of New York Press

Published by
State University of New York Press, Albany

©1988 State University of New York

All rights reserved

Printed in the United States of America

For information, address State University of New York
Press, State University Plaza, Albany, N.Y., 12246

Library of Congress Cataloging in Publication Data

New directions in budget theory.

    (SUNY series in public administration)
    Includes index.
    1. Budget.   I. Rubin, Irene.   II. Series.
HJ2005.N48   1987   350.72′2   87-9977
ISBN 0-88706-624-0
ISBN 0-88706-625-9 (pbk.)

10 9 8 7 6 5 4 3

To Norm, my brother

Contents

Acknowledgments

I would like to thank Allen Schick, Lance LeLoup, and Herbert Rubin who read and critiqued earlier drafts of the chapters I wrote, and the anonymous readers for SUNY Press who read the entire manuscript and made helpful comments. Particular thanks are due to all the contributors for their creativity, their time, and their interest. I would work with any of them again, at any time, and I hope they would think the same of me.

Introduction

IRENE S. RUBIN

Budgets and Budget Theory

Politicians look to budgeting as a source of political power and control over policy. Budgets allocate resources to particular people, companies, places, and interest groups, so that if politicians can influence the budget allocations, they can enhance their political support. Politicians also frequently attempt to influence broader budget policies, such as how low the unemployment rate should be or how much spending there should be for police relative to social services.

The public looks to budgeting because it wants to know where its money is going. Citizens also are concerned about who pays taxes and how much they pay. They sometimes get sufficiently excited about taxation to pass referenda to limit taxes or spending.

Bureaucrats are interested in budgeting because they have major responsibilities in preparing budgets and administering them. They estimate revenues and draw up proposals for spending. Bureaucrats often play a role in evaluating budget proposals. When they do, one of their concerns is the adequacy of funds to achieve stated goals.

Budgeting, thus, is a complex field of study. Budgeting involves interaction over time between political and technical concerns, between politicians and bureaucrats. It takes place within popular and resource constraints, which have to be estimated. It involves a tension between spending for constituents and overall expenditure control that can take a variety of institutional forms.

The aim of the scholar is to describe this complexity in a way that is realistic yet comprehensible and comprehensive. Unfortunately, scholars have tended to approach the study of budgeting in a somewhat piecemeal manner. The reasons for this are varied. One reason is that budgets can be studied appropriately by a variety of disciplines, including public administration, political science, accounting, and economics. Scholars from each discipline tend to approach the subject solely from their own academic perspectives, which creates considerable fragmentation. A second reason is that the size of the budget and the concern of the public creates considerable demand for policy related studies. Some scholars go after the policy problems as they arise, without a coherent long-term agenda and with no way of putting together the results of different studies. Third, budgets themselves are fragmented; different parts of the budget seem to have very different characteristics. A theory that describes one part of the budget often fails to describe other parts.

More progress would be made in understanding and explaining budgeting if the field had better theories. Theories define key problems, specify the assumptions that guide research, and provide a framework for accumulating knowledge. Perhaps most important, theories are the source of hypotheses to be tested. These hypotheses help keep the research effort organized, so that knowledge can accumulate in meaningful ways.

The need for new and improved budget theory has been highlighted by the demise of an old, widely used theory, incrementalism. It is time to examine the usefulness, coverage and meaning of budgetary concepts; it is time to look at assumptions and see how different results are likely to be found as researchers shift from one set of assumptions to another. It is time to generate newer research hypotheses and explore a variety of methodological tools. The first steps toward a new theory may create only fragments of a theory in the short run, but they should make research more vibrant, fresher, and more powerfully descriptive.

This book explores the current state of budget theory, with its variety of new assumptions, hypotheses, and research approaches. The authors hope to stimulate more thought on budget theory and generate fresh ideas for research to replace the older paradigm of incrementalism. More ambitiously, the goal of the book is to begin to lay the groundwork for future theory and research in budgeting, to show a unity of themes, areas of agreement and disagreement, and test the appropriateness of some of the new assumptions.

The Demise of Incrementalism

The need for a new budget theory became urgent with the demise of incrementalism. Incrementalism as a budget theory was simultaneously too global, too narrow, and too difficult to prove or disprove.

Incrementalism was too global because it was derived from perceived characteristics of human nature. For example, the theory argued that people are of limited intelligence and have only limited time to devote to budgetary matters. Because of these limitations, those who review budget proposals are unable to deal with comparisons among all expenditures in a budget, so they developed simplifying rules, the major one being that they examine only the differences between last year's budget and this year's proposals. Last year's budget constitutes the base, and the difference between last year's budget and this year's is the increment. As a consequence, agency heads develop budget strategies that will expand the base by almost any means, on the assumption the base will probably never be examined again.

Stated with this degree of baldness, the proposition appears overstated and seems to constrain rather than stimulate research questions. In retrospect, one would want to know, how limited is human (and hence legislative) intelligence? If each individual's attention is limited, does it make any difference how many individuals review the budget? Or how they divide up the work? Or how many years experience they have? Surely individual limitations can be mitigated. One can agree with the self-evident notion that people have limited intelligence and time and that complex budgets often are approached by using simplifying rules without concluding that budget reviewers look only at increments. When and how decision makers simplify a complex reality and with what effect, are questions that should have been asked, by incrementalists. But this theory tended to focus more on the routines and commonalities of budgeting than on the variations and conditional truths.

Incrementalists argued that not only do people in general and politicians in particular have limited intelligence and short attention spans, they also dislike and avoid conflict in a political arena. To avoid conflict, politicians avoid making choices between programs. Since politicians do not take from one program to give to another, the amount of change possible in any given year is very limited. Human nature does not change, so budget processes generated by human nature do not change, and hence budget outcomes are likely to be fairly predictable, and changes are likely to be small. Again, superficially, it is easy to agree with the argument that politicians who have to work with each other over years are likely to try to avoid polarizing conflicts, but the argument is not specific enough to describe a complex reality.

Empirical findings have not been consistent with incremental theory.[1] Studies have shown the budget base is not stable (different budget actors define the base differently and change their definitions from year to year); legislators look at things other than the increment; they sometimes compare different forms of expenditures and choose more of one and less of another; agencies' budget shares change over time; and somehow conflict is expressed and handled in a political, budgetary arena, at least at times. Incrementalism has not done a very good job of explaining these findings because its initial assumptions about human nature or political nature were overstated and their implications overly deterministic.

Since incrementalism did not work very well as a descriptive model, the response was to stretch the theory to cover the new empirical findings. Incremental increases could be nearly any size, and over time budget shares could change by adding up what were essentially incremental changes from year to year. The clarity of the incremental hypotheses, which had been a major part of their attraction, disappeared, because it was no longer clear whether the theory was predicting change or stability, nor was it clear what was or was not an incremental change.

The theory was too elastic in another sense as well. Like much of public administration theory, it had a normative component. Incrementalism was better than the alternatives and should be maintained in the face of reforms.[2] As a statement of what should be rather than what was, incrementalism could not be confirmed or disconfirmed.

At the same time that parts of the theory were too broad, other aspects made it too narrow. It focused only on the part of the budget process repeated annually and on the agency's request, executive review, and congressional approval. It ignored the role of authorizations, revenue, and entitlements; it ignored the differences between budgeting at different levels of hierarchy, and the effects of environment on budgetary processes.

Incrementalism has not paid much attention to the role of the department heads nor later (after the 1974 congressional budget reform act) did it give much weight to the budgeting committees in Congress. The theory has not focused attention on continuing resolutions, supplemental appropriations, or other forms of omnibus legislation. Each of the ignored parts of the process functions in an integrative fashion. As there was no role for this function of budgeting in the theory, these centripetal processes got short shrift. As a result of this selective focus, much of budgeting was left out of incrementalist theory.

Through the 1970s evidence accumulated that various parts of the theoretical edifice of incrementalism had little or no foundation. Even its own proponents began to go off in other theoretical directions, recognizing that change was not simply a random shock in an otherwise deterministic system.[3] By 1984, when Wildavsky's famous incrementalist study, *Politics of the Budgetary Process*, was reissued, there was a long disclaimer in his prologue:

> The applicability of the basic concepts in the Politics of the Budgetary Process depends on the extent to which its basic presuppositions—the norms of balance, comprehensiveness and annualarity—hold true. If the budgetary process of the mid 1960's and the 1970's continues into the future, with denigration of predictability, limits and collective concern, the book will become, at best a faithful record of a time long since gone. (p.xxx)

Wildavsky argued that incrementalism could only be reinstated through reforms that restore the norms. He remained hopeful that the past would return but made no claim to the present descriptiveness of his landmark work on incrementalism.

The hammer blows of fine critical studies and the grudging yielding of Wildavsky himself have done much to make students of budgeting discontent with the state of budget theory. But, creating a new budget theory to take its place has been a difficult task. Some scholars along the way have become discouraged and wondered whether the task was possible.

The Possibility of Budget Theory

One major problem in developing a budget theory is that budgeting has a tendency to get coopted by other intellectual fields, to be defined as a subset or example of the larger process or area of study. Thus, budgeting has been declared at times to be the same as the study of politics or to be a subset of the study of legislative behavior. Or, it may be claimed at times as illustrative of the decision-making portion of organization theory or management. A second and possibly related problem is that other disciplines approach budgeting with their own theoretical apparatus and methodology, creating multidisciplinary rather than interdisciplinary studies. When this happens it is not clear what is supposed to be the theoretical core of budgeting, apart from the theory of economics or political science or sociology or accounting. Both of these issues can be addressed and do not present insuperable obstacles to creating a budget theory.

Budgeting is a distinct area, easily recognizable from legislative or executive behavior or politics in general. First of all, it is a *process* not an institution, and it cuts across institutions. There is going to be a budget document somewhere in the process, and this document will contain a projection of revenues and expenditures and attempt to match them for some future time period. The process of drawing up the plan and implementing it constitutes budgeting, and it does not look like any other process. A budget hearing is usually labeled as such, and a budget office is usually called a budget office, though it may do more than budgeting. The observable pattern stands out from the background. Studying executive behavior may indicate something about budgeting, as may legislative behavior, but added up the two do not equal the budget process.

While it is fairly clear that executive behavior is not the same as budgeting and does not explain it fully, it is less obvious that budgeting is not so generally overlapped by politics that to study politics is to study budgeting as well. Such a broad equation of budgeting with politics makes theory very difficult, especially since *politics* is such a general term. Fortunately, the formulation is slightly off, and the reality is easier to work with.

To begin with, budgeting is not exclusively political, no matter how politics is defined. Budgeting is both political and technical, which is part of what makes it so interesting. How do the two parts merge? How much of the technical can be politicized without loss of function? For example, how much can revenue projections be distorted before users respond by generating newer and more impartial sources of information or various discount factors? Also, how much of the political can be treated technically without loss of political accountability and policy direction? How does the political or technical become more dominant at one stage or another of the process?

Second, one can learn about politics in general by studying politics in specific in the budgetary process, but one cannot learn about budgeting in specific by studying politics in general. Budgeting generates and reflects different aspects of politics at different stages of the process. The specifics of budget politics translate into different sets of actors at different stages of budgeting. Interest groups may be intensely involved at one stage and have little to do with another stage. Many small specialized interest groups or even individual companies may fight over tax advantages, while a few interest groups representing large classes of society (such as labor or business) may fight about the appropriateness of running a deficit during a recession. One may get a very different view of politics depending on which budgeting issue one examines. When congressional representatives are acting on appropriations they may be most concerned with constituency benefits and norms of logrolling, but when they deal with issues of the total scope of the budget and the appropriateness of cutting expenditures or raising revenues to balance the budget, they may be motivated more by ideology and line up more along party lines. Different concepts of representation may be evoked at different stages of budget consideration.

The politics of changing a budget process is likely to be largely internal to government, with most citizens and interest groups uninvolved. Academic specialists, think tanks, or past officials may provide advice; politicians interested in process or good government may be involved. This is a side of politicians and politics that has not been widely publicized. Other political actors may get involved because they think a particular structure will facilitate certain desired outcomes or strengthen their own activities. This kind of internal jockeying is another aspect of politics.

In short, there is not one kind of politics, there are many. By studying them through the budgetary process, one can put them in proximity with each other and watch their interaction in a way that may not be obvious from other vantage points. One can avoid the one-sided views that result from observing only distributive politics or only the politics of process. It is much easier to study politics from the vantage point of the budget than to study budgeting from the vantage point of politics.

The problem of multidisciplinary, rather than interdisciplinary, approaches to budgeting is less easy to handle, since the problem results to some extent from the structure of universities, especially the discipline basis of graduate training and the reward system that recognizes work done only in one's own discipline. Those trained in only one academic discipline are likely to approach budgeting from the premise and within the theory of their own discipline. Accountants approach budgeting from the perspective of how well budgets represent assets and liabilities; economists want to know how public sector allocations resemble or differ from market allocations, and they wonder about the equity of budgetary outcomes and the neutrality of taxation. Political scientists want to know who gets what and why. Public administrators want to know whether all the appropriate alternatives were considered in making the decision. None of this adds up to meaningful budgetary research agendas. Multidisciplinary work has no cumulative focus.

One must be familiar with a variety of disciplines to study budget processes. The economists typically do the revenue projections and models of the economy; the public administrators draw up budget estimates; politics comes in when policy is inserted into the budget; and the accountants come in to record expenditures and evaluate the financial outcomes. To practice good budget theory and research, one must be familiar with these stages of the budget and these disciplines, but it is important not to import the assumptions of these fields and their theories along with the insights from their work.

So, from where do we get our questions, if not from the economists or accountants, each doing their own work? Budget questions really tend to be interdisciplinary. For example, how is the size of a deficit perceived to affect the economy, and how does that perception influence the budgetary process and outcomes? How does the projection of the economy interacting with political policy influence the distribution of expenditures? How do political and technical concerns combine at different stages of budgetary process? One can generate a very long list. These questions might be of interest to different disciplines, but they belong to budgeting.

Some of the questions might be best approached with economic tools, or with political science tools, or accounting tools, or a combination of several tools. Budgeting is not a discipline and does not have its own tools. It is a process, and like almost any process, one can generate a theory to describe it. One can use economics or political science or accounting without losing the uniqueness of budgeting, as long as one focuses on process, broadly defined, and leaves behind the theory that comes with the disciplines.

Where Have We Been? Where Are We Going?

If we look at current budget theory in the context of its own history, we can determine some trends that may be suggestive of where budget theory and budget research are likely to go over the next few years.

A continuing theme in budget theory has been the importance of process. In describing process, there has been evolution from a description of fixed roles and uniform processes to exploring varieties of budgetary processes across both space and time. Second, the scope of what is examined as the budget process has been increasing in several ways, to include different resources and actors, and more distinct stages of budgeting.[4]

Although concern for process has been part of budget theory for many years, public administration and political science have viewed budget processes somewhat differently. Public administration has approached the issue of budgeting without much theory but with the assumption that process is important and affects outcomes. Budgeting is defined as a technical skill, but outcomes can be influenced by political choices or political interference, which are likely to run up costs and may cause a violation of the technical requirement of a balance between revenue and expenditure. The purpose of budget process is to structure decisions so that technical skills predominate and the requirements of balance and control are met.[5]

Traditional public administration has always included a component of historical analysis, tracing institutional and legislative changes. For example, the history of the Office of Management and Budget or the history of the 1921 Budget and Accounting Act have held a prominent place in budgeting literature.[6] This historical literature assumes that budget processes change and that the roles of actors change. A normative element still exists in some of this literature, that that change is toward a reformist goal or away from it; neutral competence is good, excessive political influence over the budget (or over the budget office) is bad and may lead to technically bad outcomes.[7]

Political scientists approached the topic of budgeting from a rather different angle. They were interested particularly in who got what from the budget, its distributional aspects. To address their real interests, political scientists had to ask not only who benefited, but why some people or interest groups got a smaller or larger share. That question focused attention on budget processes, especially on the distribution of power over budget outcomes. This theme fits in with research on the sources and nature of agency power, the roles and access of interest groups, and the nature of representation in legislative bodies.[8]

More recently, interest has shifted to exploring the environmental factors contributing to changes in budget processes and examining the effects of changing processes on outcomes. Major themes in this literature include the effects on budget processes of the nature of the economy, and the effects of the expenditures and debt created by wars and depressions.[9]

The change of budget processes in Congress in 1974 stimulated an examination of the relationship between budget processes and budget outcomes, especially in terms of the size of total expenditures and the level of debt. This issue continues to generate research but as yet has not generated definitive answers.[10] Research will have to expand to include more of the historical and cross-sectional variation among states and local governments, and possibly across nations, to get better answers to the question of the impact of budget processes on budget outcomes.

The spectacle of the changing budget process at the national level has absorbed many budget theorists and researchers. The story is still unfolding, so methodology has shifted more from documentary analysis to interviews. The urgency of trying to explain the budget process under the Gramm Rudman Hollings Deficit Reduction Law (December 1985) has kept the issue of changing budget processes at the forefront and put pressure on budget theorists to come up with the concepts and analyses that will make current developments intelligible. There is additional pressure on budget specialists to give advice on what should be done.

For example, one question being asked is who should have the power to discipline legislators' desires to serve constituents. Does it make any difference if those desires are bridled through internal legislative controls, constitutional limits, or enhanced executive powers? From the perspective of political science, the alternatives are radically different. The distribution of power is markedly different between branches of government given one solution or another. Changes of such magnitude ought not be made without a good feeling for the consequences.

One way to get such a sense of possible consequences is to look at the experience of the states. We have long looked to the states for ideas on how to deal with federal government problems, but what I am suggesting goes beyond picking a state with a model program and implementing it at the federal level. In-depth exploration of what happened in a range of states, the ones that adopted changes and the ones that did not, is likely to yield useful information about the relation of process to outcomes. This kind of study has been done in a piecemeal fashion but needs more systematic work, with more explicit focus.[11]

Such analysis might produce some useful hesitation about implementing some particular changes at the federal level. If we look at the historical conditions that gave rise to the generally strong budget powers of the governors, it is clear that strong budget powers were often given to the governors in the context of highly fragmented executive structures and weak legislatures. Adding very strong budget powers to the President of the United States in a much more integrated executive branch with a more active and competent legislature may yield very different results.

While it seems likely that budgetary processes and their changes will retain their central role in budget theory over the next few years, the scope of those processes are likely to change. The initial conception of budget processes included advice from a budget office to agencies about how to draw up the budget, agency budget submission, some kind of executive review, and then legislative examination and approval. Our experience in watching budgetary processes indicates that this conception has been too narrow.

First, our image of who plays a role in budgeting has expanded. We now more explicitly include interest groups, cabinet level officials (both in their roles as department heads and as a collective policy and appeal body), the chief executive's staff, and legislative committees other than appropriations committees. In the future, more attention needs to focus on the members of each house, or the council acting as a body, and their actions to amend or approve expenditures, raise debt ceilings, or group money legislation in various ways. More attention needs to be paid to conference committees, especially when they write new legislation (which may be more common at the state level), and to the strategies of writing legislation so that certain parts will be open to compromise at conferences. More attention needs to be paid to the role of oversight and evaluation in major funding decisions. At the federal level, the role of the General Accounting Office in budgets—not just in audits—needs to be explored.

Some of these issues have been ignored because they have been considered legislative behavior rather than budget behavior. But the budget process should determine what we study; those involved routinely may do something else and only poke their noses into the budget; however, when they do so, they become budget actors.

Second, the concept of the budget process is likely to expand by including earlier and later steps in the decision making. The implications of revenue for budgeting, for example, are likely to be more systematically included in budget processes, so that revenue decisions, revenue constraints, and revenue estimations formally are included in the process. The politics of revenue estimation especially invites further research. More attention is currently being paid to budget implementation,[12] but this stage of the budget process has not yet been formally integrated into the concept of budget process. It is not yet clear that what happens during implementation is part of what goes before, not just the result of an accident, an error, or an uncontrollable change in the economy.

Third, the scope of budget process will have to expand to include different forms of expenditure including trust funds, loans, personnel allocations, regulations, in-kind transfers, and tax expenditures. Differences among program funds and operating lines (salaries and expenditures) need to be sorted out because they are treated differently by budget actors. Capital expenditures need to be looked at separately, especially at the state and local level, where the concept is more meaningful. Capital expenditures vary from year to year, in content and amount, making them by definition nonincremental, and they tend to attract the most direct political pressure at the local level, where the rest of the budget may seem apolitical. Similarly, earmarked funds, such as intergovernmental revenues, may be subject to very different budgeting processes. It is important to realize that there may be more than one budget process going on, with different characteristics in each one.

As budget theory becomes both more extensive in what it includes and more precise about what it is studying, it is likely to become fragmented. We might develop separate theories for the allocation of personnel and money; or different theories of capital and operating budgets. Such fragmentation may seem annoying initially, but ideally we are moving toward a differentiated theory that tries to specify the circumstances under which its generalizations hold.

The Chapters in This Book

The first two chapters in this book are by Lance Leloup and Naomi Caiden. They describe what we have learned from observing the budget process in recent years. These chapters focus on change, developing concepts that describe variations in budgetary processes over time. They define the meaningful range of change in budget processes.

Lance LeLoup's chapter, "From Microbudgeting to Macro-budgeting," describes and evaluates the growth of top-down (as opposed to bottom-up) budgeting in the Congress and the executive branch and argues that budget theory has kept up with these changes.

Naomi Caiden's essay, "Shaping Things to Come" briefly surveys major historical changes in budgeting and describes the expansion of budget functions of the 1970s as having produced a new type of budgeting—super-budgets. Super-budgets are affected by multiple interacting systems, such as the intergovernmental system, the economic system, and the political-bureaucratic system. These interacting systems create rigidity, instability, and complexity. Super-budgeters have to manage these other systems as well as traditional budget concerns.

The third chapter, "An Inquiry into the Possibility of a Budgetary Theory" by Allen Schick, begins by distinguishing budget processes from the rest of the political process, and then offers a link between changes in budgetary process and budget outcomes. The important dimension of change for Schick is whether budget processes strengthen those who put claims on the budget for resources or whether they strengthen those who try to conserve resources. He makes no assumptions about who is filling the role of claimant or conserver.

Peter Benda and Charles Levine's chapter approaches the issue of changing process over time by dealing more directly with who plays what budgetary role. They attack the problem from an institutional and historical perspective, arguing that functions may be added to an office over time but may not ever become institutionalized. For a budgeting office, like the OMB, a function that is regular and recurs every year will squeeze out occasional or nonregular processes, like management improvement, even though the two functions may be connected logically. This essay suggests that the budgetary roles of institutional actors may evolve in fairly constrained ways and that the similarity of the work cycle may be more important than the relatedness of the substance of the work.

While the first four chapters deal with change and how to describe it, the next four deal primarily with the appropriate scope of budget theory. Straussman's chapter deals with the differences between regular appropriations and entitlements, arguing that the scope of budgeting must include entitlement spending. Rubin's chapter argues that room in theory should be found for occasional actors, because they may play very important budget roles at certain intervals. Horton and Brecher argue that interest groups need to be reincorporated more formally into budgeting and that, even if we cannot always see them directly, we can infer their existence and successes. Joe White's chapter looks at scope a little differently; he argues that the scope of budgeting functions is too broad. Presumably, he would narrow somewhat the scope of budget theory along with the scope of budget functions.

Jeffrey Straussman's piece describes the concept of rights-based budgeting, which means that some program expenditures are made because there is a societal belief that people are entitled to that level of service by some moral or legal right. For example, people may have a right to a minimal level of income so that they do not starve. Straussman argues that rights-based budgeting is incompatible with traditional budget theory. A new theory needs to be devised that will include these "uncontrollable" portions of the budget; Straussman shows some of the ways this might be done.

Irene Rubin's chapter describes some occasional actors in the budget process, the authorizing committees, and tries to explain why such committees occasionally get involved in the budget and with what effect. Integrating authorizing committees into the budget process provides at least one mechanism for linking interest groups directly into the budget process and also provides a locus for the resolution of conflicts of interests over budgetary matters. Occasional actors may improve dramatically the quality of decision making, spending years in review of programs and then feeding the results into the budget process. The occasional role of authorizing committees in the budget process links oversight and budget changes.

Charles Brecher and Ray Horton link the community power debate to budget analysis, arguing that, for New York City, budgets are reflections of policy choices, that there have been shifts in shares of the budget, and that these shifts reflected the changing power distribution in the community. They argue that budgets ought to be used more as a tool to analyze shifts in community power.

Joe White's chapter "What Budgeting Cannot Do," argues that the budget processes at the national level have been asked to do too much. Budgets can perform successfully only a limited range of functions. Some functions that the budget is asked to perform are contradictory. It is also possible to put too many functions on the budget process, even if they are not contradictory. Furthermore, some particular functions may be impossible for the budget process to handle. White worries about the possibility of overload and collapse of the budget process. He addresses many of the same kinds of change that Naomi Caiden addresses but comes up with different concepts and conclusions.

Looked at together, the chapters demonstrate some common themes. The authors assume that process affects outcomes, that environment affects process, and that budgets reflect policy. The chapters also assume that change occurs both in budgeting processes and outcomes and that these changes need to be explained. The new direction in budget theory, thus, is a reemphasis on change rather than on constancy or regularity.

No single methodological paradigm is suggested in these chapters, but there is a common emphasis on process, on capturing the richness and variety of streams of events that may stretch over years, and on devising the conceptual tools that make this flow intellectually manageable and comprehensible. The pieces take a historical perspective to capture the variation in process and outcomes over time. This emphasis on richness of data emphasized case studies, institutional analysis over time, and time series analysis for quantitative data.

Common themes and approaches do not constitute a theory, however. We still have a long way to go before we achieve the unity and appeal of a single explanatory theory, but getting there is going to be an absorbing, stimulating, and enjoyable task. The essays in this collection provide a start in that direction.

Conclusions

Budget theory is possible, and we have made considerable progress toward a new theory in the past eight years. Our definition of appropriate research problems has become sharper and our list of new assumptions more explicit. Our conceptual armory has improved, and our ability to describe budgetary processes and their changes has improved commensurately. But, we still tend to be guided and stimulated more by immediate policy problems than theory. Fortunately, those policy problems have led to and will continue to lead to fruitful research, but the need for a widely agreed on theoretical framework is clear, if we are to organize our research efforts so that the results cumulate.

In building our theory, we need to avoid importing the theories of the disciplines that contribute to budgeting and focus on budgetary processes as the core issue. We may have to build such a theory in stages, examining first the major sources of variation, such as variation over time, between levels of government or levels of hierarchy, between capital and operating budgets, between own source and intergovernmental revenues, and between general fund and other funds. After studying their characteristics, we can gradually draw them together in one theory. We have learned the hard way that beginning with broad generalities about human nature and then working down to inferences about budget behavior is not a useful strategy.

Notes

1. Some studies that do not support the incrementalist theory are cited in LeLoup's essay, "The Myth of Incrementalism: Analytic Choices in Budgetary Theory" *Polity* 10 No. 4, (Summer 1978): 488–509. He includes John Bailey and Robert O'Connor, "Operationalizing Incrementalism: Measuring the Muddles" *PAR* 35 (January/February 1975): 60–66; William Moreland, "A Non-Incremental Perspective on Budgetary Political Actions" in *Policy Making in the Federal Executive Branch*, eds. R. Ripley and G. Franklin (New York: Free Press, 1975); Lance LeLoup, "Agency Policy Actions: Determinants of Non-Incremental Change" ibid.; John Wanat, "The Bases of Budgetary Incrementalism" *American Political Science Review* 68 (September 1974) 1121–28; Lance LeLoup and William Moreland, "Agency Strategies and Executive Review: The Hidden Politics of Budgeting" *PAR* 38 (May/June 1978) 232–39; John Gist, "Increment and Base in the Congressional Appropriations Process" *American Journal of*

Political Science 21 (May 1977) 341–52; P. B. Natchez and I. C. Bupp, "Policy and Priority in the Budgetary Process" *American Political Science Review* 67 (September 1973) 951–63; Arnold Kanter, "Congress and the Defense Budget, 1960–1970" *American Political Science Review* 66 (March 1972) 129–43.

2. Arnold Meltsner and Aaron Wildavsky, for example, argue that Planning Program Budgeting systems for cities are both too expensive to implement (regardless of the potential savings) and make expenditures too visible, enhancing the level of community conflict. See "Leave City Budgeting Alone! A Survey Case Study and Recommendations for Reform" in *Financing the Metropolis: Public Policy in Urban Economies*, ed. John P. Crecine Urban Affairs Annual Reviews, 4, (Beverly Hills: Sage, 1970). Meltsner and Wildavsky argue for continued line item budgeting, with selected performance measures where appropriate to enhance the control function.

3. Michael Davis, Michael Dempster, and Aaron Wildavsky, "A Theory of the Budgetary Process" *American Political Science Review* 60 (September 1966).

4. LeLoup summarizes the major themes of these changes in his 1978 essay, "The Myth of Incrementalism."

5. The executive budget reforms and the city manager reforms generally were bred as an antidote to political machines, excessive expenditures on capital projects, and lack of financial control. They were seen as an antidote to legislative branch pork-barrel projects. The emphasis on keeping political interest groups out of the budget process was particularly evident in the literature on the city manager reform. These reforms and these values continued in the public administration literature for many years.

6. A good recent example of this tradition in public administration is Frederick Mosher's *A Tale of Two Agencies: A Comparative Analysis of the General Accounting Office and the Office of Management and Budget* (Baton Rouge: Louisiana State University, 1984). On the 1921 Budget and Accounting Act, see Louis Fisher, *Presidential Spending Power* (Princeton, N.J.: Princeton University Press, 1975), 31–35.

7. See for example, Mosher, *A Tale of Two Agencies*, 129–35. I have overdrawn the issue in comparison to Mosher's more subtle argument, but he makes it clear that successful functioning of OMB depends on maintaining a modicum of neutral competence. Too much political responsiveness or proactive policy formulation and implementation is harmful to the agency.

8. Much of the political science literature was developed separately but had clear budgetary implications. Francis Rourke, for example, talks about the sources of agency power in general, but he notes that agencies may start programs at a low level and through bureaucratic momentum "transform small commitments into larger ones." He used the commitment to the H bomb as an exam-

ple. *Bureaucracy, Politics and Public Policy*, 3d ed. (Boston: Little, Brown & Co., 1984), 34. Martha Derthick made a similar point about the cost of program expansion in social security, begun gradually by the Social Security Administration and then mushrooming into a very expensive program. *Policy Making for Social Security* (Washington, D.C.: Brookings, 1979). The discussion of the nature of representation has blended into discussion of deficit control and legislative spending control. See, for example, Kenneth A. Shepsle and Barry Weingast, "Legislative Politics and Budget Outcomes" in *Federal Budget Policy in the 1980's* eds. Gregory Mills and John Palmer, (Washington, D.C.: The Urban Institute, 1984), 343–67. See also Kenneth Shepsle, "The Congressional Budget Process: Diagnosis, Prescription, Prognosis" in *Congressional Budgeting*, eds. W. Thomas Wander, F. Ted Herbert, and Gary W. Copeland, (Baltimore: Johns Hopkins, 1984) 190–218.

9. Two authors who demonstrate clear links between historical events, such as war and debt levels, and budgeting processes are Allen Schick and Naomi Caiden. See for example, Allen Schick, "The Whole and the Parts: Piecemeal and Integrated Approaches to Congressional Budgeting" ms, 1986; and Naomi Caiden, "Negative Financial Management: *A Backward Look at Fiscal Stress"* in *Fiscal Stress and Public Policy* eds., Charles Levine and Irene Rubin (Beverly Hills, Calif.: Sage 1980) 135–158.

10. There has been a lively debate in the literature on whether the 1974 congressional Budget Reform Act is neutral or has a spending bias. Louis Fisher argues that the act has a bias toward increased expenditures. "The Budget Act of 1974: A Further Loss of Spending Control" in *Congressional Budgeting*, eds. Wander, Hebert, and Copeland, 179–89. Schick has argued that the process is essentially neutral. See for example, "The Evolution of Congressional Budgeting" in *Crisis in the Budget Process: Exercising Political Choice*, ed. Allen Schick (Washington D.C.: American Enterprise Institute, 1986), 23. The arguments are hard to weigh, since the amount of federal spending is sensitive not only to the budget process but also to the vagaries of the economy and to the impact of decisions made many years earlier.

11. Glenn Abney and Thomas Lauth have made a start on measuring political process at the state and local level, with implications for budgeting. For example, they look at the frequency with which legislators approach executive agencies with requests. But, they do not measure the impact of the budget process on budget outcomes; *The Politics of State and City Administration* (Albany, N.Y.: SUNY Press, 1986). There are scattered references in historical literature to the relationship of budget process (and form of government) to spending levels. See, for example, William T. Huchinson, *Lowden of Illinois: The Life of Frank O. Lowden*, vol. 1, *City and State* (Chicago: University of Chicago Press, 1957), chapter 13; or M. Craig Brown and Charles Hallaby, "Bosses, Reform and the

Socioeconomic Bases of Urban Expenditures, 1890-1940," in Terrence McDonald and Sally Ward, *The Politics of Urban Fiscal Policy* (Beverly Hills, Calif.: Sage, 1986), 69-99.

12. See for example, Irene Rubin, "Retrenchment and Flexibility in Public Organizations" in *Fiscal Stress and Public Policy* eds. Charles Levine and Irene Rubin, (Beverly Hills, Calif.: Sage, 1980) 159-78; George E. Hale and S. Douglass, "The Politics of Budget Execution: Financial Manipulation in State and Local Government" *Administration and Society* 9 (November 1977): 367-78; George Hale, "State Budget Execution: The Legislature's Role," *National Civic Review* 66, no. 66 (June 1977): 284-90; Frank Draper and Bernard Pitsvada "Limitations in Federal Budget Execution" *Government Accountants Journal* 30, no. 3 (Fall 1981): 15-25. Irene Rubin, *Shrinking the Federal Government* (New York: Longman, 1985), also has a considerable amount of material on budget implementation. See also Fisher, *Presidential Spending Power*.

Chapter 1
From Microbudgeting to Macrobudgeting: Evolution in Theory and Practice

LANCE T. LELOUP

Introduction

Budgeting in the United States has been transformed during the past two decades. Macrobudgeting—high level decisions on spending, revenue and deficit aggregates and relative budget shares, often made from the top down—has become increasingly more prevalent in both the legislative and executive branches. Microbudgeting—intermediate level decisions on agencies, programs, and line-items, usually made from the bottom up—remains a critical if less compelling part of the budget process. Political science theories about the budgetary process have been transformed as well: All but the most diehard incrementalists now generally recognize the critical importance of macro-level decisions in explaining the politics of outcomes of budgeting. But how complete has been the transition from micro- to macrobudgeting? How thoroughly have political scientists revised the concepts and theories to explain budgetary politics?

A decade ago, a chorus of protest arose against incrementalism, both in practice and theory. In the political arena, executive branch reformers pursued changes to make budgeting more rational, such as planning programming budgeting, management by objectives, and zero-base budgeting. Congressional reformers passed the Budget and Impoundment Control Act of 1974 in an attempt to make legislative budgeting more comprehensive and responsible.[1] Within the academic community, a number of budget theorists criticized incrementalism on a host of normative, conceptual, and empirical grounds.[2] What has happened in the subsequent ten years?

Change has been both swift and dramatic, yet criticism of budgeting hardly has been muted. No critique of macrobudgeting in the 1980s has been more devastating than that by President Reagan's former budget director, David Stockman. His book, *The Triumph of Politics*, is a testament to the disappointing performance of top-down budgeting in carrying out the Reagan Revolution.[3] Despite his highly ideological criteria for evaluation, Stockman's recollections reveal a litany of constraints, limitations, and the imperfections of macrobudgeting. Other, perhaps more credible, observers of the budget practices of the Reagan Administration reached comparable conclusions concerning the ineffectiveness of macrobudgeting.[4]

Political scientists have not been much kinder in evaluating the performance and adaptation of budgetary theory to the world of macro-level budgeting. Bozeman and Straussman, in assessing the state of "shrinking" budget theory, argue that political scientists have been slow to respond to the transition from micro- to macrobudgeting, concluding that, "events are rapidly overcoming budgeting theory."[5] Is this a fair characterization?

This paper attempts to assess the state of budgeting and budgetary theory as a result of the apparent reorientation from microbudgeting to macrobudgeting. Several key questions will be pursued.

(1) How did incrementalism, as a paradigm of budgeting, begin to crumble and collapse in the 1970s as a result of the macro-versus micro-level of analysis concerns?

(2) In the decade following the passage of the 1974 Budget Act, how much had Congress actually reoriented itself from microbudgeting to macrobudgeting?

(3) Even though the President has historically been concerned with budget totals, how much of a transition from microbudgeting to macrobudgeting has occurred in the executive branch, particularly in the 1980s?

(4) How have budget scholars responded to the transition from microbudgeting to macrobudgeting? Is there theory after incrementalism?

(5) Has macrobudgeting failed? How permanent are recent changes? Can micro- and macrobudgeting be balanced in theory or practice?

I begin by examining the theory of incrementalism and its challenge by those concerned with macro-level issues.

Microbudgeting: The Rise and Fall of Incrementalism

Incrementalism as a theory of the national budgetary process had become dominant by the mid-1960s. Made theoretically and empirically elegant by the landmark work of Aaron Wildavsky, in *The Politics of the Budgetary Process*, and Richard Fenno, in *The Power of the Purse*, incrementalism became a powerful paradigm in political science.[6] Charles Lindblom had earlier been influential in claiming that incrementalism (or "muddling through")—limited, noncomprehensive change representing mutual adjustment through successive limited comparisons—was the most common method of policy making. Applying the theory specifically to the politics of national budgeting, Wildavsky and Fenno described the interaction of agencies and Congress and the resulting appropriations decisions. Wildavsky explained; "Budgeting is incremental, not comprehensive. The beginning of wisdom about an agency budget is that it is almost never actively reviewed as a whole every year. . . . Instead, it is based on last year's budget with special attention given to a narrow range of increases or decreases.[7]

In this stable and predictable process, participants play definitive roles. Agencies play the role of advocate, attempting to maintain their budget base and gain small increases. The appropriations subcommittees in Congress play the role of guardian, attempting to protect the public purse by making cuts in requests. Incremental decision making results in incremental budgetary outcomes.[8] Annual increases in spending in the range of 5–10 percent were cited as confirmation of the inherently incremental nature of budgeting.

The empirical evidence supporting incrementalism was elevated by the mathematical representation of the budget process using regression equations. Davis, Dempster, and Wildavsky modeled appropriations outcomes in Congress for fifty-six domestic agencies from 1946–1963.[9] Two dominant decision rules were found, one for agencies and one for appropriations committees. Agencies took a fixed percentage increase in their previous year's appropriation to formulate this year's request. Appropriations committees took a fixed percentage cut in the request to calculate the final appropriation. These two simple decision rules summarized the process and results of incrementalism: the "striking regularities of the budgetary process."[10] The incremental paradigm was pushed one step further in attempts to use econometric modeling to actually predict budgetary outcomes.[11] For the first time, external factors, such as economic and political forces, were included in the model, but they resulted in little change in the assumptions of the model or the conclusions derived from it.

At its zenith, the theory of budgetary incrementalism extended far beyond the bounds of national budgeting in the United States. Other scholars applied it to American states,[12] municipal budgeting,[13] school district budgeting,[14] foreign nations,[15] the United Nations, the World Health Organization, and the International Labor Organization.[16] But despite its widespread acceptance, many scholars were increasingly critical.

By the mid-1970s, incrementalism was attacked for its normative perspective, interpretation of results, and its basic analytical framework. In "The Myth of Incrementalism," I summarized many of the diverse criticisms of incrementalism and attempted to show that analytical choices in developing the theory, although appearing logical, actually structured both the findings and conclusions, assuring that all budgets would always be "incremental."

Observers noted that incrementalism was theoretically linked to pluralism and, as such, defended (or rationalized) the results of group bargaining as morally superior to any other process.[17] Other critics noted the confusion between incrementalism in decision making and incremental outcomes.[18] Questioning the interpretation of data on budget change, they suggested that much greater variation in budget outcomes could be observed in the incrementalist's own data. Bailey and O'Connor concluded that, "when incremental is defined as bargaining, we are aware of no empirical case of a budgetary process which is nonincremental."[19] Other scholars questioned the interpretation of the regression equations, suggesting that the high correlations in the regression models were the result of not controlling for collinearity in the data.[20] John Wanat found that the magnitude of correlations in randomly generated data were as high as those reported and did not validly support the existence of fixed decision rules.[21] The assumption of a single dominant decision rule for agencies was challenged. A study by LeLoup and Moreland found dramatic variation in agency behavior in the executive budget formulation process and the inadequacy of using requests in the president's budget as an indication of agency desires.[22] The cumulative impact of these studies was to arrive at a conclusion that incremental assumptions colored the interpretation of budget results. Reanalyzing the incrementalist's own data, it was possible to support a much more diverse set of conclusions.

The theory of incremental budgeting was based on a series of analytical choices that initially passed unnoticed but had the effect of severely limiting the applicability of the theory.[23] One of the first analytical choices was the level of aggregation. Incrementalism looked at budgets by agency rather than by function or by broad aggregates, such as defense or entitlements, or by smaller program components within agency budgets. No distinctions were made between controllable and uncontrollable components of the budget base, making incremental descriptions of calculations rather unrealistic.[24] A second analytical choice concerned time and the object of analysis. Only annual appropriations were examined, ignoring multiyear spending decisions that would reveal significant change over time. Entitlements, revenues, interest on debt, and other nonappropriations spending actions were ignored. Finally, the choice of independent and dependent variables had the effect of ensuring that incrementalism would be found. By including total agency requests and final appropriations in the models rather than percentage change, for example, high correlations virtually were assured. Different results occurred when alternative dependent and independent variables were used to model the budgetary process.[25]

Incrementalism is essentially a theory of microbudgeting: It concentrates on the parts, not the whole. It defines budgeting as a bottom-up process of making marginal adjustments in budgets, based on the stable roles of participants and political bargaining that results in minimal changes in budgets from year to year. Looking back a decade later, it is clear that most of the criticism of incrementalism stemmed from its total disregard for macrobudgeting. Incrementalism virtually ignored the role in budgeting played by the President, who, in the 1960s, was the major actor concerned with macrobudgeting. OMB was relevant to incrementalism only in terms of its relations with individual agencies·and programs, not in its role of assembling the budget as a package for the President. Congress, lacking any mechanism for considering the budget as a whole, was the essence of incremental microbudgeting. Goals for fiscal policy or the macro-level tradeoff between defense and domestic priorities were simply excluded from incremental theory. By the mid-1970s, it was clear that incrementalism was a tautology that could not be disproven because budgets simply did not change dramatically from year to year. But, as social science theory, the paradigm left analysts without an adequate base for explaining past budgets, let alone predicting the dramatic budget developments of the 1970s and 1980s. Incrementalism disintegrated as a paradigm because its view of the budgetary world increasingly became irrelevant to the reality of national budgeting. The scholarly criticism was a process of discovering its theoretical limitations as its irrelevance in practice became more obvious. But, with the demise of incrementalism, what was to take its place? How would macro-level analysis of budgeting be included in a theory? Before taking up that question, it is necessary to examine the changes in budgeting practice in the legislative and executive branches.

From Microbudgeting to Macrobudgeting in Congress

Preoccupation with incremental appropriations led political scientists, budget analysts, and decision makers to ignore critical changes in the 1960s and 1970s that would eventually drive macrobudgeting to center stage in the 1980s. Perhaps no change was more important or initially more overlooked than the expansion of entitlements. The passage of the Medicare Act of 1965 would have profound budgetary implications over the ensuing decades. Expansion of the program to include the disabled in 1974, other increases in eligible beneficiaries, and rapid increases in health care costs shot total medical insurance spending up to nearly 8 percent of all outlays by the 1980s. The growth of new entitlements, such as food stamps, had critical long-term results. Other important entitlement changes included large increases in Social Security benefits in the early 1970s and the decision to index benefit levels beginning in 1975. Key budgetary developments included the growth of tax expenditures and off-budget credit activities. Both allowed policy makers to allocate tangible but less visible benefits to achieve a variety of goals outside of the normal appropriations process. An expanded definition of what constituted relevant budget decisions was needed to understand the evolving practice of budgeting.

Table 1-1 examines some of the characteristics of microbudgeting and macrobudgeting in Congress. As we will see, macro-level budgeting in Congress caused severe strains with the more traditional appropriations and authorizations processes.

The Budget and Impoundment Control Act of 1974 stands as the critical step taken by Congress to engage in macrobudgeting.[26] Although the drafters of budget reform in Congress had very different goals and ideological objectives leading them to support the bill, a desire to increase Congress' overall control of budget totals was a common thread. Republicans and fiscally conservative Democrats wanted a budget process that would restrain spending, that would force members to vote for budget aggregates and go on record for or against deficits. Liberals in Congress saw budget reform as an opportunity to engage in a debate on national priorities, to use the functional breakdowns to compare total national resources going to defense versus domestic needs.[27] Still other reformers wanted Congress to play a more meaningful role in determining fiscal policy. To accomplish this, Congress had to have more control

Table 1-1.

Characteristics of Microbudgeting and Macrobudgeting
in Congress.

	Microbudgeting	*Macrobudgeting*
Key Actors	Authorizing and appropriations committees and subcommittees	Budget committees and party leaders
Legislation	Individual bills	Budget resolutions, reconciliation instructions, tax and spending "packages"
Budgetary Process	Fragmented, bottom up	Centralized, top down
Reforms	Strengthening appropriations, authorizing committees; sunset laws	Budget Act of 1974; Balanced Budget and Emergency Deficit Control Act of 1985

over aggregate levels of taxing and spending than they had before. For all of these diverse goals—reducing spending, improving fiscal planning, or comparing national priorities—significant movement from micro- to macrobudgeting was needed.

Budget reform in 1974 took important steps in that direction. The Budget Act created two new budget committees and gave them the responsibility of approving budget resolutions that would shape the overall parameters of the budget. Budget resolutions would include total spending, revenues, deficit, debt, and functional subtotals. The act also created a strict timetable for congressional budgeting and moved the fiscal year so Congress would have more time. On paper, Congress had a framework for macrobudgeting.

The new budget process, however, did not replace the traditional authorization and appropriations processes with an effective system of top-down budgeting to make macro-level decisions. In fact, the budget committees, whose responsibilities were superimposed on top of the old taxing and spending committee jurisdictions, remained relatively weak compared to the more established committees. As a result, many were disappointed with the performance of the congressional budget process in the 1970s. The Budget Act did not restrain spending significantly or eliminate deficits. The House and Senate budget panels were christened "adding machine" committees since, instead of enforcing discipline on the standing committees, they largely accommodated their spending and programmatic desires.[28] National priorities were infrequently debated and rarely changed. And, there was little evidence that Congress played a significantly enhanced role in shaping the fiscal policy of the nation. In fact, as the budget became more vulnerable to changes in the economy, it appeared that the economy was driving the budget not vice versa.

Despite the disappointment with the budget process, by 1980 it became clear that Congress at least could perform the mechanics of macrobudgeting. Congress approved budget resolutions specifying totals, even if it did not fundamentally reshape the budget from the top down. Members became much more comfortable dealing with budget aggregates, more used to confronting economic assumptions, better able to compare proportions of GNP, and more sensitive to multiyear expenditure and revenue trends. These changes were of more than symbolic value: The tools were in place to foster the move toward macrobudgeting in the 1980s.

The year 1981 was a landmark in recent political history. The adoption of President Reagan's far reaching budget and economic plan had important procedural and policy consequences for Congress. In terms of procedure, the use of the previously overlooked reconciliation provisions resulted, temporarily, in a form of highly centralized, top-down budgeting. Used at the beginning of the budget calendar, reconciliation allowed a conservative majority to make significant multiyear cuts in domestic spending, not only in discretionary appropriations, but in entitlements and other budget authority as well.[29] In terms of policy, the "rosy scenario" economic assumptions on which the budget was built allowed policy makers in both branches to plunge ahead with major tax cuts and a defense buildup.[30] Even with the major cuts in domestic spending huge structural budget deficits resulted: The debt doubled from $1 trillion in 1981 to over $2 trillion by 1986. The profound political pressure created by the massive deficits would dominate budgetary politics in the 1980s and finally result in the passage of a mandatory deficit reduction process. The controversial Gramm-Rudman (The Balanced Budget and Emergency Deficit Control Act of 1985) legislation not only attempted to force automatic cuts in the budget, but also revised and updated the congressional budget process.

Analysis of the congressional budget process since 1975 requires far more space than is available here. In terms of the evolution of budget practice, a number of developments in Congress in the 1980s have fostered a movement towards macrobudgeting. Several key trends can be identified.

Reconciliation Has Been Institutionalized

Reconciliation, despite its perception by many members as a process used by the President against Congress, has been used regularly in subsequent years. Gramm-Rudman furthered centralization by institutionalizing reconciliation at the beginning of the budget process. Several other factors have helped increase the centralization of the budget process.

The Budget Committees and Party Leaders Are More Powerful

The movement towards macrobudgeting has led to a change in the power structure of Congress. Without overstating the case, the leaders of both the House and Senate, working through the Budget Committees, have become more powerful vis a vis the standing committees, which remain primarily oriented to microbudgeting. Enforcement procedures have been strengthened, particularly in the Senate under Gramm-Rudman, adding some real teeth to the budget process for the first time.

Budget-Related Legislation Is Increasingly "Packaged" Together

The trend towards packaging—lumping together assorted taxing, appropriating, authorizing, and debt limitation bills into a single piece of legislation—is unmistakable. While packaging may correctly be seen as a response to the breakdown of some parts of the congressional budget process, its effect is to reinforce centralization and foster macrobudgeting. When various components of budgeting are put together in a package, more pressure exists to pass the legislation, and to pass it without crippling amendments. Clearly, the massive budget deficits have put tremendous strains on the budget process, fostering more centralized approaches to decision making than Congress would have previously tolerated. The imminence of stalemate and political gridlock has actually resulted in a grudging acceptance of some top-down budgeting within Congress.

Relations Between the President and Congress Have Evolved to Negotiating Budget Aggregates

The experience of 1981, where Congress acted to give the President essentially what he wanted, was short-lived. Because of the shifting short-term political strategies of the Reagan White House, legislative-executive relations have been highly volatile in the 1980s. What has emerged, however, is more oriented towards macrobudgeting than at

any previous time. The leaders of the two branches now generally
negotiate budgets at the macro level: overall decisions on the relative size
of defense, domestic discretionary, and entitlement spending; deficits;
and revenues. Congressional consideration of the budget has come a long
way from the 1960s.

Changes in congressional budgeting since the mid-1970s have made
incrementalism largely irrelevant in explaining budget outcomes. The
range of decisions where incrementalism might even be applicable is
restricted to discretionary domestic programs, now less than 16 percent
of outlays. Yet, as will be noted in the conclusion, the transformation
from micro- to macrobudgeting has been neither successful nor complete. Despite the more established legacy of macrobudgeting in the
presidency, the next section will show an increasing orientation to
macrobudgeting in the executive branch as well.

Enhancing Macrobudgeting in the Executive Branch

Unlike Congress, which avoided direct decisions on budget aggregates until the 1970s, the President has been concerned with totals
since the passage of the Budget and Accounting Act of 1921. With the advent of Keynesian economics and discretionary fiscal policy during the
Roosevelt Administration in the 1930s, budget totals took on additional
importance. Yet presidential budgeting remained largely a bottom-up
process, with presidents having difficulty shaping the budget from the
top-down, especially if they wanted to cut back. Table 1-2 compares
some of the characteristics of macrobudgeting and microbudgeting in the
executive branch. Even Eisenhower complained about the inflexibility of
the budget when he took office in 1953.[31] Despite the difficulties of top-
down budgeting, for many decades presidents were the only actors in the
process concerned with macrobudgeting. Presidents have long noticed
total spending and deficits and made decisions based on those concerns.
Lyndon Johnson's retreat to the LBJ ranch in December of 1963 to pare
the fiscal year 1965 budget below the symbolic $100 billion level is one of
the better known cases.[32]

The constraints on presidential budgeting seemed even greater in the
1970s.[33] Nixon, Ford, and Carter all found increasing difficulties in solv-
ing macroeconomic and macrobudgetary problems with a system
oriented primarily to microbudgeting. With changes in the composition
of the budget, such as the growth of entitlements, totals seemed more difficult to control than ever. Fiscal policy, once seen as the most effective

Table 1-2.

Characteristics of Microbudgeting and Macrobudgeting
in the Executive Branch.

	Microbudgeting	*Macrobudgeting*
Key Actors	Agencies, OMB budget examiners	President, White House staff, OMB Director
Policy Focus	Agency budgets, programs, annual marginal changes	Aggregates, multiyear projections, budget shares, percent of GNP, economic assumptions
Budget Process	Fragmented, bottom up	Centralized, top down
Reforms	Program budgeting, PPB, MBO, ZBB	Implementing top-down budgeting

weapon in the government's economic arsenal, seemed increasingly impotent. Instead of the budget stabilizing the economy, the economy was increasingly destabilizing the budget. Executive branch budget reforms, such as planning program budgeting (PPB), management by objective (MBO), and zero-base budgeting (ZBB), had mixed if unspectacular records in terms of individual agencies and programs but did nothing to help the President manage increasingly pressing budget aggregates.

As with the Congress, executive branch budgeting went through dramatic changes in the 1980s. Led by Budget Director David Stockman, the Reagan Administration engaged in an unprecedented exercise of top-down budgeting in the executive branch. The supply-side revolution envisioned by Stockman was sufficiently compatible with Ronald Reagan's strong commitment to reduce domestic spending and lower taxes to convince the President to give Stockman a green light. Stockman was well prepared. He and Phill Gramm, then Democratic Representative from Texas, had prepared a comprehensive list of proposed cuts in both discretionary and entitlement spending in the previous Congress. Although most of Stockman's energies were initially focused on Congress, with the help of a revitalized OMB, agency budgets were also targets of the assault. Many agency old timers, used to playing the budget game from the bottom up, were stunned at the new rules of the game. Instead of trying to protect the base and make marginal increases in appropriations, agencies were trying to prevent wholesale erosion of their agencies through program reduction, consolidation, and elimination, while coping with hiring freezes and mandated staff reductions.

In 1981 and 1982, normal agency budget practices were replaced with a top-down process. Under Stockman, OMB gave specific instructions on budget preparation.³⁴ Opportunities to appeal were limited and time constraints were harsh. Regular policy analysis, program evaluation data, and substantive alternatives characteristic of microbudgeting were not used in determining the cuts. Many decisions were made in the White House without any agency participation.³⁵ With the appointment of political executives who largely supported the President, agency officials simply had to run their agencies under adverse conditions rather than trying to fight the cuts.³⁶ After the first two years, however, more traditional political alliances began to reassert themselves and budgeting returned to more normal practices. But many major cuts had already been made and many agencies had considerably less discretion in the budgetary process than before 1981.

Even when top-down budgeting, as practiced in the first two years of the Reagan Administration, faded, macrobudgeting did not. Stockman effectively continued to set the agenda within the administration and on Capitol Hill by defining issues in macro terms. Congressman Richard Bolling (D-Mo.), former head of the House Rules Committee complained, "The papers were always their papers, the figures were always their figures. I kept saying that I had to have a whole package and look at the detail. I was looking for the smaller pieces."³⁷ The necessity for this emphasis was exacerbated by the massive deficits, but in part it reflected the degree to which macrobudgeting was beginning to become institutionalized.

The defense budget process in the 1980s reflects the shift from micro- to macro-level concerns. Defense issues were cast in macro terms—percentage real growth, percent of GNP, percent of outlays—not in program, agency, or department terms.³⁸ Defense analyst Richard Stubbing describes it:

> The largest peacetime increase in defense in history was the product of an agreement between a few key Republican senators and the administration. . . . There was little Office of Secretary of Defense or OMB budget review; the task of adding the extra money was simply assigned to the three military departments, all of which had long standing shopping lists. There was no balancing of individual department requests; potentially important national needs like sealift and airlift were not high on the Navy and Air Force lists and consequently received short shrift. And thus we embarked on a massive defense buildup.³⁹

The role of the OMB shifted as well. One of the most marked changes was a shift in its orientation from agencies to Congress, monitoring the progress of proposed budget cuts in a host of committees and subcommittees.[40] While the Stockman era brought a boost in morale to staffers, changes in the OMB's role also brought new strains. The shift to top-down budgeting changed the relationship between budget examiners and agency officials from negotiation to implementation of decisions made at a higher level. The politicization that started long before the Reagan Administration seemed complete.[41]

Even though the presidency had always been more concerned with macrobudgeting than any other institution, a further shift from microbudgeting to macrobudgeting is observable in the 1980s. Within the White House, the budget occupied much of the President's valuable time. Macrobudgetary issues—protecting the tax cut and the defense buildup while trying to reduce the deficit—continued to dominate throughout the 1980s. Microbudgetary issues remained important but were always debated in the shadow of the totals. Yet, the transition from micro- to macrobudgeting raises many difficult issues: the apparent failure of top-down budgeting, the balance between micro- and macro-level decisions, and assessing the permanence of the observed changes. Before considering these crucial questions, let us examine the assertion that budgetary theory has lagged far behind events.

From Micro to Macro Analysis: Is There Theory After Incrementalism?

Bozeman and Straussmen observe that "a 'new' budgetary process has been evolving since the passage of the Congressional Budget and Impoundment Control Act," but lament the failure of budgetary theory to keep pace with the changes.[42] A brief survey of recent developments in budgetary theory and some related areas of inquiry will allow us to draw our own conclusions about how well political science and public administration has responded to the movement from microbudgeting to macrobudgeting.

Because the implications for macrobudgeting were so obvious with the passage of the Budget Act in 1974, students of the congressional budget process were attentive to it. Works by Schick, Ippolito, LeLoup, Fisher, Ellwood, Thurber and others examined various aspects of the new budget process.[43] Most of these studies were published by 1981.

Although some differences exist in author's results and conclusions, several characteristics are shared among their studies. None uses incrementalism as the theoretical base for explaining how congressional budgeting works. Virtually all of the studies confront in some way the conflict between microbudgeting in Congress (the traditional authorization and appropriations process) and macrobudgeting (the budget process). Despite differences in assessments of how well the process has worked, the various studies share the underlying premise that congressional budgeting is a struggle between the whole and the parts.

A somewhat different theoretical perspective on congressional budgeting is provided by the public choice or rational expectations approach. As typified by the work of Shepsle and Weingast, an assertion is made that the root of fiscal problems, particularly outlay growth and deficit spending, lies in the electoral orientation and internal fragmentation of Congress.[44] While containing many provocative insights, evidence suggests that their conclusions are overdrawn.[45] Nonetheless, this approach makes an important theoretical contribution by linking reelection-minded behavior at the micro level to aggregate budget results. Research on budgeting in Congress may not have generated a unified theory of budgeting to replace incrementalism, but conceptually it clearly has kept pace with observed changes in practice.

Related to theories about budgeting is the political business cycle hypothesis. Since the mid-1970s a number of studies have tested the assertion that political decision makers use their economic policy tools, including the budget, to enhance their electoral chances by stimulating the economy and rewarding certain constituent groups just before the next election.[46] Initial empirical findings revealed that target variables like employment, growth, and inflation fluctuate in a cyclical fashion generally consistent with the hypothesis. Empirical results examining economic instruments that officials actually control, however, reveal virtually no association between fiscal policy manipulation and elections.[47] In terms of our particular inquiry here, the key characteristic to budgetary theory is the obvious macro focus of the research. Both proponents and opponents of the political business cycle hypothesis conceptualize taxing and spending decisions at the macro level of analysis.

Conceptualization of the federal budget process has undergone rapid change in the past decade. Naiomi Caiden has made several important contributions to the reconceptualization of budgeting. In "The Myth of the Annual Budget", Caiden amplifies the theme that annual budgeting, one of the analytical choices underlying the theory of incrementalism, poorly reflects the reality of the 1980s.[48] Noting the changes in the composition of the budget, problems of inflexibility and controllability, Caiden concludes that "the annual unified budget is pass-ing and is being replaced by a different mode of handling public financial policy making and administration."[49] Caiden more explicitly deals with the enhanced role of macrobudgeting in "The New Rules of the Federal Budget Game."[50] She notes the vulnerability of the budget to economy and economic assumptions, the rise of packaging as a legislative tech-nique for dealing with taxing and spending, and the increased orientation to cutting rather than increasing expenditures. All of these new premises reflect the changes in practice since the mid-1970s.

Allen Schick's chapter in this book reflects his attempt to come up with a broadly applicable theory of budgeting. His previous works, however, already reflect the basic reconceptualization of budgeting in the post-incremental era. Budgeting as "the war between the parts and the whole" reflects the importance of both levels of budgeting. His work clarifies the difficulties presidents face in effectively practicing macrobudgeting and some of the failures of top-down budgeting in the Reagan era.[51] Schick's analysis of the congressional budget process reflects the transformation of congressional budgeting, both through for-mal and informal adaptation. He has made several other recent contribu-tions to the development of budget theory. Examination of congressional attempts to increase controls over off-budget or "nonconventional ex-penditure," such as the credit budget and tax expenditures, helps to redefine the boundaries of what are considered relevant budgetary deci-sions.[52] Finally, his article, "Macro-Budgetary Adaptations to Fiscal Stress in Industrialized Democracies" reflects the most comprehensive comparative study of budgeting in a decade.[53] He finds that the shift in emphasis from micro- to macrobudgeting in response to economic prob-lems and budget deficits has not been limited to the United States. Around the world, other nations have adopted macro-level strategies to reduce expenditures: developing new fiscal norms; creating ceilings, targets, advance limits; practicing multiyear budgeting; changing budget preparation; and generally strengthening budget conservers. Schick describes the critical relationship between micro- and macrobudgeting:

> Fiscal norms, spending targets, multiyear controls and other con-straints do not suffice to reorient budgeting from growth to retrench-ment. It is also necessary for the government to follow up these macro actions with restrictive budget decisions on specific programs. If micro budgeting continues to be geared to growth, government might find its overall budget objectives undermined.[54]

Not only has federal budgeting been largely reconceptualized in the post-incremental era, but empirical models of the budget have adopted many of the changes. The most important contributions in developing mathematical models of the macrobudget process have been made by Mark Kamlet and David Mowrey.[55] In a number of articles published since 1980, they incorporated conceptual changes in their models and tested them with data from an extensive budget archive developed by John Crecine at the University of Pittsburgh. Kamlet and Mowrey include several critical new elements in the models. Unlike their incremental predecessors, their models encompass both microbudgeting and macrobudgeting, and comparisons of their relative importance. Both top-down and bottom-up processes are examined. The authors test for the interdependence between, for example, domestic and defense spending, as well as between spending and revenues. Both political and economic variables are included, as well as differences between legislative and executive processes. Kamlet and Mowrey's research also considers the differences between budget authority and outlays in budgeting. Their model partially tests the political business cycle hypothesis as well.

The results of their research require careful interpretation and many of the findings are intriguing but tentative. They found little support for the political business cycle hypotheses: Rather than pursuing expansionist fiscal policies in the year preceding the election, outlays are held down during the campaign.[56] In terms of macro-level budgeting, they found that, while spending is subject to a revenue constraint and the existing tax structure, tax policy is not responsive to spending pressure. Kamlet and Mowrey conclude that economic variables have a significant impact on budget outcomes, while political variables have relatively less. An important result of their model is that uncontrollable spending and defense as well as discretionary domestic spending are subject to the macrobudgetary calculations. Perhaps the main weaknesses of their research, which they readily acknowledge, is the very high level of aggregation and the long time periods necessary to adequately specify the models. Political variables are not measured very effectively and their criticism of congressional budgeting emulating executive budgeting seem to be based primarily on value judgements. Yet, despite the difficulties, they have made a significant contribution in developing realistic models of the reconceptualized budget process.

A number of other studies, both conceptual and empirical, have added to our understanding of budgetary behavior and outcomes. This brief review identifies major contributions and is by no means comprehensive. It should be abundantly clear, however, that budgetary theory has done a remarkable job of "keeping up with events." In fact, it has done more than that. Although no unified paradigm of budgeting has emerged in the way incrementalism did, most scholars now agree on the major elements in the reconceptualization of budgeting: differentiated types of spending and spending authority, interdependence and tradeoffs at the aggregate level, annual and multiyear decisions with varying degrees of controllability, vulnerability to macroeconomic performance and economic projections, and a growing preoccupation with macrobudgeting by decision makers requiring the use of top-down budgeting in the face of fiscal stress. Budget theory has progressed in recent years and the foundation for the reconceptualization was laid by the original critiques of incrementalism a decade ago.

In the conclusion to "The Myth of Incrementalism" I wrote, "In all probability incrementalism will remain in prevalent use regardless of findings to the contrary; it is a truism that government changes only marginally from year to year."[57] Despite the rapid theoretical progress of the past decade, incrementalism remains an irresistible description of the budgetary process for some. Joseph White, in an otherwise perceptive review of recent publications on the budget, reveals that incrementalism can still be used to describe any budget change, large or small, at any level of decision making. He writes, "The current debate over defense, centering on the size of the current year's increase . . . illustrates that incrementalist simplifications are alive and well. . . . Both the successes and failures of the Reagan years reveal the uses of incrementalism in calculation and conflict management."[58]

Perhaps an even more astounding demonstration that incrementalism can be all things to all people is found in a *Public Administration Review* article by Pitsvada and Draper entitled, "Making Sense of the Federal Budget the Old Fashioned Way—Incrementally." Despite the many critiques of incrementalism, they believe that, "on balance, incrementalism still remains the best method of explaining and understanding budgets."[59] They identify several changes in budgeting in recent years that have, "added to rather than reduced the tendency toward incrementalism."[60] Ironically, many of these are the same factors that generally have been identified as making incrementalism irrelevant! Included are indexing and inflation, multiyear budgeting, continuing resolutions (packaging), and the use of budget baselines based on complex estimation procedures. It is hard to imagine how indexed entitlements, long-term spending commitments, and the increasing orientation to macrobudgeting have reinforced incrementalism. It is clear that to some, the term *incrementalism* still means no more than "the government changes only marginally from year to year."

From Microbudgeting to Macrobudgeting: An Assessment

Let me summarize what I have attempted to establish in the preceding pages. First, incrementalism as a paradigm of budgeting—that is, a meaningful, reasonably comprehensive explanatory theory not a tautology—began to erode in the 1970s. Events and the practice of budgeting changed, while critics found many key elements of budgeting ignored or dismissed by incrementalism. Second, the practice of budgeting underwent observable changes in recent years, moving from a process primarily of microbudgeting to one where macrobudgeting was of great concern. The change was more noticeable in the Congress with the passage of the 1974 budget act, but emphasis on macrobudgeting increased in the executive branch as well, particularly in the 1980s. Third, contrary to some assertions, budgetary theory responded remarkably quickly and well. We have witnessed a substantial reconceptualization of budgetary processes and outcomes in a relatively short period of time.

The basic conceptualization of budgeting has shifted from a cycle of micro-level, incremental executive requests and legislative actions to a complex series of political responses to short-term economic changes and projections of relatively inflexible long-term trends in outlays and revenues. Key questions now concern how to balance micro decisions within macro-level parameters. No grand theory of budgeting has emerged, but we are much closer to explaining and realistically modeling the budgetary process in the United States than we were a decade ago. Yet many critical questions remain. One is the dismal performance, some say the failure, of macrobudgeting in practice, both in the legislative and executive branches. A second question surrounds our understanding of the relationship between macro- and microbudgeting. And, despite all the evidence, just how much of a transformation from micro- to macrobudgeting really has occurred? Is macrobudgeting a temporary phenomenon or has a permanent change in budgeting taken place?

The Failure of Macrobudgeting in Practice

A fairly strong case can be made that macrobudgeting has been a dismal failure both in the Congress and the executive branch. The Reagan Administration, despite using unrealistic economic projections, demonstrated remarkable political skill in getting Congress to approve the budget changes. The result was a decade of massive structural deficits. The trend towards macrobudgeting was obviously hastened by the deficit crisis, forcing the White House and Congress to constantly deal with the unmanageable aggregates. Gramm-Rudman, with its radical solution to deficit reduction, is a testament to the frustrating demands of macrobudgeting.

Despite the problems with macrobudgeting in attempting to deal with deficits, it has not been a complete failure. The experience with top-down budgeting in the presidency, even though it has not been institutionalized, will have a profound effect on the thinking of future presidents. The experience in Congress with reconciliation, packaging, and procedural innovation tending to centralize power likewise will have a profound effect on future congresses. The advent and inevitability of macrobudgeting reflects an end of innocence for national decision makers, who can never return to the simpler days of microbudgeting. Budgeting at the aggregate level is relatively new and, as such, somewhat experimental. The experiment is still going on. The criticism heaped upon macrobudgeting as practiced in the 1980s should not diminish the significance of the change. Allen Schick's comparison of similar macro-level responses in other democratic nations should make this even clearer. Now, the highest priority is to better integrate micro- and macrobudgeting in both theory and practice.

Balancing Microbudgeting and Macrobudgeting

It should be clear that a complete transformation from microbudgeting to macrobudgeting has not taken place. Far from it. In some ways, concern with agencies, programs, and line items remains as important as ever. The scholarly emphasis placed on macrobudgeting reflects, in part, an effort to compensate for the imbalance in budgeting and budgetary theory in earlier years. Given the activities of the federal government, microbudgeting has to remain a central, dominant focus.

Gramm-Rudman enacted into law a comprehensive budget reform package that had been formulated in the House in 1984. It represents Congress' latest attempt to balance macro- and microbudgeting. Those with macro level responsibilities, the budget committees and the party leaders, appear to have been strengthened at the expense of the microbudgeting authorizing and appropriating committees. The top-down budgeting of the early years of the Reagan Administration did not balance micro- and macrobudgeting well. Authoritarian, heavy-handed budget slashing may have served the short-term needs of shaping and manipulating the aggregates, as well as the ideological agenda of the budget director, but it served the President and everyone else poorly in the long run. The lack of careful policy analysis, the failure to ascertain justifiable cuts versus unwarranted cuts now appears to be the legacy of top-down budgeting. The challenge for a future President will be to balance the demands of macrobudgeting with a more careful, discriminating continuation of the best practices of microbudgeting.

Finally, how permanent are the changes that have been observed in recent years? Some have suggested that Congress is simply in a regular cycle that alternates from centralization to decentralization and that recent centralizing changes are no more than a temporary response to deficits. Schick suggested that the use of top-down budgeting in the White House has actually weakened presidential capacity in budgeting in the long run.[61] Heclo believes the Stockman years and OMB's role in top-down budgeting will negatively affect that agency and the presidency in the long run.[62] Despite the problems, there is no going back all the way. Congress may be on a cycle of centralization-decentralization but it is occurring on a trend line moving towards macrobudgeting. The President has more constraints, but they will only foster his orientation towards macrobudgeting and his desire to implement top-down budgeting. The events of the 1980s may seem anomolous, from the personality of the President, to the huge deficits, to the peculiarities of the world economy. But, to a far greater extent than is generally acknowledged, I suspect, the increased orientation towards macrobudgeting is more permanent than temporary.

Notes

1. See Allen Schick, *Congress and Money*, (Washington, D.C.: Urban Institute Press, 1980); and Lance T. LeLoup, *The Fiscal Congress* (Westport, Conn,: Greenwood Press, 1980).

2. Randall B. Ripley and Grace R. Franklin, eds., *Policy Making in the Federal Executive Branch* (New York: Free Press, 1975); John R. Gist, "Mandatory Expenditures and the Defense Sector: Theory of Budgetary Incrementalism," *Sage Professional Papers in American Politics*, vol. 2, series 04-020 (Beverly Hills, Calif.: Sage, 1976); Lance T. LeLoup, "The Myth of Incrementalism: Analytic Choices in Budgetary Theory," *Polity* 10, no. 4 (summer 1978): 488–509.

3. David Stockman, *The Triumph of Politics* (New York: Harper and Row, 1986).

4. Hugh Heclo, "Executive Budget Making," in *Federal Budget Policy in the 1980s*, Gregory Mills and John Palmer (Washington, D.C.: Urban Institute, 1984), 255–91; and Allen Schick, "The Budget as an Instrument of Presidential

Policy," in *The Reagan Presidency and the Governing of America*, Lester M. Salamon and Michael S. Lund (Washington, D.C.: Urban Institute, 1985), 91–125.

5. Barry Bozeman and Jeffrey D. Straussman, "Shrinking Budgets and the Shrinkage of Budget Theory," *Public Administration Review* 42, no. 6, (November–December 1982): 515.

6. Aaron Wildavsky, *The Politics of the Budgetary Process*, (Boston: Little, Brown & Co., 1964); and Richard C. Fenno, *The Power of the Purse* (Boston: Little, Brown & Co., 1965).

7. Wildavsky, *Budgetary Process*, 15.

8. John Bailey and Robert O'Connor, "Operationalizing Incrementalism: Measuring the Muddles," *Public Administration Review* 35, (January–February 1975): 60–66.

9. Michael Davis, Michael Dempster, and Aaron Wildavsky, "A Theory of the Budgetary Process," *American Political Science Review* 60 (September 1966).

10. Ibid., 529.

11. Michael Davis, Michael Dempster, and Aaron Wildavsky, "Toward A Predictive Theory of Government Expenditure: U.S. Domestic Appropriations," *British Journal of Political Science* (October 1974): 419–52.

12. For example, Thomas Anton, *The Politics of State Expenditure in Illinois*, (Urbana: University of Illinois Press, 1966).

13. John Crecine, "A Computer Simulation Model of Municipal Budgeting," *Management Science* (July 1967): 786–815.

14. Donald A. Gerwin, *Budgeting Public Funds: The Decision Process in an Urban School District* (Madison: University of Wisconsin Press, 1969).

15. Andrew Cowart, Tore Hansen, and Karl-Erik Brofoss, "Budgetary Strategies and Success at Multiple Decision Levels in the Norwegian Urban Setting," *American Political Science Review* 69 (June 1975): 543–58.

16. Francis Hoole, Brian Job, and Harvey Tucker, "Incremental Budgeting in International Organizations," *American Political Science Review* 70 (May 1976): 273–301.

17. Allen Schick, "Systems Politics and Systems Budgeting," *Public Administration Review* 29 (March–April 1969): 137–51.

18. Bailey and O'Connor, "Operationalizing Incrementalism 60.

19. Ibid., 65.

20. Gist "Mandatory Expenditures," 13–14; William Moreland, "A Nonincremental Perspective on Budgetary Policy Actions," in *Policy Making in the Federal Executive Branch*, Ripley and Franklin, eds., Chapter 3.

21. John Wanat, "The Bases of Budgetary Incrementalism," *American Political Science Review* 68 (September 1974): 1221–28.

22. Lance T. LeLoup and William Moreland, "Agency Strategies and Executive Review: The Hidden Politics of Budgeting," *Public Administration Review* (May–June 1978): 232–39.

23. LeLoup, "Myth of Incrementalism."

24. Gist, "Mandatory Expenditures," 15; Wanat, "Bases of Budgetary Incrementalism," 1225.

25. LeLoup and Moreland, "Agency Strategies."

26. LeLoup, *Fiscal Congress*; Schick, *Congress and Money*.

27. LeLoup, *Fiscal Congress*, 16–31.

28. Dennis Ippolito, *Congressional Spending* (Ithaca, N.Y.: Cornell University Press, 1981).

29. Lance T. LeLoup, "After The Blitz: Reagan and the U.S. Congressional Budget Process," *Legislative Studies Quarterly* 7, no. 3 (August 1982): 331–39; and Allen Schick, *Reconciliation and the Congressional Budget* (Washington D.C.: American Enterprise Institute, 1981).

30. Stockman, *Triumph of Politics*, 96–99.

31. Dwight D. Eisenhower, *Mandates for Change: 1953–1956* (Garden City, N.Y.: Doubleday, 1963), 296.

32. Lyndon B. Johnson, *The Vantage Point* (New York: Holt, 1971), 36.

33. Schick, "Budget as an Instrument," 99–102.

34. Joseph S. Wholey, "Executive Agency Retrenchment," in Mills and Palmer, *Federal Budget Policy*, 300.

35. Ibid., 301.

36. Irene S. Rubin, *Shrinking the Federal Government: The Effect of Cutbacks on Five Federal Agencies* (New York: Longman, 1985).

37. Quoted in Laurence I. Barrett, *Gambling With History* (New York: Doubleday, 1983), 358.

38. Stockman, *Triumph of Politics*, 276–99; and Richard Stubbing, "The Defense Budget" in Mills and Palmer, *Federal Budget Policy*.

39. Stubbing, "Defense Budget," 101.

40. Heclo, "Executive Budget Making," 263–64.

41. Shelly Lynne Tompkin, "Playing Politics in OMB: Civil Servants Join the Game," *Presidential Studies Quarterly* 15, no. 1 (Winter 1985): 158–70; Hugh Heclo, "OMB and the Presidency—The Problem of Neutral Competency," *The Public Interest* 28 (Winter 1975): 89.

42. Bozeman and Straussman, "Shrinking Budgets," 509.

43. In addition to Schick, *Congress and Money*, LeLoup, *Fiscal Congress*, and Ippolito, *Congressional Spending*, see: John Ellwood and James Thurber, "The Politics of the Congressional Budget Process Reconsidered," in Lawrence Dodd and Bruce I. Oppenheimer *Congress Reconsidered*, (Washington D.C.: CQ Press, 1981), 246–75; Louis Fisher, "Ten Years of the Budget Act: Still Searching for Controls," *Public Budgeting and Finance* 5, no. 3 (Autumn 1985).

44. Kenneth Shepsle and Barry Weingast, "Legislative Politics and Budget Outcomes," in Mills and Palmer, *Federal Budget Policy*, 343–66.

45. R. Douglas Arnold, *Congress and the Bureaucracy* (New Haven, Conn.: Yale University Press, 1979); John Ellwood, "Comments on Shepsle and Weingast," in Mills and Palmer, *Federal Budget Policy* 368–78.

46. Douglas A. Hibbs, "Political Parties and Macroeconomic Policy," *American Political Science Review* 71 (December 1977): 1467–87; C. Duncan MacRae, "A Political Model of the Business Cycle," *Journal of Political Economy* 85: 239–63; Edward Tufte, *Political Control of the Economy*, (Princeton, N.J.: Princeton University Press, 1978).

47. D. Golden and J. Poterba, "The Price of Popularity: The Political Business Cycle Reexamined," *American Journal of Political Science* 24: 696–714; Michael Lewis-Beck and Tom Rice, "Government Growth in the United States," *Journal of Politics* (February 1985).

48. Naomi Caiden, "The Myth of the Annual Budget," *Public Administration Review* 42, no. 6 (November–December 1982): 516–23.

49. Ibid., 522.

50. Naomi Caiden, "The New Rules of the Federal Budget Game," *Public Administration Review* 44, no. 2 (March–April 1984): 109–17.

51. Schick, "Budget as an Instrument."

52. Allen Schick, "Controlling Nonconventional Expenditure: Tax Expenditures and Loans," *Public Budgeting and Finance* 6, no 1 (Spring 1986): 3–19.

53. Allen Schick, "Macro-Budgetary Adaptations to Fiscal Stress in Industrialized Democracies," *Public Administration Review* 46, no. 2 (March–April 1986): 124–34.

54. Ibid., 133.

55. Mark S. Kamlet and David C. Mowery, "The Budgetary Base in Federal Resource Allocation," *American Journal of Political Science* 24, (November

1980); "Budgetary Side-Payments and Government Growth: 1953–1968," *American Journal of Political Science* 27 (November 1983); "Influences on Executive and Congressional Budgetary Priorities, 1955–1981" *American Political Science Review* 81 no. 1 (March 1987): 155–78.

56. Kamlet and Mowrey, "Influences on Executive and Congressional Priorities;" 162.

57. LeLoup, "Myth of Incrementalism," 505.

58. Joseph White, "Much Ado About Everything: Making Sense of Federal Budgeting," *Public Administration Review* 45 no. 5 (September–October 1985): 623–30.

59. Bernard T. Pitsvada and Frank D. Draper, "Making Sense of the Federal Budget the Old Fashioned Way—Incrementally," *Public Administration Review* 44, no. 5 (September–October 1984): 401–06.

60. Ibid., 402.

61. Schick, "Budget as an Instrument."

62. Heclo, "Executive Budget Making."

Chapter 2
Shaping Things to Come Super-Budgeters as Heroes (and Heroines) in the Late-Twentieth Century

Naomi Caiden

Long ago, when people wanted to discern the shape of things to come, they looked to the stars; today they look at the budget. And they are right, because budgets represent choices made in the present that will determine and influence decisions of the future. Further, the processes through which budgets are made reflect the nature of politics and administration of the times, delineating and circumscribing the possibilities and constraints of societal action. Future historians will find budgets and budget processes rich sources for the discovery of fateful turning points, accumulating changes, the emergence of the new, and the waning of the old.

But without the benefit of their hindsight, we have much greater difficulty in projecting contemporary budget events and trends. The future may be shaped by the present, but we do not really understand the present, let alone the future. To relate cause and effect, to distinguish the significant from the trivial, to establish normative criteria for performance, to conceptualize changes still in progress—all these are subject to uncertainty and debate.

How might we characterize the nature of public budgeting in the last quarter of the twentieth century? And, what indicators are presently visible for future developments? The processes by which public authorities have raised revenues and allocated expenditures have not been static. In response to economic, social, and ideological changes, budget conceptions and practices have also changed. Expectations of budget functions have expanded, and budget institutions have adapted to meet them. Currently, perceptions of dysfunction dominate discussions of budget processes, and older concepts seem maladapted to contemporary circumstances. Budgets are now closely entwined with economic trends, and relationships are not fully understood. Budget processes are a primary focus for the resolution of societal conflicts. Budgets reflect the varied functions of governments and the ways they respond to public demands. They have become the focus of the crucial debate on the role of governments in contemporary society. In a word, budgeting has become super-budgeting. Small wonder that the original budget conception, first put into practice at national level in early nineteenth century Europe, has not been equal to these expanded expectations, and that it has undergone and is still undergoing transformation.

Great Expectations: The Development of Budget Purposes

Budgets are such a familiar piece of the governmental scenery that it is hard to imagine a world without them. But they emerged only at the beginning of the nineteenth century from a European prebudgetary environment that handled government finances through a diversified system of separate accounts and funds, often in private hands.[1] The system stressed private power and cash flow to the exclusion of public accountability, administrative control, and equitable taxation. It relied heavily upon a flow of diverse expedients, the mingling of private and public interests, and decentralized administration. It was constrained not only by the low level of technical development in accounting and communications but by the refusal of the head of state to share power. Accountable to no one, these monarchs could not enforce accountability to themselves. Fascinating as they are, the details need not concern us here: What is important is the length of time this system persisted, the extent to which it was accepted as normal and appropriate, and the fact that the more it was perfected, the further it moved from what are now regarded as basic norms of financial control, accountability, efficiency, and effectiveness. The better it became, the worse it became, until finally reform was implemented (initially in France with the restoration of the monarchy after the Napoleonic Wars).

Budgets radically transformed the handling of government finances. The main ideas were the advance assessment of the funds required by each agency, Legislative assent, control of the disbursement of monies, and audit to ensure that all expenditures were made legally and properly. Classical budgetary theory relied on the principles of annuality, unity, appropriation, and audit, which have formed a framework defining budget structure to this day. The difference made by this simple device was enormous: For the first time governments could actually see what they were doing, plan revenue and expenditure policies in advance, control and enforce financial decisions, and compare one year's totals with another. An example of the marvelous flexibility of the budget tool may be drawn from the second half of the nineteenth century in Britain, where it allowed cohesive revenue policies, successful economy campaigns (Gladstone's famous "cheese parings and candle-ends"), and annual debates focusing on incremental changes and based upon real knowledge of revenue yields, experience of past needs, and considerations of equity and efficiency.[2]

Actually, it has to be admitted that things did not really work all that well. René Stourm's classic *Le Budget* is full of chidings against European governments that one way or another failed to live up to budgetary principles.[3] From a later perspective it now seems clear that success in accomplishing the annual budget depended not only on the commitment and will of those involved but on a set of conditions that would not always be available. The system envisaged a hierarchical bureaucracy engaged in direct and fairly limited functions, whose scope and direction lay within its control. Despite legislative involvement, access to budgetary decisions was narrowed by constitutional limits and restricted franchise, while conflicts were lessened through broad agreement among cohesive parties. Predictability was enhanced by relative social and economic stability, and uncertainties were cushioned by economic growth, a rising level of prosperity, and expanding revenues. While undoubtedly serving a far broader set of interests than the prebudgetary system, and incorporating values of control, accountability, legitimacy, and regularity, budgeting also might have been regarded as in some sense an insulated, autonomous system. Introduce a war, a depression, a determined defense build up, even a modest pension scheme—and the whole system was likely to disintegrate into crisis; prolonged conflict, crisis management, and cash flow once again taking the place of deliberate annual decision making.

But the general idea of budgeting—advance appropriation, control and check of expenditures—was a strong enough foundation upon which to build further budgeting functions. In the early years of the twentieth century, the attainment of government efficiency through an "executive budget" was popularized, particularly in the United States.[4] Budget reformers conceived the United States federal budget as a work plan and financial program. Later administrative theorists saw the purpose of a budget system as providing in financial terms for planning, information, and control, establishing an integrated financial program in harmony with long-range and general economic policies.[5]

The major conceptual expansion of the purpose of national budgets came with the embracing of Keynesian economic theory. In the United States, the passage of the Employment Act of 1946 committed the federal government to the promotion of "maximum employment, production and purchasing power." The federal budget became the major mechanism through which this goal might be attained. Fiscal policy involved the manipulation of budgetary surpluses and deficits to influence the national economy so as to maintain full employment, stable prices, and economic growth. The purpose behind budgeting took a quantum leap from the financing of government activities to responsibility for national economic well being, based upon expert knowledge and advice.

Yet, even this was not the end of the story. Ideas of public responsibility for general social welfare stretch back many centuries, and piecemeal measures were already in place in various forms in many countries. In the twentieth century, these ideas crystallized into the conception of the welfare state, which embodied the conception of community responsibility for basic individual security, equalization of opportunity, public provision of standard amenities, and general enhancement of quality of life. The partial incorporation of such ideas into public policy in the United States in the 1960s also involved the concept of structural social change; in particular, racial equality, elimination of geographically related poverty, and revitalization of urban areas. Budgets were now concerned with program effectiveness, equity goals, and the achievement of public purposes.

A decade later, budgeting was called upon to make further adaptations. For many Western industrialized countries, the 1970s were watershed years, which marked revision of assumptions of unlimited growth and assured resources for public purposes. Constraints and uncertainties focused and sharpened budget conflicts, while entrenched budget commitments narrowed room for compromise and maneuver. Budgets appeared vulnerable to economic fluctuation and limited in their ability to adapt. The larger issues of the nature and extent of public revenue mobilization and the ends and means of public activities found expression in an expanded concept of budget capacity,[6] whose linked elements included the following:

> Planning: capacity to respond to long-term developments and make appropriate adaptations in the light of current projections of the future implications of present decisions;

> Flexibility: capacity to cope with short-term economic fluctuations, including capability to make viable economic assump-

tions and accurate predictions of budget performance, to monitor closely revenue and expenditure trends, and to take compensatory action;

Economic guidance: capacity to maintain economic stability while maximizing economic growth and minimizing inflation and unemployment;

Integration: capacity to control budget totals and make individual budgetary decisions consistent with their framework, as the basis for viable fiscal and economic policymaking;

Evaluation: capacity to evaluate and control highly dispersed activities, many of which are conducted outside the direct ambit of the federal bureaucracy.

It might be expected that, as demands upon budgeting expanded, processes would adapt to fulfill them. Normative theory supplied optimal techniques, many of which were incorporated into practice; but, on the whole, new purposes were not easily accommodated. For one thing, the sheer number and scope of these purposes seemed overwhelming, involving commitments to economic guidance, societal change, individual well being, program accomplishment, resolution of demands and priorities—quite apart from financial viability.[7] All these went well beyond mere procedural considerations. For another, the consistency of all these purposes was open to question. In particular, the demands for long-term commitment and short-term adaptation might appear difficult to achieve simultaneously. In addition, circumstances, to say the least, were not optimal: The times, it seemed, were "out of joint," baffling and entangling even the best of budgeters in their quest for the orderly planning and control that lie at the heart of successful budgeting. But, most of all, the very expansion of the budgetary role translated into substantive policies, practices, and procedures had unexpected consequences, transforming budgeting into "super-budgeting." Super-budgeting represented a response to the multidimensional demands upon public budgeting, but since wish is not accomplishment, super-budgets, too, have their own characteristics.

An Age of Super-Budgeting

While budget purposes expanded, budgeting in practice also developed. Some of these developments were internal, relating to greater analytical and managerial capacity. Others concerned the penetration of the public sector into larger areas of society and economy, increasing the

scope and variety of public budgets. But the major change lay in a shift
of emphasis from budgeting as process to budgeting as a system. It is this
transformed concept of budgeting that I have called *super-budgeting.*

The overriding characteristic of super-budgets is that they are integral parts of systems, which to a large measure structure their processes
and determine their outcomes. Super-budgeting in the last quarter of the
twentieth century is affected by multiple, interacting systems, which produce the rigidity, instability, and complexity so frequently referred to in
budgeting literature. Super-budgeters are successful insofar as they are
able to understand, adapt to, work within, or even master the dynamics
of those systems. I shall discuss their accommodations in the next section. First, I need to explore the nature of the systems affecting super-
budgeting and their consequences.

Super-budgets are conceived less as documents or even autonomous
processes than as systems, interacting with other systems. At their core
lies the fundamental revenue mobilization and expenditure function, but
they are also an integral part of other systems, including the intergovernmental system, the economic system, and the political-bureaucratic
system. To some extent, this always has been true of any public financial
administration, even in prebudgetary systems, such as that of pre-
Revolutionary France. What converts budgeting to super-budgeting is
the degree of integration of these systems and their direct and immediate
impact upon budgetary decision-making processes and outcomes.

Budgeting is more than technique. Budgets express societal decisions
regarding the levels and sources of public revenue mobilization and the
purposes supported by public expenditures. Where these decisions are
more or less settled, they may become "non-decisions";[8] or changes may
be accommodated incrementally;[9] or there may be agreement for
automatic processes to take over, such as automatic indexing or bracket
creep.[10] But, where there is serious dissension, budgeting has to include
overt revenue policies: Arguments about efficiency and equity become
integral parts of the decision-making process. Budgetary discussions
come to incorporate the philosophical values of what should be financed
publicly, and at what level. Budgeting becomes super-budgeting, whose
primary concern is who should benefit and who should pay.

As Keynesian economics has taught us, such decisions are not whol-
ly autonomous. The balance between revenues and expenditures in
economic systems where public expenditures represent over one-third of
gross national product has a large impact on the level of national
economic activity. Revenue policies help determine incentives; expenditure policies subsidize some activities, create employment, and support
large public works systems benefiting the private sector. Conversely,

economics also determines budgets: Economic cycles and fluctuations directly affect revenue yields, and many expenditures are tied to both national and international economic conditions. Where determination of budget outcomes is tied closely to behavior of the economic system, budgeters must become super-budgeters to stay ahead of the game. Where governments do less and influence more, super-budgeters are concerned with the indirect as well as the direct effects of their decisions.

Super-budgeters work within organizations but, to a considerable extent, they are concerned with what goes on in other organizations at different levels of government. Phone any local government policy maker in the United States and the odds are you will find that he or she is in Washington, or Sacramento, or Albany! Intergovernmental money and mandates are an important part of financing any government function, and their ramifications go beyond the actual sums received to encompass questions of control, effectiveness, and prediction. Super-budgeters learn to operate in a complex intergovernmental system, where actions in one area produce reverberations through the whole.

Finally, just as budgets are by definition "political things," super-budgets are politicized budgets, through which private and public interests vie to attain their goals. Super-budgets are distributive and redistributive budgets, the focus of bureau-political processes that define the formal and informal rules by which decisions are made. The sharper the conflicts, the more that fundamental questions have to be resolved, the greater the access to the budget process; and the less defined the rules, the more vulnerable is the budget system to breakdown and disintegration. Super-budgeters act upon a political stage, according to political incentives and sanctions.

Of course, there is no sharp line at which budgeting is transformed into super-budgeting. Rather, we may envisage a continuum from a point where a budgeter works in a relatively autonomous manner, within definable boundaries and according to settled rules, to a situation where the super-budgeter operates as an integral element of multiple, interacting systems directly affecting decision making, where concerns lie as much outside as inside the organization and where basic issues have to be resolved as part of the budget process.

The characteristics of super-budgeting in Western industrialized countries have become familiar. They follow directly from pursuit of the enhanced goals of budgeting. Because of entrenched commitments, budgets tend to be rigid and policy adjustments are difficult to make. The close relationship with national and local economies also entails a high degree of instability. The scope and variety of government activities makes for a complexity in operations.

The rigidity of super-budgets is a much mentioned feature of contemporary governments. The United States budget, in which over three-quarters of the expenditures are counted as "relatively uncontrollable," is a case in point. These expenditures represent what Ysander and Robinson have called "a rather rigid system of commitments and responsibilities with little leeway for intramarginal adjustments and reorientations."[11] They consist of payments resulting from past decisions, including individual entitlements, contracts and grants, and interest payments, all of which are difficult to control in the short term.

Super-budgets are rigid in other ways, too. Richard Rose has drawn attention to the role of inertia in decision making on taxes.[12] Others, such as Mancur Olson, have noted the tendency of vested interests to deadlock politically to prevent changes in the status quo: The more open the budget system to established interests, the more likely may be political stalemate.[13]

Yet, the sources of rigidity are also those of stability, allowing, as Allen Schick has pointed out, individuals, corporations, and governments to depend on commitments and make plans.[14] But, paradoxically, super-budgets are also unstable budgets, their instability stemming from the identical factors that produce rigidity. In seeking to master the economy, super-budgeters often find themselves its victims. The behavior of many budget variables, such as unemployment payments, benefits indexed to the cost of living, and revenues, is related directly to that of the economy as a whole. Super-budgets are sensitive, and a volatile economy produces volatile budget figures, which are difficult to predict. The levels of revenues, expenditures, and deficits are dependent on assumptions, whose accuracy is often open to question. At worst, figures become political numbers that seem to fly off the page even as the budgeter (let alone the citizen) tries to grasp their derivation and significance. At best, they may be problematic guesstimates, verifiable only with hindsight.

Budgetary instability also goes beyond the economic dimension. Political stalemates, polarization, and interest group fragmentation prevent formation of stable majorities. Passage of super-budgets often depends on shifting coalitions, each of which has to be put together painstakingly to support carefully crafted packages. The regular cycles that were a hallmark of budget processes are now subject to disruptions and delays, and the next fiscal year often rolls around without resolution of the previous year's issues.

Finally, super-budgets are complex and are not easily described as a single type. Some of the complexity arises from the varied financial measures used by contemporary governments that no longer rely on direct expenditures to achieve their goals.[15] Loans and loan guarantees, tax expenditures or tax preferences, and regulatory actions form a body of "nonconventional" expenditures that do not lend themselves to counting let alone controlling through conventional budget means. The exigencies of government borrowing and cash flow management form an arcane area on their own. In addition, the super-budget system as a whole is characterized by a very wide variety of budgets rarely recognized by the budget literature, which commonly deals with only national and city budgets. In the United States, for example, there are county budgets closely controlled in form by state governments and characterized by a large proportion of "pass through" funding; public enterprise budgets that are largely self-sustaining in nature; contract budgets based on fixed fee for service or reimbursement; intergovernmental arrangements; and a variety of public-private partnerships. All these have their own structures and dynamics to be mastered by the super-budgeters.

By this point, the reader will wonder why I have omitted what appears as the most salient characteristic of contemporary public budgeting—ubiquitous revenue constraints forcing cutbacks at all levels of government. It is true that many of the features related in the preceding paragraphs have emerged in response to pressures for subtraction in many systems accustomed to addition (although not all areas of public budgeting have suffered from revenue constraints, which in any case, are a relative concept). But, I also would argue that these features lay, as it were, below the surface, masked by what Aaron Wildavsky and I elsewhere have referred to as a complex functional redundancy that acted to cushion uncertainties, smooth compromises, obviate unpleasant decisions, and in general, keep things running.[16] With its disappearance, underlying problems were starkly revealed, and super-budgeters found they had to invent new procedures, strategies, and tactics to enable change, provide stability, and simplify intolerable complexities.

Shaping Things to Come

Super-budgeters do not sit idly by, enduring "the slings and arrows of outrageous fortune." Temperamentally, they are more inclined to "take arms against a sea of troubles," but since the environments within which they work are not uniform, it is difficult to summarize their tactics and strategies. Many of their practices are incorporated in current texts that stress analytical techniques and control systems, but others have only slowly become apparent. The following trends, which have been gleaned from the literature and conversations with super-budgeters, may be taken as representative, though not comprehensive or universal, reactions to their predicament.

Formulas

The use of formulas in budgeting is not new.[17] Tax rates may be regarded as formulas, for example. Formulas represent the application of a single standard, such as a percentage, to a variety of given circumstances. Their purposes are many and increasing. They may be used for distributive purposes, determining eligibility of receivers of payments and the amount they are paid, as in individual entitlements. They also may be used as targeting instruments, to calculate need or hardship, as in the use of revenue sharing and other federal grant instruments.

Formulas are employed for allocative purposes, too. A common use is to assume a projected rate of inflation and factor this automatically into budget projections, where it becomes part of the "base" for argument and negotiation. Another is to devise a set of relationships based upon a single standard budget unit, for example, full-time equivalent faculty or students in educational administration: The growth or decline in the aggregate unit then "derives" a variety of subsequent budget figures, such as staffing, overheads, equipment, or space. In this way, formulas easily become management tools, as responsibility centers within organizations are allocated formula performance targets, which are used as surrogates for efficiency and effectiveness. Similarly, formulas may become negotiating instruments, used not only for "costing out" exercises but as a facet of a "sideways" view of the budget concentration on aggregates rather than programs.[18] Finally, formulas may be used as constitutional limits on expenditures and taxes, as they have been in many states and localities as the result of popular initiative. The archetypical formula, of course, is the Gramm-Rudman-Hollings Act, which seeks to reduce the entire United States federal budget to formula!

The popularity of formulas in conditions of high complexity and politicization is not difficult to understand. Formulas provide simple and stable decision rules for complex and variable situations. They resolve problems of priorities without constantly reopening conflicts and reduce political problems to technical vocabulary. Formulas are super-tools for super-budgeters; moreover, they are easily converted to use with computers.

Recreating Redundancy

"We live," one local budget official told me recently, "by the increment." Of course, he is one of the lucky ones. As long-term com-

mitments crowd out new possibilities and projected expenditures appear
to outrun feasible expected revenues, cutbacks are the order of the day in
many jurisdictions, but super-budgeters generally hate cutbacks and
strive to recreate redundancy. Whether quickly or slowly, most budgets
grow from year to year and the challenge usually is met. In a recent class
exercise in which students were asked to simulate the following year's
budgets on the basis of interviews with local budget officials, virtually all
discovered sources of redundancy. One common device was the imposition of "salary savings," usable throughout the year for contingencies.
Another was the imposition of fees to cover shortfalls and even provide
for future projected operational deficits. The optimal handling of cash
flow was also crucial, while redundancy was additionally created by projections, such as those for inflation, built into the budget. Further opportunities for creating redundancy arise from the complexities of debt
management and manipulation of revenue bonds.[19] Obviously, where
budgeters find themselves prey to outside forces, from systems beyond
their control, they need to find redundancy to defend themselves against
uncertainties and maintain stability in operation.

Privatization

Much has been written about the privatization of government activities, particularly about the contracting with private companies for
public functions and the imposition of service fees upon citizens. But
these do not really encompass the extent to which public organizations
now see themselves as operating in quasi-markets, and super-budgeters
have become public entrepreneurs. Within organizations, it has become
increasingly common to "allocate" costs to subunits or expect them to
shoulder a certain proportion of workload according to some efficiency
ranking. The effect is to create a market within the organization in which
areas that "pay their way" are favored with resources over those that do
not. External private contract bids are used as standards for cost estimation, on a pure efficiency basis. The cost of services is expected more and
more to be covered by fees. The recent financial statement of a large
county listed more than thirty different service fees, the yield of many of
which was projected to increase by as much as 50 percent in the following year. In similar vein, the United States Customs Service recently announced a $5 fee for customs inspection of arriving passengers.

Super-budgeters' interests extend beyond simply financing services.
They also are concerned with revenue bases, which means the economic
development of their jurisdictions' areas. They, thus, are deeply involved
in the raising of bond revenues for a variety of purposes including shop-
ping and auto malls, residential developments, and the attraction of

commercial and industrial enterprise generally. The mingling of public and private sectors reinforces their interdependence and the extent to which public organizations increasingly behave as market organizations.

Financial Management

Recent budgeting texts record the extent to which budgeting has become financial management. Whereas, previously, stress was on processes of resource allocation and budget execution went virtually unmentioned, now the emphasis has been almost reversed. As many as half the chapters of typical texts are concerned with such topics as auditing, risk management, cash flow, debt management, fiscal impact analysis, and revenue and expenditure analysis. On a more general level, observers of the federal government report that more and more policies are being initiated and implemented on an administrative level.[20] From a budgeting perspective it appears that budgetary policy, in many cases has been moved downward to the more technical level of what Herbert Kaufman has called "neutral competence."[21] It is as if, in reaction to the buffeting of interdependence, super-budgeters have moved to protect their core and to convert their organizations to self-sustaining systems, rugged enough to endure policital storms, economic exigencies, and the shocks administered by contiguous systems beyond their control.

These strategies and practices by no means include all those resorted to by super-budgeters, of whom the variety of their situations is a characteristic feature. In general, their reactions have been to modify rigidity to provide room for change, gain stability and simplify complexity. They try to reduce their vulnerability to the impact of systems beyond their control, even as they attempt to understand them and work within them. How else would we expect them to behave? Like the best of heroes and heroines, they rise to adversity, and should we find room for criticism, do we not all share blame for the world we have created for them? But, as historians of the future, we need to go one step further and, transcending the feats of individuals, inquire into the consequences of their actions and the implications of super-budgeting for budget capacity.

Forward or Backward

In the eighteenth century age of enlightenment, people were fond of asking whether things had become better or worse, and from such questioning emerged the idea of progress. Our analysis has moved from prebudgeting to budgeting to super-budgeting. Each of these modes of organizing government finances in some way was related to its environment but also incorporated dysfunctions that, gradually or suddenly, contributed to its supersession. Does super-budgeting represent progress or is it an aberration leading to a dead end? Is it a genuine development or a retrogression?

To gain some perspective, it may be helpful to employ part of a model I used previously to explain distinctions among historical patterns of budgeting.[22] Employing three variables, it was possible to extrapolate nine different patterns of budgeting that corresponded to actual historical types. Of particular interest are the two patterns labeled here *prebudgetary* and *budgetary*. The former, prevalent in absolutist European monarchies, succeeded in raising relatively large amounts of revenue, despite low accountability and administrative control. The latter achieved accountability through bureaucratic processes and structures answerable directly or indirectly to legitimately constituted legislatures. I also suggested that at some time a third kind of budgeting might emerge, characterized by high revenue mobilization and high accountability, achieved by some means different from the bureaucratic processes upon which these currently depended. This third type might correspond to super-budgeting. Schematically, the patterns might be represented in Figure 2-1.

	Revenue Mobilization	Accountability	Administrative Control
Prebudgeting	High	Low	Low
Budgeting	High	High	High
Super-budgeting	High	High	Low

Figure 2-1. *Patterns of Budgeting.*

Classical budgeting achieved accountability through administrative control; i.e., hierarchical, bureaucratic organization. It was based on the confining principles of annuality, unity, appropriation, and audit, which were sufficient to control financial administration where the aim was accountability and the functions of revenue collection and disbursement were carried out directly by the same controlling authority. In the twentieth century, these principles came to be breached more often than observed, the purposes of budgeting expanded, and budgeting in any one organization became highly dependent on external developments beyond bureaucratic control. The key question is whether a new form of

accountability, not dependent on that control, has developed or is
emerging. There are two interpretations: one optimistic; one pessimistic.

The optimistic interpretation sees public budgeting in a decentralized mode, taking ideas of public choice as its general guide.[23] According
to this view, big government, legitimated in large part by the idea of centralized responsibility, has failed. In its place has arisen a variety of arrangements that rely either on direct democratic voting measures or
quasi-market solutions to the question of what public services should be
provided and at what cost. Bureaucracies are dissolved into a series of
contracts with private or not-for-profit organizations, on the one hand,
and a series of technocratic expert functions (e.g., cash management, risk
management), on the other. Even the largest units, such as the federal
government, would tend to shed functions and to exercise others in a
diversified fashion, dividing up its budget into discrete sections (e.g.,
social security, defense) that would run on a more or less automatic
course controlled through periodic political interventions to ensure adaptations to new circumstances. Applications of new information management techniques obviate the need for bureaucratic centralization as a
means of budget control. Current dysfunctions represent a transition to
this new mode of public budgeting more adapted to postindustrial conditions.

A more pessimistic interpretation would be that the loss of administrative control represents a retrogression to the prebudgetary situation. Revenue mobilization remains high, but it is achieved in the face of
sullen resistance from the tax payers and raised in a complex, indirect,
and regressive manner. Budgets are fragmented into a wide variety of
separate accounts and funds, over which there is little or no control.
Caught in a vice between spiraling demands for expenditures and concessions on all sides and inadequate revenue bases, authorities turn to expedients, juggling cash flow, short-term and long-term debt, and a maze of
fees and charges. Policy decision to influence events is impossible, so that
public expenditures serve private purposes at the expense of public
needs. Public and private interests are commingled with inevitable opportunities for systemic corruption. Budgeting is reduced to a desperate
struggle to maintain financial viability, and the capacity to achieve any
of its expanded functions is limited, together with the loss of accountability upon which they were originally built.

Future historians, like super-budgeters, hedge their bets. I leave the
reader to come to his or her own conclusions. Our present perspective is
a limited one that will enlarge only with the passage of time. But, the
future is shaped by the ideas, decisions, and actions of the present: To
the extent that we can try to understand the developments of our times,

the greater are the chances that we might discern the outlines of that future.

Notes

1. For a description of prebudgeting in Europe, see Naomi Caiden, "Patterns of Budgeting: The Experience of France 987-1830, (Ph.D. diss., School of Public Administration, University of Southern California, 1978); Naomi Caiden, "Negative Financial Management: A Backward Look at Fiscal Stress" in *Fiscal Stress and Public Policy*, Charles Levine and Irene Rubin, eds., (Beverly Hills, Calif.: Sage, 1980): 135-158; Naomi Caiden, "Patterns of Budgeting," *Public Administration Review* 38, (November-December 1978): 539-44.

2. See Naomi Caiden, "The Financial Revolution: The Transformation of Public Resource Mobilization Capacity in Major European States in the Nineteenth Century" (unpublished ms., Los Angeles, 1981).

3. René Stourm, *The Budget* (New York: D. Appleton, 1917).

4. William Willoughby, *The Problem of a National Budget* (New York: D. Appleton, 1918), 132.

5. "Report of the President's Committee on Administrative Management," *Public Budgeting and Finance* 1 (Spring 1981): 85.

6. Naomi Caiden, "The Capacity to Budget: Adaptations in the Federal Budget Process of the United States of America," completed for the Organization for Economic Cooperation and Development Study on the Capacity to Budget, 1984, 2.

7. Aaron Wildavsky, "A Budget for All Seasons: Why the Traditional Budget Lasts," *Public Administration Review* 28 (November-December 1978): 501-09.

8. Allen Schick, *Congress and Money* (Washington, D.C.: Urban Institute, 1980): 338.

9. Aaron Wildavsky, *The Politics of the Budgetary Process*, 4th ed. (Boston: Little, Brown & Co., 1985).

10. Naomi Caiden, "The Politics of Subtraction" in *Making Economic Policy in Congress*, Allen Schick, ed. (Washington, D.C.: American Enterprise Institute, 1984): 103.

11. Bengt-Christer Ysander and Ann Robinson, "The Inflexibility of Contemporary Budgets," *Public Budgeting and Finance* 2 (Autumn 1982): 7.

12. Richard Rose, "Maximizing Tax Revenue While Minimizing Political Costs," *Journal of Public Policy* 5, Part 3 (August 1985): 289-320.

13. Mancur Olson, *The Rise and Decline of Nations; Economic Growth, Stagflation and Social Rigidities* (Cambridge, Mass.: Harvard University Press, 1983).

14. Allen Schick, *Congress and Money*, 572.

15. Allen Schick, "Controlling Nonconventional Expenditure: Tax Expenditures and Loans," *Public Budgeting and Finance* 6 (Spring 1986): 3–19. Aaron Wildavsky, "Keeping Kosher: The Epistemology of Tax Expenditures," *Journal of Public Policy* 5, Part 3 (August 1985): 413–31.

16. Naomi Caiden and Aaron Wildavsky, *Planning and Budgeting in Poor Countries* (New Brunswick, N.J.: Transaction Books, 1980): 45–65.

17. See also Naomi Caiden, "The New Rules of the Federal Budget Game," *Public Administration Review* (March–April 1984): 100–30.

18. Robert Bailey, *The Crisis Regime; The MAC, the EFCB, and the Political Impact of the New York City Financial Crisis* (Albany, N.Y.: SUNY Press, 1984).

19. Naomi Caiden and Jeffrey Chapman, "Constraint and Uncertainty: Budgeting in California," *Public Budgeting and Finance* 2 (Winter 1982): 111–29.

20. Richard Nathan, *The Administrative Presidency* (New York: John Wiley, 1983).

21. Herbert Kaufman, "Administrative Decentralization and Political Power," *Public Administration Review* 29 (January–February 1969): 3–15.

22. Naomi Caiden, "Patterns of Budgeting."

23. See Elinor Ostrom and Vincent Ostrom, "Public Choice: A Different Approach to the Study of Public Administration," *Public Administration Review* (March–April 1971): 302–16.

Chapter 3
An Inquiry into the Possibility of a Budgetary Theory

ALLEN SCHICK

Political science has been vexed by the lack of a budgetary theory ever since V.O. Key noted this gap in his famous 1940 article.[1] In the ensuing half century, a vast accumulation of data, hypotheses, explanations, and case studies has been amassed. Much more is known about the conduct of budgeting than earlier, and a multiplicity of theories vie for scholarly attention and statistical support. But, there still is no theory of budgeting that fits diverse political settings and economic conditions. One scholar has recently suggested that "in this field, theory is most appropriately stated in the negative. . . . The issues and alternatives confronted in public budgeting lack a common denominator."[2]

This paper makes one more try at a theory of budgeting. As an inquiry into the possibility of a theory, the paper explores how such a theory might be constructed. It offers the building blocks of a theory and a few hypotheses, not a complete construct or testable propositions. Whether these elements can be assembled into a theory is a matter to be determined empirically, by the uses to which they are put.

Why Previous Efforts Failed

The approach taken in this paper diverges from previous efforts to devise a theory of budgeting in three important ways: (1) It seeks an empirical rather than a normative theory; (2) it seeks a theory that pertains specifically to budgeting rather than to more general social behavior; and (3) it focuses on generic characteristics of budgeting, not on ancillary features.

Normative or Empirical Theory?

Key and others have sought a normative theory that, in his words, would answer the question: "On what basis shall it be decided to allocate x dollars to activity A instead of activity B?"[3] This question is not for budgeting to answer, however, for it depends on the core values of politics. A theory that determines which allocations should be made would have to be a theory that allocates power and other political values as well. Key recognized the futility of seeking a normative theory by concluding that "the most advantageous utilization of public funds resolves itself into a matter of value preferences between ends lacking a common denominator. As such, the question is a problem in political philosophy."[4]

Nevertheless, the quest for a normative theory has continued in each of the three main fields in which budgeting functions: public administration, economics, and political science. Since its emergence as a distinctive field a century ago, public administration has sought the "one best way" to perform budgeting and other administrative activities.[5] The long parade of budgetary reforms—performance budgeting, program budgeting, planning-programming-budgeting, and zero-base budgeting—attests to the normative inclinations of public administration. But, the disappointing results of these reforms suggests that the norms underlying them are incompatible with broader political values.[6]

Economics masks its normative tendencies in quantitative method. Cost-benefit analysis, the most prominent application of economic theory to budgetary choice, has efficiency as its core value, but efficiency cannot be a sufficient basis for budgetary allocation. Cost-benefit analysis answers Key's question in the easy cases, when (as often occurs) efficiency is consonant with political values. In the hard cases, when values collide, efficiency is not an adequate guide for allocation.

Political science has diverse normative tendencies, but its concept of budgeting has been most strongly influenced by pluralist values. These values are rooted in the rules rather than the results of politics: If the process is right—usually taken to mean group and party competition—then the allocations flowing from it also are deemed to be the right ones. This approach has the big advantage of obviating the need for substantive norms to determine budget outcomes. Process as the value has been vigorously advocated by Aaron Wildavsky, whose theory of incrementalism is both a statement of how budgeting works and a prescription for how the process should work.[7] Incrementalism combines value judgment and description, so that its normative facets sometimes are assumed to be validated if observed behavior conforms to the descriptive theory. But incrementalism's hold on budgeting has stemmed more from its normative claims than its factual basis. Wildavsky argues that an incremental process is to be valued because it moderates conflict, reduces search and transaction costs, stabilizes budgetary roles and expectations, reduces the amount of time that busy officials must spend on budgeting, and facilitates remedial action to correct mistakes. These "goods" are not the only ones that might be valued in budgeting. The process that has these qualities also favors old claims over new ones, reinforces unequal distributions of private power and public money, and has the characteristic biases and shortcomings of pluralism. If one were to assess budgeting's substantive outcomes, rather than just the process by which allocations are made, incrementalism might be found wanting. Even if descriptive incrementalism were confirmed by the evidence, normative incrementalism would still be open to challenge by alternative value structures.

The fact that each of these fields invests budgeting with its own values has important implications for budgetary theory. Budgeting is not so much a field in its own right as a subset of more general social disciplines.[8] Each field views budgeting through distinctive norms. From his normative perspective, Wildavsky can claim that "the 'study of budgeting' is just another expression for the 'study of politics.' "[9] The problem is that the same can be claimed of all the values attributed to budgeting. There is an economic theory of budgeting and an administrative theory, as well as less well-developed theories grounded in other social disciplines. Normatively, the paucity of budgetary theory arises out of the pluralism of budgetary theories.

For a theory of budgeting to be common to a multiplicity of fields, it must be stated in descriptive terms. It must transform Key's question into On what basis is it decided to allocate x dollars to activity A instead of activity B? Even so, each discipline will add its particular perspective and define this question in terms indigenous to it. Several fields can, despite their differences, share the elements of a budget theory, but each combines the elements, and considers other features, in ways that comport with its peculiar method(s) of inquiry. Beyond the elements, the political theory of budgeting will differ from the economic or administrative theory.

Special Theory

An elemental theory would have to explain budgeting in terms that are peculiar to it; otherwise, the elements would not be inherent to budgeting but would belong to some other, more general class of behavior. And that more general behavior would not fit all the fields in which budgeting can be said to operate.

This condition rules out descriptive incrementalism as a theoretical basis of budgeting. The essential features of incrementalism—stable behavior, gradual change, actions based mostly on past decisions, and limited search for alternatives—characterizes most continuing social behavior. Most individuals live their personal and professional lives incrementally; so, too, do most firms and other organizations. It is a rare Albert Schweitzer who in midlife leaps from music to medicine, from the conservatory to the jungle. For most firms, next year's products and markets are this year's plus or minus a few.

If all one knew of budgeting was that it is incremental, one would know little indeed. Incrementalsm says more about what budgeting is not than about what it is. It tells us that budget makers do not reexamine each item each year nor do they canvass all possible options or compare all programs against one another in a competition for public funds. Much of what is known about incrementalism comes from statistical studies of budgeting. Because budget increments are easy to measure, over the past two decades, a small army of quantifiers has correlated changes in budget requests, appropriations, and other budgetary inputs or outputs with all sorts of political and economic conditions. But these studies have yielded little knowledge concerning the size and distribution of increments; why some programs get more than others; and why budget shares change over time.

To understand how budgeting works, one must have a theory more specific than incrementalism that begins with the distinctive features of budgeting not with broader social behavior.

Basic Theory

Over the decades, budgeting has accumulated uses and practices that are not essential, though they have become closely identified with it. Through many years of accretion, various administrative and political uses have been added to budgeting, probably to take advantage of its action-forcing potency and its command of the public purse. As a result, budgeting has become a leveraged process, in which the essential functions are sometimes seen as subordinate to other ends. At one time or another, budgeting has been used to plan government programs and objectives, manage agencies and coordinate their activities, steer the economy and redistribute income, evaluate performance, and prevent illegal or imprudent expenditure. Some of these features were examined by me nearly two decades ago in an article analyzing the development of budgeting in the United States.[10] These features are among budgeting's most conspicuous activities and the ones reformers usually concentrate on when they seek to improve the process. Although these ancillary characteristics often are quite useful, budgeting can exist without them, and concentrating on them impedes theory building. Because these features vary with time and place, budgeting has not always been used for economic management and is not used everywhere for program planning, they cannot be the basis for a general theory of budgeting. If one wishes to study how budgeting is conducted in a particular government, it is necessary to take into account the various activities and purposes linked to it. But, to build a generic theory, one must first strip away the nonessential characteristics, until all that are left are the irreducible elements found in every budget system.

The Elements of Budgeting

We begin, therefore, by identifying the smallest number of actions that can be said to constitute budgeting, wherever it is conducted. It can be observed that budgeting always entails a request for funds and an allocation of funds. Budgeting, thus, has at least two basic elements: claiming and allocating resources. Budgeting does not occur in the absence of either of these functions; it might occur if these were the only processes at work. Claiming and allocating resources take place both when expenditures are being increased and when they are being cut back. They occur in big governments with complex budget systems and in small governments with simple processes. Claiming and allocating are performed by rich and poor countries, in mature democracies as well as in less democratic countries and socialist regimes.

Budgeting is usually thought of as a process for claiming and allocating money, but any physical resource in scarce supply can be allocated by means of the budget. In World War II, for example, the U.S. government utilized a budget process, which was a precursor of program budgeting introduced after the war, for allocating strategic materials and production capacity. Narrowing the concept of budgeting to material resources distinguishes it from other processes in which nonphysical resources are claimed and allocated. Social systems allocate status, legal systems allocate rights, political systems allocate power. Each of these allocations can exert a strong influence on budgetary outcomes. But, if budgeting were defined broadly to encompass these and other non-material values, it would lose its distinctiveness, and a theory of budgeting would not be possible.

The concept of budgeting has to be narrowed in yet another way. Budgeting is not the only means by which money and other material resources are claimed and allocated. Markets perform these functions, as do other social relationships. What distinguishes budgeting is that resources are claimed and allocated according to rules and procedures established for this purpose. Budgeting is the process that prescribes how, when, and by whom claims are to be made and resources distributed. Take away this process and budgeting does not exist in the sense that it is commonly understood. The rules do not have to spell out every procedure, nor do they have to deal with substantive matters, but they have to be sufficiently formed as to constitute a process. In contrast to budgeting, markets lack allocative rules; exchanges are made solely according to the consent of participants.[11] Claims and allocations also are made by war, other acts of violence, threats, ad hoc decisions, and other exchanges that are differentiated from budgeting by the absence of process.

The fact that budgeting's core characteristics—claiming and allocating resources—are found where there is no budget process suggests that formulation of a budgetary theory is likely to be a difficult, if not impossible task. In specifying process as one of budgeting's defining elements, one comes perilously close to arguing that budgeting is whatever it is deemed to be.

Claiming is the easier of the basic functions to identify and label. A budget claim is any request for resources made according to the rules and procedures of the process. Claims are typically submitted by administrative agencies, but the process can provide for them to be presented through other channels as well. However, there have to be claims for there to be a budget; if no one wants money, there is no need to allocate it through a budgetary process.

The second function arises out of a common, perhaps universal, characteristic of budget claims: They add up to more than is available. Budgeting would not exist if all claims were satisfied; asking for resources would suffice for getting them. If, on the other hand, no claims were satisfied, there also would be no budget process. Budgeting can occur at any point between these extremes, that is, whenever some—but not all—claims are satisfied. This is a rather common occurrence, which is why budgeting is such a widespread practice.

The fact that some claims are denied and others approved suggests an additional activity between the claiming and allocation of resources. The activity that intervenes between claims and allocations and leads to partial satisfaction of claims is something other than full rejection or approval. For want of a better term, this activity is labeled here *conserving*.

In the conserving function, productive claims are not opposed, but other ones are. What is a good claim is mostly a matter of judgment, which is exactly what occurs in the process of budgeting.

Claiming and conserving are generic functions, separable from the particular roles of budget participants. Spending agencies usually behave as claimants, but most have procedures to conserve the resources available to them. Agencies often reject some claims made by their subdivisions or by outsiders. Thus, the same agency is sometimes a claimant and sometimes a conserver. Similarly, the central budget office has a lead role in conserving resources, but it occasionally serves as a claimant for uses that it favors. It is not uncommon for the budget office to argue that some programs should be given more funds than have been requested.

The interaction of claiming and conserving activities in the budget process emanates in allocations that approve some claims and not others. The allocations, thus, are usually in the form of rations: They are limited in amount. (An important question in development of a budgetary theory pertains to open-ended allocations, such as expenditures in time of war or emergency or for entitlements.) Rationing is necessitated by the fact that claims exceed resources, the ubiquitous condition of budgeting.

Linking and Using the Elements

Of what use is the understanding that budgeting consists of conserving and claiming activities, conducted according to rules and procedures, which emanate in rations? Not very much, unless we can specify the relationship between claiming and conserving on the one hand and rations on the other.

This might be an impossible task, for budgeting is open to all the influences, conditions, and subtleties of political, economic, and social behavior. Just about anything can affect the vigor, skill, and success with which resources are claimed and conserved. A theory of budgeting that accounts for everything that affects the critical functions of budgeting would have to reach far beyond the budget process itself to much of the human condition.

One way out of this difficulty might be to consider how economics deals with a parallel problem in explaining market behavior. Both markets and budgets ration resources, the former by means of prices, the latter through authoritative decisions. In both, rationing is the result of interaction among contending forces: supply and demand in markets, claiming and conserving in budgets. Markets, no less than budget processes, are open systems, affected by all of life's influences on the volume and variety of supply and demand. Economists cut through the complications of the market by working back from its results. Without understanding all the factors that motivate people and organizations to produce and consume, they reason that in perfect markets, prices accurately and efficiently reflect the balance between supply and demand. Economists also know that real markets are not perfect, and they have developed a plethora of theories and gathered considerable data on how people behave under different market conditions. The fact that they still do not understand much about the working of the market—a fact demonstrated by contemporary disputes between supplysiders and demand managers—has not barred economists from making good use of the bits and pieces of theory and data that they have.

Development of a budgetary theory along the lines pursued in market economics suggests a number of propositions that might merit further consideration.

> *Proposition 1.* In a perfect budget process, rations reflect the balance between claims and conservation. Anything that alters the relative strength of these functions will change budget outcomes.

Many input-output analyses and other statistical studies of budget outcomes are predicated on the assumption that changes in the strength of claims and conservation affect budget decisions. The political changes that have been examined for their effects on budget results include election cycles and results, shifts in public opinion, and differences between Democrats and Republicans. These political changes influence budget decisions by strengthening or weakening claimants and conservers.

> *Proposition 2.* Stronger claims receive larger allocations than weaker ones. As a result, the budget shares of claimants change over time.

This proposition also underlies much budgetary theory and research. Incrementalism, for example, is a condition in which older claims are stronger than new ones, and therefore they get a larger share of budget allocations.

> *Proposition 3.* The process of budgeting affects the relative strength of the claiming and conserving functions; changes in the process intentionally or unintentionally alter their relative strength and thereby change budget allocations.

Claiming and conserving are carried out according to the rules and procedures of the budget process. These are not neutral but affect the relative strength of budgeting's two essential functions. The process can strengthen or weaken claims and make it easier or harder to conserve resources. In so doing, it inevitably affects budget outcomes. During the postwar era of government growth, for example, budgeting in the United States and elsewhere was modified to strengthen claims. The changes included a reorientation from inputs to outputs, emphasis on plans and programs, and the development of multiyear budgets. In recent years, the adjustments made to strengthen the conserving functions have included across the board cuts and other cutback tactics, reinstitution of inputs controls, and a reorientation of multiyear budgets from plans to projections.

In assessing process changes, it is important to keep in mind that these are often made for reasons not directly related to budgeting's claiming and conserving functions. It has been noted that over the years budgeting has taken on a number of ancillary functions, and these, rather than the claiming and conserving aspects, might be the object of change. Moreover, the effects of process on budget outcomes may not always turn out as intended.

> *Proposition 4.* A budget process is imperfect if allocations fail to reflect the relative strength of claiming and conserving. Allocations can be above the level necessary to balance these functions because of *sticky expenditure* (a concept adapted from "sticky prices" in economics).

The possibility that budget allocations might not reflect the relative strength of the claiming and conserving functions is suggested by two related conditions in contemporary budgeting. One is the growth and intractability of what has been labeled (or mislabeled) "uncontrollable" spending for entitlements and other items. The other has been the continuing rise of government spending in the face of seemingly strong efforts to curtail expenditures. This has happened in the United States where, despite Ronald Reagan's professed commitment to decrease the federal government, national expenditure claims a higher share of GNP than it did in 1981, when he entered office. It could be that the spending trend reflects the fact that (1) claims on expenditure continue to be strong and/or (2) that the conserving function is weaker than White House rhetoric suggests. Nevertheless, a theory of budgeting has to make room for imperfections in the process which lead to allocations that are at variance with the balance between claiming and conserving.

The Possibility of Budgetary Theory

This inquiry was undertaken to explore the possibility of a descriptive theory derived from the special characteristics of budgeting and expressed in generic terms. The paper suggests one (not the only, and perhaps not the most productive) way of assembling and linking the elements of a budgetary theory. At this stage, the inquiry has not progressed very far, and the verdict must be suspended as to whether a theory is possible.[12]

Having carried the inquiry to this point, I must profess to stronger doubts that I had at the outset concerning the possibility and utility of a budgetary theory. The difficulties encountered in composing this introductory statement leave me with three tentative conclusions.

(1) It may be more illuminating to examine budgeting as a subset of other fields than as a field in its own right. More might be gleaned from studying budgeting as a political process than as a distinct process upon which politics and other forces impinge.

(2) The rudiments offered in this paper might be more useful as a construct for organizing the study of budgetary processes and outcomes than as a causal theory of budgetary choice.

(3) The most fruitful application of these elements might be to study the internal processes of budgeting rather than the larger questions of political, economic, and social behavior.

Notes

1. See V.O. Key, Jr. "The Lack of a Budgetary Theory," *American Political Science Review* 34 (1940): 1137–44.

2. John E. Dawson, *A Model for Systemic Budgeting*, (Santa Monica, Calif.: RAND Corporation, 1985) 3.

3. Key, "Budgeting Theory," 1138.

4. Ibid., 1143.

5. Dwight Waldo, *The Administrative State: A Study of the Political Theory of American Public Administration* (New York: Roland Press, 1948) is a penetrating analysis of the normative basis of this discipline.

6. Political incompatibility is not the only reason for the failure of these reforms, but it is the one stressed by Aaron Wildavsky in *The Politics of the Budgetary Process* (Boston: Little, Brown & Co., 1964).

7. Some of the comments on incrementalism in this section are adapted from Allen Schick, "Incremental Budgeting in a Decremental Age," *Policy Sciences* 16 (1983): 1–25.

8. In addition to the three fields briefly discussed in this paper (public administration, political science, and economics), budgeting can be considered from the perspectives of other—perhaps all—fields of social study: sociology, psychology, anthropology, etc.

9. Wildavsky, *"Budgetary Process,* 126.

10. In "The Road to PPB: The Stages of Budget Reform," *Public Administration Review* (1966): 243–58, I identified control, management, and planning as the functions that explain budgetary development in the United States.

11. In order for markets to function, there have to be social or legal rules governing property, contract, and other terms of exchange; but, markets do not have formal procedures that describe how the exchange is to be carried out.

12. The term is taken from Key, "Budgetary Theory," 1137.

Chapter 4
The Assignment and Institutionalization of Functions at OMB: Lessons from Two Cases in Work Force Management

PETER M. BENDA
AND
CHARLES H. LEVINE

The assignment of responsibility for coordinating administrative functions is an often overlooked but important aspect of federal management. Indeed, since the creation of the Bureau of the Budget (BOB) in 1921, decisions about whether to assign a particular administrative function to units which, like BOB/OMB, are located in the Executive Office of the President, to staff agencies that are not officially part of the EOP structure, such as the General Services Administration (GSA) and the Office of Personnel Management (OPM), or to the line departments and agencies, have perplexed those concerned with promoting effective government-wide management improvement efforts.[1] Part of the difficulty in assigning responsibility for different functions stems from the problem of projecting the likely consequences of different choices (i.e., what would happen if responsibility were given to OPM rather than OMB, to GSA rather than OPM, etc.). Simply put, the theory of administrative functional assignment in the executive branch is not very well developed, despite the extensive efforts of the Brownlow and Hoover Commissions and several subsequent groups to develop such a doctrine. Therefore, the informed judgment of a relatively small group of people with broad, first-hand experience in central management generally is all we have to go on in making these decisions.

70

A second aspect of the functional assignment problem is the fact that, for a variety of reasons, some functions appear to become "institutionalized," i.e., well accepted by the particular organization to which they are assigned, while others never become incorporated in a stable and routine way in that same agency's operations.[2] Thus, the long-term effectiveness of the choices or decisions made appears to depend to a significant extent on the receptivity of the agency to the function being assigned to it, as well as on the power of other agencies in its environment that may make claims for control of that function. The functional assignment question therefore has significant political implications as well as important consequences for government-wide managerial effectiveness, but little codified knowledge is available to help decisionmakers make these choices wisely.

Issues of functional assignment and institutionalization have figured prominently in the area of personnel administration for some time, especially where matters of "work-force management" have been concerned. In theory, the concept of work-force management implies a comprehensive and integrated approach to determining "the number of people and the skills necessary to accomplish an organization's objectives, and the actions necessary to obtain, develop and motivate the work force."[3] While many business firms have develped such human resources planning systems, work-force management in the federal government has been carried out in piecemeal fashion, with various responsibilities allocated both horizontally (among OMB, OPM, and GSA) and vertically (between the central management agencies and the line departments). According to the president's Private Sector Survey on Cost Control (the Grace Commission): "Work force requirements . . . have received little attention in Government because budget decisions are usually overriding, [because] there is a lack of leadership from the Office of Personnel Management (OPM), and [because] there is insufficient information to develop complete and integrated systems."[4] The fragmentation and gaps in the work-force management system, the commission charged, has given rise to a host of problems in the federal government's personnel practices, including misallocations of personnel, a lack of attention to the improvement of worker productivity, excessive overtime costs, thousands of unnecessary temporary positions as well as excessive managerial positions, and inadequate training and development programs.[5]

To rectify this state of affairs, the Grace Commission recommended "that OPM develop an adequate work force planning policy to be used by Federal agencies and that OMB develop and coordinate government-wide programs to improve productivity."[6] This recommendation was forwarded as part of a large structural reorganization of the central management agencies proposed by the Grace Commission—the Office of Federal Management (OFM)—to build integrated management policies and systems in the federal government generally. No matter what reception its OFM plan receives,[7] the commission's proposal to divide responsibility between OPM and OMB along the lines just outlined seems to reflect an unresolved ambiguity about what role each of these agencies might best play in helping to improve work-force management capabilities in the federal government. The commission emphasized the need for human resource planning procedures that would allow for uniform decision making throughout the federal government. But, there is little evidence that its proposal would substantially alleviate the jurisdictional problems arising from the division of responsibilities between OMB and OPM (before 1978, the Civil Service Commission) that have often impeded efforts to reform the work-force management system in the past. The central question is this: On what basis should the assignment of work-force management responsibilities be predicated? In particular, what role should OMB play in this context?

In this essay, we explore this issue by focusing on two of the many functions that might be said to fall under the rubric of work-force management: control of work-force size and executive development. While BOB/OMB has long exercised principal responsibility for the first of these functions, authority for overseeing and administering government-wide executive development programs sometimes has been shared by OMB and the CSC/OPM, at other times regarded as properly the exclusive province of one or the other of these agencies. By using these two case studies as "foils," we hope to draw some general conclusions about the considerations that seem to militate for or against the "institutionalization" of work-force management functions at OMB. The lessons to be learned from these experiences are suggestive of the problems that future initiatives to strengthen the work-force management system are likely to encounter.

Work-Force Size

Of the various functions BOB/OMB has assumed for federal personnel policy and administration, its responsibility for the control of work-force size is clearly of longest standing. All presidents since World War II have favored constraints on the overall level of federal civilian employment and looked to BOB/OMB to play the lead role in monitoring and enforcing limitations on staffing levels throughout the executive branch. For more than four decades, as part of its annual review of agency budget requests, BOB/OMB has established "employment ceilings," specifying the maximum allowable personnel resources available to a department or agency in a given fiscal year. At various points since 1968, BOB/OMB has also been directed to oversee implementation of a number of governmentwide "hiring freezes," or restrictions on employment mandated by the Congress or the President.[8] However, the annual establishment by OMB of personnel ceilings for each agency clearly constitutes the "predominate method of control over employment" in the federal government,[9] and this will be our primary focus here.

OMB's Administration of Personnel Ceilings: Background and Recent Developments

BOB/OMB's formal responsibility for monitoring the size of the federal work force dates from 1942. In that year, Congress enacted Public Law 77–821, an act that required department and agency heads to justify their personnel levels to the director of the Bureau of the Budget and authorized the BOB to reduce the number of personnel found to be in excess of minimum requirements. The BOB also was empowered to establish personnel ceilings for the individual departments and agencies in two subsequent enactments, the Federal Employees Pay Act of 1945 and Public Law 79–360 of 1946.[10] But the statutory basis for this practice lapsed with the repeal of all statutory personnel ceilings in the Budget and Accounting Procedures Act of 1950 (P.L. 81–784) and has not been renewed.[11]

Despite the absence of any express statutory authorization to undergird the practice, the use of personnel ceilings to control agency employment has continued uninterrupted as a matter of executive branch policy since 1951. In June of that year, the Budget Bureau issued Circular A–44, which advised department and agency heads that the President stressed the importance of conserving manpower and would hold them responsible for giving this objective top priority. Circular A–44 was later superceded by Circular A–64 (Revised) of June 28, 1965 ("Position Management Systems and Employment Ceilings"), which set forth procedures and concepts regarding personnel ceilings and emphasized that:

> Consistent with the policy of reducing Government costs . . . the President expects each agency head to pursue vigorously the efforts of his agency to achieve lower employment levels and increased productivity . . . and to assure strict observance of the employment ceilings.

Circular A–64 (Revised) was amended in January 1970 to require detailed justifications on requests for ceiling adjustments "in cases where Federal employees are used in lieu of service contracts for the performance of required services." It otherwise underwent no significant modification until 1980 and remained in effect until July 1983, at which time those provisions of Circular A-64 (Revised) pertaining to employment ceilings were superceded by portions of Circular A-11 ("Preparation and Submission of Budget Estimates"). The current administrative policy on personnel ceilings is set forth in Circular A-11 (Revised), Section 13 and Appendix C.

As this overview suggests, responsibility for administering the ceiling control device has long since been "institutionalized" as a basic component of OMB's function.[12] It is important to note, however, that while the basic process whereby ceilings are established has remained much the same under each of the circulars referred to earlier,[13] in fiscal year 1982, a significant change was implemented in the manner in which OMB determines and monitors an agency's use of its annual "maximum personnel resources."

By virtue of the 1980 amendment to Circular A-64 (Revised), in fiscal year 1982, the OMB switched its method of accounting for federal employees from the traditional "head count" or "end of year" ceiling system to a new "full-time equivalent" (FTE) system. The head count or end of year system had two distinguishing features, as the alternative designations suggest. First, the limitations on direct work strength specified in the ceilings—which were of two types, one ceiling on full-time permanent (FTP) employees, the other on total employment, including temporary, part-time, and intermittent hirees—were spelled simply in terms of the number of permissible employees or positions; i.e., no more than x slots available for full-time permanent employees. Second, these limitations were applicable only on the last day of the fiscal year; that is, an agency could exceed its specified quotas in either or both categories so long as its year-end figures remained within the prescribed bounds.

The FTE ceiling system, which the Carter Administration had instructed OMB and the Civil Service Commission (now OPM) to begin on a trial basis in 1977, incorporates changes along both these dimensions. First, rather than being predicated on the number of employees or positions per se as in the end of year system, it is based on the total number of employee *work years* deemed necessary to achieve agency missions and objectives. Second, the specification of a maximum number of workhours for use by agency employees provides a "bank account" from which each hour worked by those employees can be deducted.[14] Hence, the FTE system affords a means whereby an agency's deployment of its personnel resources can be monitored throughout the fiscal year rather than only on the last day of the fiscal year.

OMB supported the switch to the FTE system, in no small measure because its adoption would force agencies to closely monitor staff hiring and usage on a continuous, year-round basis. However, the primary impetus for the change came from elsewhere. Although they did not (and were not intended to) provide a corrective to all the criticisms raised against the use of personnel ceilings as such, the changes introduced in fiscal year 1982 are best understood when viewed in light of the larger dispute about the use and effectiveness of ceiling controls that has been going on for quite some time.

Ceilings: Arguments Pro and Con

Traditionally, BOB/OMB has maintained that personnel ceilings provide a necessary control over what otherwise might be an explosive growth in federal employment, a growth the agency alleges could not be curbed by budgetary restrictions alone. Proponents contend that the use of ceilings encourages efficiency and cost-effectiveness in government by focusing management concern on program priorities, budget and staff allocations, and means of effectively utilizing available personnel. Limitations on full-time permanent employment in the agencies have been defended on the grounds that they help reduce the costs associated with the federal government's underwriting of employee retirement and health benefits while encouraging agencies to develop and utilize a more flexible work force; i.e., one with a higher proportion of part-time and temporary employees. In addition, personnel ceilings are said to be of beneficial effect in encouraging agencies to consider alternative, less expensive means of carrying out their program objectives and responsibilities; for example, through the temporary employment of private contractors to provide certain services.

Critics, however, have taken issue with the traditional arguments on behalf of personnel ceilings, contending that ceilings do not control costs or promote efficiency and generally have deleterious effects on agency operations. One of the most persistent of these critics has been the General Accounting Office (GAO). In a series of reports issued over the past decade and a half, the GAO has pressed its view that personnel ceilings constitute a barrier to effective personnel management in the federal government and that normal funding or program limitations provide an alternative and equally or more effective means of controlling agency employment levels.[15] The additional controls imposed by ceilings, the GAO has argued, "deprive agency management of options for accomplishing essential work through the most efficient and economical use of the most appropriate types of manpower in specific circumstances."[16]

Other critics, including various congressional committees and presidential advisory groups, have echoed many of the concerns that prompted the GAO to call for the abolition of ceiling controls. Among the central claims traditionally made by those opposed to the use of personnel ceilings, four interrelated arguments deserve brief mention here:

Argument 1. Restraints on the size of the federal work force have been imposed without regard to the government's workload.

Critics contend that while objections to the proliferation of federal units and programs or their respective budgets may be justified, a far less substantial case can be lodged against the size or growth of the federal work force. The federal share of total civilian government employment has in fact declined significantly over the past three decades (from 37.2 percent in 1954 to 17.5 percent in 1984), but there has been no corresponding moratorium on adding to the government's workload. The imposition of ceilings therefore forces agencies to exploit other ways of doing their job, e.g., by using private contractors.

Argument 2. Ceilings create a misleading illusion of control in that restraints on the size of the federal work force do not necessarily control the costs of government.

This constitutes one of the chief objections to the use of personnel ceilings. If agencies need more personnel than allowed by their assigned ceilings, they must acquire the additional resources by other means, i.e., through contracts with private firms or through grants to institutions and state and local government. "These people are neither included in personnel ceilings nor counted as part of the Federal work force," the GAO has observed, but "regardless of the source of manpower, the Federal government ultimately bears the cost."[17]

Argument 3. Personnel ceilings create an incentive for hiring out irrespective of cost, efficiency, or personnel considerations.

Express prohibitions against using contractors to circumvent or avoid ceilings have been incorporated into the administrative policy on employment ceilings since Circular A-64 (revised) of June 1965, a policy that has been reiterated in Circular A-76 on contracting. "Nevertheless, it has been established that this violation does occur and that the use of contracting as a principal means of coping with personnel ceilings, hiring freezes, and other contributors to staffing shortages may be pervasive in executive brance agencies."[18]

Argument 4. Because they may result in insufficient resources to perform work required, the imposition of ceilings may have adverse consequences on agency productivity and efficiency.

In an appendix to a 1977 report on personnel ceilings, the GAO provided a number of examples to illustrate how the use of ceilings had resulted in the reduction of agency services and the deferment or outright cancellation of work.[19]

As suggested by the lack of any significant changes in the nature or operation of the ceiling system for many years, OMB maintained that compelling counterarguments could be brought to bear against the claims of critics. For example, OMB has argued that many of the problems agency officials, the GAO, and others have attributed to OMB-devised restrictions on personnel usage (e.g., reduced services, deferred work, overtime costs, etc.) have in fact been due to "inadequate or inflexible internal personnel management practices rather than . . . employment ceilings."[20] Other objections have been dismissed in similar fashion. For example, commenting on a draft version of the 1977 report in which the GAO reiterated its claim that personnel ceilings do not promote less costly government because the taxpayer "must ultimately bear the cost" of alternative sources of personnel, OMB observed: "Although previous GAO reports . . . have emphasized the need to consider the full cost of employee benefits (e.g., retirement), the draft report does not recognize the substantial hidden costs associated with the use of Federal employees."[21] On a higher plane, OMB on occasion has been inclined to suggest that, even if it could conclusively demonstrate the merit of the arguments on cost grounds made by the GAO and others, these objections basically are beside the point: "employment ceilings exist to constrain increases, primarily because of the proper concern of the President, many members of Congress, and the public in the number of employees on the Federal payroll, *regardless of any other considerations.*"[22] (emphasis supplied).

The recent adoption of the FTE system evidently has not in the least induced OMB to change its basic position on personnel ceilings. OMB continues to maintain that direct staffing limitations are necessary to ensure that the size of the direct federal work force is controlled, and the fact that the FTE system has obviated many of the traditional objections to the ceiling control device may only have strengthened its resolve in this context.[23]

The Lessons of Institutionalization

Recognition that the dispute as to the advisability of relying upon personnel ceilings to control staffing is likely to continue substantially unabated, however, is not the most important conclusion to be drawn from the story of ceiling management at OMB, at least for immediate purposes. Our primary concern in this essay is to explore the factors that have militated for or against the institutionalization of work-force management functions at OMB. When viewed from this broader perspective, there is a more important lesson to be gleaned: Whatever misgivings may have been or may in the future be entertained about the effectiveness of one technique or another to ensure that the size of the federal work force is controlled, no one has seriously questioned the proposition that employment levels should be no larger than is necessary to accomplish agency missions. More significantly, no one has questioned the idea that, of the various central management agencies, OMB ought to have primary responsibility for seeing that efforts are made to keep staffing levels within appropriate bounds.

The GAO arguably has been the most persistent and vociferous opponent of the use of personnel ceilings. Nonetheless, as is revealed in ex-Comptroller General Staats' formulation of what the GAO regards as the most appropriate alternative to employment ceilings, it has not challenged the basic legitimacy of OMB's role in monitoring the size of the federal work force:

> The basic framework for a practical and effective alternative . . . exists in the budget process. What is lacking is confidence in the soundness of agencies' estimates [of their personnel needs] and in agency managers' willingness to adhere to their estimates. . . .
>
> With OMB's direction, the agencies could develop methods for preparing sound estimates of the minimum manpower requirements needed to accomplish all types of authorized programs and activities. The agencies should fully document the processes and data used and make this information available to OMB and concerned congressional committees for evaluation.
>
> Since the budget process takes place every year and budget examiners and congressional committees and subcommittees monitor agency activities during the year, agency managers would be obliged to develop realistic estimates and avoid deviating substantially from them without approval.[24]

It is obvious that the GAO's position is predicated on the premise that the control of levels and types of personnel used is properly, at least in the first instance, a function of line management in the departments and agencies—a premise that OMB for its part has been reluctant to embrace quite so wholeheartedly. Nevertheless, the GAO's proposed alternative to centrally mandated personnel ceilings does not challenge the basic assumption that, by virtue of the central position it occupies in the budget process, OMB has the best vantage point from which to supervise a range of agency activities, including their adherence to personnel targets.

The very considerations that seem to argue for OMB's retention of the work-force size component of the work-force management function, however, might militate against the assignment to OMB of other components of that function. Such would seem to be the principal lesson of the story of executive development efforts in the federal government, to which we now turn.

Executive Personnel Development

It has long been recognized that the presence of able, prepared, and committed executives has a critical bearing on the federal government's capacity to manage public programs effectively. In the view of many commentators, however, the government's performance in executive personnel development to date has been sadly lacking. While a number of historic problems have contributed to the failure to devise a reasonably systematic, governmentwide approach to executive personnel planning and training, one important source of difficulty has been the recurrent controversy that has surrounded the question of who should have charge of such endeavors. Indeed, the pattern of divided responsibility and role conflict between OMB and the Civil Service Commission/Office of Personnel Management, which has characterized so much of federal personnel policy and administration, has been particularly pronounced in this arena.

Executive Development:
Early History Through the Nixon Administration

The authority of the Civil Service Commission with respect to executive personnel development dates from the Government Employees Training Act of 1958 (P.L. 85–807), which charged the commission with responsibility for administering and overseeing all federal employee training programs.[25] In 1963 and 1966, respectively, the commission established Executive Seminar Centers in Kings Point, N.Y., and Berkeley, Calif., aimed at middle managers (GS 14–15s),[26] and in 1968 it set up the Federal Executive Institute (FEI) at Charlottesville, Va., which sponsored a Senior Executive Education program to train GS 16–18s and their equivalents, the so-called supergrades.[27] Some criticisms were expressed as to the quality and appropriateness of the curricula in the programs offered at these centers.[28] Nonetheless, the basic authority of the CSC over executive development matters went largely uncontested throughout the 1960s.

A major break in this context occurred with the transformation of the Bureau of the Budget into the Office of Management and Budget by means of Reorganization Plan No. 2 of 1970. Citing what it termed the "primitive state" of executive personnel planning and development in the federal government, the President's Advisory Committee on Executive Organization (the Ash Council) had recommended to President Nixon that a new division be established within a refashioned BOB to "take the lead in developing and evaluating programs to recruit, train, motivate, deploy and evaluate top executives."[29]

This intrusion upon what had been the exclusive prerogative of the Civil Service Commission was vigorously denounced by Chairman of the CSC Robert E. Hampton in a private March 1970 memo to Presidential Assistant John Erlichman. The Ash Council proposal also was attacked by several witnesses who appeared before a subcommittee of the House Committee on Government Operations during consideration of Reorganization Plan No. 2. A number of objections to the council's proposal were cited; e.g., that it would downgrade the authority and responsibility of the CSC by imposing OMB as a layer between it and the President, thus denying him essential advice on personnel management from the most knowledgable source; that it would risk setting up a "political patronage system," in which appointments and promotions to top career positions would be politically motivated, thereby endangering the nonpolitical nature of the civil service and jeopardizing the merit system; and that it would produce confusion and increase costs by assigning two separate agencies apparent ultimate administrative jurisdiction over federal employee personnel policies.[30]

In response to these allegations, administration spokesmen claimed that OMB's role would be to supplement the commission's executive development efforts and to coordinate the federal government's many different personnel systems, and that no infringement of the CSC's executive personnel management function was implied or intended.[31] These assurances evidently did little to assuage a majority of the Government Operations Committee, which, in its report on Reorganization Plan No. 2, voiced concern that the proposal "could be used as a basis for downgrading the statutory authority of the Civil Service Commission, endangering the nonpolitical nature of the civil service, and making the civil service system subservient to the Executive Office of the President."[32] However, the committee's resolution to disapprove the plan was not endorsed by the House, and shortly after OMB commenced operations in July 1970, it served notice of its intention to assume an active role in federal personnel management by announcing the establishment of a Division of Executive Development and Labor Relations (EDLR).

The establishment of this new division, of course, did not in and of itself, ensure that OMB would assume the "lead role" in executive development envisaged for it by the Ash Council. At the very least, the controversy surrounding that council's proposal to vest increased authority for executive development matters in OMB had alerted the latter to the need to work cooperatively with the CSC in these matters,[33] and in fact, the OMB for some time continued to play a role secondary to the CSC in this arena. For example, OMB contributed only marginally to the development of the Nixon Administration's ambitious 1971 proposal for the establishment of a Federal Executive Service (FES). The impetus for the FES proposal, which would have brought 7000 career and non-career executives at GS levels 16–18 (and their equivalents) under a single system in order to ensure the more effective development and utilization of executive resources, was provided almost exclusively by the Civil Service Commission's Bureau of Executive Manpower.[34] Moreover, while OMB's contemplated role in this scheme was not extensive,[35] the precariousness of its newly commissioned executive development function was dramatically underscored when the Senate Committee on Post Office and Civil Service, in its report on S. 1682, took exception to the notion that the agency had *any* legitimate role to play in administration of the proposed FES. Professing to view "with some concern" what it termed OMB's "intrusion" into the "substantive business, unrelated to budgetary matters, of Departments and agencies," the committee moved to strike a provision mandating collaboration between OMB and the CSC in certain aspects of FES administration and to make the commission "solely accountable" for the program.[36]

Although Congress never enacted the Nixon Administration's FES proposal into law,[37] the Senate Post Office and Civil Service Committee report on S. 1682 illustrates some of the external obstacles that would confront OMB in its efforts to become more actively involved in executive development matters. Not all the obstacles were external in nature, however. The fact that OMB continued to play a role secondary to the CSC in this context during the period immediately following the 1970 reorganization is largely attributable to the influence of the agency's first director, Charles Shultz. An economist by training, Shultz reportedly was considerably more concerned about the labor relations side of federal personnel policy than about executive development.[38] Given Schultz's priorities and the fact that the background of the first director of the Executive Development and Labor Relations division, David P. Taylor, was in labor relations, it is hardly surprising that the staff of about twenty professionals, who constituted EDLR initially, concentrated primarily on labor relations matters.[39] Congressional failure to act on the FES proposal did not deter the CSC and OMB from jointly undertaking to build executive development programs in the various departments and agencies during 1971–1972. But the relative lack of enthusiasm on the part of top OMB officials for such ventures may have contributed to what one agency official later described as the "mixed" results of these initiatives.[40]

OMB's commitment to executive development efforts, however, increased notably under Roy Ash, Shultz's successor as OMB Director, and Frederick Malek, who joined OMB in the capacity of deputy director along with Ash in February 1972. Malek, in particular, placed special emphasis on executive development and sought to establish this as an important administration priority during President Nixon's second term.[41] Under his lead, in the spring of 1973, the OMB and CSC embarked on a more aggressive strategy to improve executive selection and development processes throughout the federal government. Among the central components of this strategy were requirements that agencies establish executive development programs and specify short-term executive development goals, and a pilot Federal Executive Development Program (FEDP) of education and interagency work experience for GS 15s.[42]

The OMB and the CSC both apparently held high expectatons for the FEPD program. According to Edward Preston, whom Ash and Malek had recruited from the IRS to head OMB's Executive Development and Labor Relations division early in 1974,[43] the central concept of this program was to take promising personnel recommended by the agencies for training to become "generalist" top-line managers and executives. However, although two or three sessions were held, involving roughly twenty-five participants, the initiative evidently did not work as well as OMB or the CSC had anticipated. Preston has suggested that the program failed to take hold for reasons that had invariably undermined similar efforts in the past: Many agencies, resisting a perceived challenge to the traditional in-house selection route where "subject-matter" specialists are promoted to positions of executive leadership, either declined to participate or proved reluctant to accept trainees previously employed elsewhere.[44] The then-executive director of the Civil Service Commission took a different view of the lack of agency enthusiasm for training executives and moving them to other agencies. In his view, the fact that political appointees tend to remain in government only for a short period (the average is under two years) means that most career executives need high competence in both subject matter and executive management in order to be effective in the career-political relationship.[45]

·Executive Development Post-Nixon: OMB's Role in Decline

With the departure of Ash and Malek shortly after President Nixon's resignation in August 1974, OMB's prominence in executive development matters receded considerably.[46] The later stages of the Nixon presidency, in fact, may be regarded as the high-water mark of OMB's role as centralized coordinator of executive development programs in the federal government. The failure to establish the FEPD on a permanent basis, however, attests to the limited effectiveness of OMB's executive development efforts even in those rare instances when they have enjoyed the support of top agency officials.

There are some grounds for speculation that the traditional resistance of the line departments and agencies to centrally coordinated executive development programs may not have been the only obstacle confronting OMB during this period. In particular, although the Civil Service Commission had collaborated with OMB in the establishment and compensation, for monitoring legislation relating to personnel matthe Nixon (and early Ford) years, there are indications that several high-placed officials within the commission were less than pleased with the secondary status accorded the CSC in executive development matters by Reorganization Plan No. 2 of 1970.

The frustration occasioned within the commission by the vesting in OMB of the "lead role" in this context was very much evident, for example, in a 1975 monograph prepared for the House Government Operations Committee by the recently retired Executive Director of the CSC, Bernard Rosen. Claiming that the stated purpose of the 1970 reorganization with respect to greater OMB involvement in personnel management had not been achieved and that the latter's performance in this arena after five years could "only be rated as weak or non-existent,"[47] Rosen recommended that legislation be enacted "to eliminate the confusion, uncertainty, and duplication inherent in Reorganization Plan No. 2 of 1970, and to clarify the Civil Service Commission's role as the central personnel agency, by terminating the Office of Management and Budget's responsibility to advise the President on the development of new programs to recruit, train, motivate, deploy, and evaluate top executives."[48]

In fact, in 1976, during the second session of the 94th Congress, legislation was introduced in the House that (while falling short of

Rosen's proposal to vest exclusive authority in this arena in the commission) was intended in part to reaffirm the CSC's role in executive development matters.[49] Hearings on H.R. 12080 disclosed support for the adoption of an even stronger provision on the part of federal employee union representatives, who maintained that OMB's increasing involvement in personnel matters had resulted in a "politicization" of the civil service and a "usurpation" of CSC functions and prerogatives.[50] However, others suggested that the strains in the relations between OMB and the Civil Service Commission, which had characterized the later Nixon years, had subsided substantially in the interim.[51] CSC Chairman Hampton, for his part, while welcoming the provision that would have reaffirmed the CSC's authority with respect to executive manpower management as a "vote of confidence in the Commission's ability in this important area," restated the position in the Executive Order that "this was a shared responsibility with the Office of Management and Budget" and added that the CSC had enjoyed "a close, constructive, and effective working relationship" with OMB in this context.[52]

No action was ever taken by Congress on H.R. 12080, which died in committee. Yet, despite Chairman Hampton's disclaimer that the sharing of executive development functions between OMB and CSC had given rise to any serious conflicts, doubts as to whether OMB had a legitimate role to play in this area evidently persisted. President Carter had entered office promising to reorganize and streamline the EOP, and members of the President's Reorganization Project (the PRP) subsequently recommended that, in partial fulfillment of this objective, certain OMB "management" functions—including its executive development function—be transferred elsewhere.[53] Neither the OMB director at the time, Bert Lance, nor Wayne Granquist, the agency's associate director for Management and Regulatory Policy, objected to this proposal, which President Carter submitted to Congress as part of Reorganization Plan No. 1 of 1977 on July 15, 1977.

Some members of Congress voiced serious misgivings about the Carter Administration's proposal to reorganize the Executive Office of the President.[54] The Senate did not act to disapprove the initiative, however, and Reorganization Plan No. 1 of 1977 subsequently went into effect on October 19 of the same year. Some six weeks thereafter, on December 5, 1977, President Carter issued Executive Order 12027. By virtue of this directive, the step urged by Rosen and others was implemented: Authority for providing "overall Executive Branch leadership, regulation, and guidance in executive personnel selection, development and management" (including the establishment and administration of programs to "select, train, develop, motivate, deploy, and evaluate the men and women who make up the top ranks of the Federal civil service") was once again made the exclusive province of the Civil Service Commission.[55]

Shortly after the issuance of Executive Order 12027, six positions that had been assigned to OMB's Executive Development and Labor Relations division were transferred to the Civil Service Commission, and the title of that OMB unit (now with a staff of about thirteen) was changed to the Federal Personnel Policy Division. Information provided by OMB to House and Senate appropriation subcommittees in the spring of 1978, during consideration of the agency's fiscal year 1979 budget request, indicated that "executive development" no longer numbered among the formal responsibilities of the division thus renamed.[56]

The Road to CSRA: OMB's Role Terminated

It would be quite misleading to conclude on this basis, however, that OMB had abruptly withdrawn from this arena entirely. For, during the same period in which these internal changes at OMB were taking shape, the wheels of civil service reform that would eventuate in the passage of the Civil Service Reform Act of 1978 (P.L. 95–454) and the establishment of the Senior Executive Service (SES) had already been set in motion. OMB played a prominent role in many phases of that reform effort. Two of the agency's top officials, Wayne Granquist and Howard Messner, occupied key positions in the Federal Personnel Management Project (or the FPMP, as it came to be called), the inter agency group formed in June 1977 under the chairmanship of Carter's CSC chairman, Alan K. ("Scotty") Campbell, to spearhead the civil service reform initiative.[57] The professional staff of OMB's Executive Development and Labor Relations division also provided assistance to several of the nine task forces formed under the FPMP to develop various options and alternatives for reforming selected aspects of the federal civil service system.[58]

Although the seven option papers produced by these task forces during the summer and fall of 1977 covered a wide array of topics—ranging from equal employment opportunity and affirmative action to federal government labor-management relations and pay and benefit systems—several of the proposals emerging from the FPMP dominated the others. The most important of these, if only because so many other FPMP recommendations hinged on its acceptance and implementation, was a proposal to abolish the Civil Service Commission and create in its stead two new entities: the Office of Personnel Management (OPM) to oversee civil service policy and administration, and the independent

Merit Systems Protection Board (MSPB) to police the merit system. (These changes were effected by means of Reorganization Plan No. 2 of 1978 of August 11, 1978.[59]) In the view of many project participants, however, the proposal to establish a Senior Executive Service along the lines initially envisaged by the 1955 Hoover Commission was a step of equal if not surpassing significance. Indeed, FPMP Chairman Campbell characterized the SES proposal as the "linchpin" of the Carter Administration's personnel reorganization effort.[60]

The basic rationale underlying the SES proposal was set forth in volume 1 of the Final Staff Report of the Federal Personnel Management project, commonly known as the Ink Report, after FPMP Executive Director Dwight A. Ink. In familiar language that underscored widespread dissatisfaction both with existing executive personnel systems and with the effectiveness of CSC-OMB efforts to foster more viable executive development programs in the federal government, the Ink Report noted: "Despite the critical need to recruit and develop executives, no fully effective, Government-wide system exists today for selecting, preparing, advancing, and managing the men and women who administer the hundreds of vital programs that affect every citizen, family, and community in the Nation."[61] The proposed SES system—which embraced all managerial positions at GS 16–18, supergrade levels and Executive Levels V and VI, approximately 9000 positions in all—was intended to redress this persistent problem in the existing management structure for the top cadre of federal employees. At the same time, it was meant to provide each agency "considerably increased latitude to establish an executive personnel management system to meet its own special needs,"[62] for example, by minimizing the often artificial distinction between career and noncareer positions.

In the section dealing with the SES, the Ink Report recommended, among other things, that individuals be required to demonstrate managerial capability before entering the Executive Service; that systematic executive development programs be required "with full attention to the necessity for bringing women, minorities, and other excluded groups into the managerial mainstream"; that the agencies establish, under the guidance of OPM, programs to provide for the continued development of those executives already entered in the Executive Service; that such programs give increased attention to long-range planning in preparing executives for positions of greater responsibility and complexity; and that greater emphasis be placed on the training of managers brought into federal service from outside the government.[63]

According to Edward Preston, the professional staff of OMB's Division of Executive Development and Labor Relations had a hand in shaping the executive development provisions of the SES proposal and subsequently helped draft portions of what became Title IV (Senior Executive Service) of the Civil Service Reform Act, which was introduced in Congress on March 3, 1978, and signed into law by President Carter on October 13 of the same year.[64] With the enactment of this legislation, however, OMB's authority over executive development programs was effectively terminated (it already had been officially rescinded by Executive Order 12027 of December 1977). As part of the general responsibility for the supervision and oversight of the Senior Executive System vested in it by CSRA, the Office of Personnel Management was directed to establish programs for the development of candidates for and within the SES along the lines recommended by the FPMP, or to "require agencies to establish such programs which meet criteria prescribed by the Office."[65] By September 1979, OPM had established an Office of Executive Personnel and Management Development (EPMD) and taken a number of preliminary steps to carry out its executive development responsibilities.[66]

During this same time period, the staff strength of the newly renamed Federal Personnel Policy Division within OMB was further reduced from its post-Executive Order 12077 level to about eight. In the latter stages of the Carter Administration and into the early Reagan years, this division retained some responsibility in the area of federal employee pay and compensation, for monitoring legislation relating to personnel matters, and for various aspects of CSRA implementation.[67] The fact that its responsibilities both with respect to executive development and labor relations policy had been gradually chipped away, however, left the unit in a vulnerable position. Finally, in July 1982, as part of a larger reorganization of OMB under Deputy Director Joseph Wright, the Federal Personnel Policy Division was abolished.[68] Most of its remaining staff and functions were transferred to the Justice, Treasury, and General Management division on the agency's budget side, while Edward Preston, who had headed EDLR/FPPD on a continuous basis from 1974 until the division's demise, assumed a position on the White House staff.

Conclusion

The two detailed case studies of OMB's role in the spheres of personnel ceilings and executive development shed some valuable light on the central question posed at the outset of this essay: namely, of the basis upon which the assignment of function to the central management agencies might best be predicated. How well a central management agency is able to fulfill a functional responsibility would seem to depend in good part on three factors or considerations: the *close identification* of the function with a primary statutory responsibility of the agency; the *close relation* of the administration of that function to other agency processes; and the *acceptance* of the assigned functional responsibility by those most immediately affected. These factors help explain why responsibility for setting and supervising personnel ceilings became institutionalized at OMB, while responsibility for executive development was unable to take hold in the agency and could not survive reorganizations and reductions in staff. These factors also stand out in four lessons that the two case studies may be said to teach us about the assignment of central management functions to OMB.

Lesson 1. The setting and supervision of personnel ceilings is a clearly defined, ongoing function that is easily tied to the budget process on a year to year basis. It deals with relatively hard numbers that can be readily converted into dollars. Therefore, it comfortably fits the mental set of the OMB budget examiners and is amenable to the practice of setting limits and targets, which is built into OMB's role in the budget process.

In contrast, executive development is a broad concept susceptible to continual changes of direction. Executive development goals are often vague, results are difficult to measure, and the product of the training goes on into the distant future. The entire process fits poorly with the year to year orientation of the budget process, which tends to drive most of OMB's activities, and the difficulty of measuring the impact of executive development due to the softness of the data also makes it fit poorly with OMB's predominant orientation.

In general, the question of how comfortably management improvement activities and procedures comport with the activities and procedures of the budget examination process seems to be a decisive one in determining the likelihood that a given management function will be institutionalized at OMB. The executive development function was always housed in the agency's "M-side," at a distance removed from the budget examiners; the inability to easily incorporate its objectives and procedures into the budget review process helps to explain why the function did not take firm hold at OMB.

Lesson 2. The manpower ceiling function has as its basic orientation the control and reduction of personnel costs through the establishment of limits on the number of employees on the federal government's payroll. Clearly, this is a rough way to constrain the costs of the work force (more subtle ways like average grade targets have also been used from time to time on a selective basis), but it does have the virtues of simplicity and harmony with OMB's budget control function. In contrast, executive development stresses building capacity, a complex process aimed at enhancing the ability of line managers to manage their agencies. This orientation stands quite opposed to the predominant cost-containment function of OMB, and as a consequence, its importance is easily diminished within the agency in the year to year struggle to balance the budget by cutting expenditures.

Lesson 3. Personnel ceilings have come to be an accepted and deeply entrenched part of the budgetary process. Because it is well institutionalized, the process enjoys authority in its own right; relatively speaking, it is insulated from broad policy changes caused by shifting presidential priorities or support within the top White House staff. In contrast, the location of the executive development function in OMB was never widely supported by the Civil Service Commission or by the departments and agencies. During its nine- to twelve-year history at OMB (depending on how one counts), the level of activity in the unit responsible for executive development rose or fell depending on the importance key presidential assistants attached to such initiatives. When interest and support eventually evaporated, the executive development unit was abolished. Finally as both a measure and cause of institutionalization, it is important to mention the authority upon which the functions rested. The personnel ceiling function was a clearly defined responsibility of OMB supported on a continuous basis by a series of circulars, while executive development efforts were more sporadic and the function was not supported in nearly so authoritative a fashion.

Lesson 4. The "inclusiveness" of a function also appears to make a difference in whether it becomes institutionalized. *Inclusiveness* refers to the extent to which there is an agreed-upon division of labor for a function both among the central management agencies and between them and the line agencies and departments. Although it is true that line officials in the departments and agencies have been known to object to the concept, centrally mandated personnel ceilings have been used for some time and the functional division of labor has become well established: OMB sets ceilings and OPM collects data in support of OMB leadership in this area. In the case of executive development, the roles of OMB, CSC/OPM, and the departments and agencies never were firmly established, in part because each felt it had a legitimate role to play in every phase of the various programs.

These four lessons may provide some useful guidance in attempting to gauge the feasibility of assigning the OMB other functions that relate to work-force management. There is every reason to expect that the agency will continue to be called on to assume responsibilities that have significant work-force implications. For example, the Reagan Administration has initiated, under OMB's overall guidance and supervision, a comprehensive, governmentwide productivity improvement program along the lines recently recommended by the Grace Commission and others.[69] Under the Carter Administration, contrarily, the Office of Personnel Management had served as the focal point for enhancing productivity,[70] and some would argue that this function is more in keeping with OPM's mission than it is with OMB's. The merits of the initiative itself aside, whether OMB will be able to institutionalize the productivity improvement function the Reagan Administration has conferred on it is a reasonable concern—all the more so for those who would look to OMB to play a lead role in improving work-force management capabilities in the federal government.[71]

The development of means and measures to improve government productivity has been a recurring problem since 1970, and the administration's program is destined to focus attention on that problem once more. Other salient issues of work-force management—for example, the availability and effectiveness of training and development programs in the federal government, particularly for the increasing numbers of political appointees being brought into government service, or the larger question of the relationship between the levels and kinds of personnel used and the organizational capacity and effectiveness of federal departments and agencies—seem likely to loom large in the future.

To date, neither OPM nor OMB has demonstrated an ability to provide sustained leadership in these important areas. Recognition of this fact has prompted many observers to conclude that the institutional framework necessary to provide a comprehensive, coordinated work-force management system for the federal government is lacking. Although some might argue that this is a vain quest, and perhaps not even a desirable one, the question of how best to go about establishing such a framework within the central management core of the executive branch is likely to engage practitioners and commentators alike for some time to come.

Notes

1. See, e.g., President's Private Sector Survey on Cost Control, *Report on Federal Management Systems* (Washington: PPSSCC, 1983), 8–11.

2. This definition of *institutionalization* is derived from that offered by Margaret Wyzsormirski, who suggested that similar criteria may be used to determine whether agencies have become "institutionalized" in the government system as a whole. See her "The De-Institutionalization of Presidential Staff Agencies," *Public Administration Review* 42, no. 5 (September–October 1982): 456, fn. 1, and the sources cited therein.

3. President's Private Sector Survey on Cost Control, J. Peter Grace, Chairman, *War on Waste* (New York: Macmillan, 1981), 228.

4. Ibid., 228–29.

5. Ibid., 229.

6. Ibid.

7. The pros and cons of the PPSSCC's Office of Federal Management proposal are reviewed in Peter M. Benda and Charles H. Levine, "OMB's Management Role: Issues of Structure and Strategy," in *Office of Management and Budget: Evolving Roles and Future Issues*, Senate Print #99–134, U.S. Senate Committee on Governmental Affairs (Washington, D.C.: U.S. Government Printing Office, 1986), 136–42.

8. Because they rely on attrition and do not require agencies to initiate reduction-in-force (RIF) actions, partial or total restrictions on hiring are generally considered to be the least disruptive means of achieving across the board reductions in the number of federal employees. Congress utilized this tool when, in Section 201 of the Revenue and Expenditure Control Act of 1968 (P.L. 90–364), it acted to restrict agency appointments to 75 percent of the number of vacancies in full-time permanent positions "during months when the total number of Federal employees exceeds the level that existed on June 30, 1966." (This restriction was repealed in 1969.) Section 311 of the Civil Service Reform Act of 1978 (P.L. 95–454) mandated that the total number of civilian employees in the executive branch during fiscal years 1979–1981 not exceed the level that existed on September 30, 1977, without, however, specifying what type of action should be taken to adjust employment figures to maintain this overall ceiling.

More frequently, governmentwide restrictions on employment have been imposed unilaterally by the President by means of executive orders or other directives. President Carter imposed three partial freezes on appointments to full-time permanent positions, and on his first day in office, President Reagan ordered a total freeze on all federal civilian hiring that lasted until mid-March 1981. The OMB's role in the implementation of these freezes was criticized by the General Accounting Office in a March 1982 report, in which the GAO voiced its longstanding opposition to the use of centrally mandated employment ceilings. See U.S. General Accounting Office, *Recent Government-Wide Hiring Freezes Prove Ineffective in Managing Federal Employment*, FPCD–82–21 (March 10, 1982).

9. U.S. General Accounting Office, *Personnel Ceilings—A Barrier to Effective Manpower Management*, FPCD-76-88 (June 2, 1977). The Congress has generally been even less disposed to mandate agency-specific employment ceilings than it has to impose such ceilings governmentwide (see note 8). However, with the exception of the last two budget cycles (fiscal years 1985 and 1986), every Department of Defense Authorization Act since 1975 has established annual ceilings on civilian employment in the Department of Defense.

10. Under Section 607 of the Federal Employees Pay Act (P.L. 79–106), executive branch agencies were required to provide the director of the BOB with all the information necessary to determine the number of full-time civilian employees for the performance of their functions. P.L. 79–390 of 1946 amended this provision to include part-time employment; it also established maximum year-end ceilings for the Departments of War and Navy and set quarterly ceilings on the aggregate employment of all other departments and agencies.

11. Although the incidence has been relatively infrequent, Congress itself has established employment ceilings on a number of occasions since 1950. See notes 8 and 9.

12. The extent to which this function has become institutionalized at OMB is reflected in the fact that, in marked contrast to the on-again/off-again pattern whereby different OMB units and divisions have been assigned various other personnel management tasks, responsibility for oversight of the ceiling system has been centered on one unit within the Budget Review Division (BRD), currently known as the Resource Systems Branch, for at least the last twenty years. A single career official, George Strauss, served as chief of this unit for approximately fifteen years, until his retirement in February 1986.

13. As noted earlier, ceilings generally are set by OMB as part of the budget formulation process. Agency estimates of direct personnel needs are incorporated in their annual budgetary submissions to OMB and are reviewed by the latter in light of "budget proposals and assumptions with regard to workload, efficiency, proposed new legislation, interagency reimbursable arrangements, and other special financing methods." After negotiation with OMB, agency requests for personnel resources are finalized for inclusion in the President's budget. Upon review of the President's budget, the Congress undertakes, as part of the authorization and appropriation process, to review agency personnel ceilings and normally spells out the intended personnel level in committee reports and floor statements. On occasion, Congress has reacted to restrictive OMB ceilings and the tendency of some agencies to accumulate large numbers of unfilled vacancies by establishing "ceiling floors," which require a minimum complement of employees for specific programs or agencies. OMB formally specifies the personnel ceilings in "allowance letters" sent to each department or agency after budget authority (BA) has been appropriated.

The ceilings thus specified are intended to provide "absolute limits" on the personnel available to an agency, although provision has been made for their adjustment during the applicable fiscal year, when congressional action or other developments clearly indicate the need for revision. Generally speaking, OMB has not sought to mandate employment limitations for specific agency programs. Rather, the department or agency has been held responsible for allocating its authorized employment levels downward until each of its operating units has been provided a ceiling. Agency officials, however, have been charged to provide their employment figures on a monthly basis to the CSC/OPM and, in the event of a ceiling violation, to submit a report outlining the factors giving rise to the violation and action taken to prevent a recurrence.

14. When the FTE system was first implemented governmentwide, the OMB continued to set two employment ceilings for each agency, as it had before. However, OMB Bulletin No. 83-5 of October 14, 1982, further modified the system by eliminating the separate ceilings on full-time permanent employment. All agencies are now given one ceiling that represents the full-time equivalent of all categories of employment.

15. Some of the relevant GAO reports include: *Impact of Employment Ceilings on Management of Civilian Personnel*, B-165959 (April 30, 1971); *Project Reflex (Resource Flexibility)—A Demonstration of Management Through the Use of Fiscal Controls Without Personnel Ceilings*, B-165959 (June 21, 1974); *Implementation and Impact of Reductions in Civilian Employment, Fiscal Year 1972*, B-180257 (July 2, 1974); *Part-Time Employment in Federal Agencies*, B-159950 (January 2, 1976); *Personnel Ceilings—A Barrier to Effective Manpower Management*, FPCD-76-88 (June 2, 1977); *Federal Workforce Planning: Time for Renewed Emphasis*, FPCD-81-4 (December 30, 1980); and, *Improving the Management and Credibility of the Federal Work Force Through Better Planning and Budgetary Controls*, FPCD-81-54 (July 17, 1981).

16. *Personnel Ceilings—A Barrier to Effective Manpower Management*, 21.

17. Ibid., 1.

18. Congressional Research Service, Alice Mosher, *The Relationship Between Federal Personnel Ceilings and Contracting Out: Policy Background and Current Issues*, Report No. 80-138-Gov. (Washington, D.C.: Congressional Research Service, August 5, 1980). Examples of contracting out to circumvent personnel ceilings are provided in this report on pp. 7-10. See also GAO, *Personnel Ceilings*, 65.

19. GAO, *Personnel Ceilings*, Appendix IV, 42-46.

20. Cited in ibid., 26.

21. Cited in ibid., 23.

22. Cited in ibid., 61-62.

23. See, for example, the remarks of an OMB spokesperson cited in U.S. GAO, *Improving the Credibility and Management of the Federal Work Force Through Better Planning and Budgetary Controls*, 16. See also ibid., 7.

24. Statement of the Comptroller General before the Subcommittee on Human Resources, House Committee on Post Office and Civil Service, September 11, 1979. Cited in ibid., 12.

25. Prior to this point, direction of such programs, to the extent they existed at all, had been the exclusive province of the individual departments and agencies. The initial mandate provided the CSC by the terms of the Government Employees Training Act was reinforced by Executive Order 11348 of April 1967, which instructed the commission "to develop [federal] employees through the establishment and operation of progressive and efficient training centers." Primary responsibility for the direction of the CSC's training and development programs, including those sponsored by each of the commission's ten regional offices, was entrusted to the Bureau of Training.

26. For background on the Executive Seminar Centers and an early assessment of their programs and operation, see John A. Rehfuss, "Executive Development: Executive Seminar Center Style," *Public Administration Review,* 30 (September–October 1970): 553–61. An additional center was later established in Oak Ridge, Tenn., and the Berkeley center was transferred to Denver, Colo., in the late 1960s.

27. Guidance for the programs sponsored by the FEI initially was provided by the Bureau of Executive Manpower, which was established in 1966 to encourage the development of and planning for top career personnel and to oversee the new Executive Assignment System, which the CSC introduced during the same year. In 1974, the FEI added to its curriculum a three-week Executive Leadership and Management program, designed to serve executives at the critical time of their initial entry into federal service.

28. See, e.g., Bob L. Wynia, "Executive Development in the Federal Government," *Public Administration Review,* 32 (July–August 1972): 313–14.

29. The Ash Council suggested that the proposed Division of Executive Personnel within OMB would "rely on the Civil Service Commission and the agencies to execute programs," thus implying that the CSC's principal role would be to implement OMB-devised executive development programs. The groundwork for this proposed downgrading of the CSC's executive development function vis a vis OMB had been laid in an earlier memo, dated August 20, 1969, in which, having noted that "the government does not have personnel policies or mechanisms which permit the mobilization of the best managerial talent in places where the needs are greatest," the council said: "While appreciating the present role of the Civil Service Commission, we believe that the President's office should take the lead in developing programs to recruit, train, motivate, and deploy top executives."

30. House Committee on Post Office and Civil Service, *The Merit System in the United States Civil Service* (Monograph prepared by Bernard Rosen), 94th Cong., 1st sess. Committee Print #94-10 (Washington, D.C.: U.S. Government Printing Office, 1975), 72–75 (hereafter cited as Rosen, *The Merit System*).

31. Ibid., 75. But cf. note 29.

32. House Committee on Government Operations, *Disapproving Reorganization Plan No. 2 of 1970.* 91st Cong., 2nd sess. House Report #91–1066 (Washington, D.C.: U.S. Government Printing Office, 1970), 15.

33. The need for cooperation had been underscored by President Nixon in his March 12, 1970, message to Congress accompanying Reorganization Plan No. 2. In it, the President had emphasized that "Under [OMB's] leadership, there will be *joint efforts* to see to it that all executive talent is well utilized" (emphasis added). This phrase may have been included in the President's message to reassure CSC Chairman Hampton, who had expressed concern about the implications of Ash Council proposal in a private memo submitted to John Erlichman a few days earlier, that the administration did not intend OMB entirely to supplant the commission's role in executive development. See Rosen, *The Merit System*, 72–73.

34. For general background on the FES, which President Nixon first proposed to Congress on February 2, 1971, see Seymour S. Berlin, "The Federal Executive Service," *Civil Service Journal*, 11 (April–June 1971): 7–13. No OMB officials testified during the first set of hearings on the proposed FES system, held before the Senate Committee on Post Office and Civil Service in May 1971. OMB Associate Director Frank Carlucci, however, did appear before the House Subcommittee on Manpower and Civil Service the following April, at which time he was questioned about OMB's role in the development of the FES proposal. Nothing in his response appeared to challenge subcommittee chairman Henderson's understanding that "basically this FES proposal was developed in the [CSC]." House Committee on Post Office and Civil Service, Subcommittee on Manpower and Civil Service, *The Federal Executive System*, Hearings on H.R. 3807, 92nd Cong., 2nd sess. (Washington, D.C.: U.S. Government Printing Office, 1972), 12–13.

35. The legislative proposal for the FES did make provision for OMB-CSC collaboration in certain areas—for example, in determining the number of FES executives to be allocated to each agency and for ensuring that the ratio of career to noncareer executives government-wide remained within prescribed limits—but all concerned (including OMB Associate Director Carlucci) appear to have understood that day to day administration as well as substantive oversight and direction of the FES would be provided by the Civil Service Commission. *Ibid.*, 73.

36. Senate Committee on Post Office and Civil Service, *Federal Executive Service.* 92nd Cong., 2nd sess. Report #92–864, to accompany S. 1682 (Washington, D.C.: U.S. Government Printing Office, 1972), 12–13.

37. Despite the fact that no action was taken in 1971 or 1972 on its FES initiative, the Nixon Administration tried again in 1974 to stimulate congressional action on a revised version of the program. In a message to Congress delivered on July 17 of that year, President Nixon proposed the establishment of an Executive Personnel System. Given that the President was forced to resign from office only

weeks later, however, it is hardly surprising that this overture never received serious consideration.

38. Interview with Edward Preston (Assistant Director of Executive Development and Labor Relations/Federal Personnel Policy, OMB, 1974–1982), on November 18, 1985.

39. The inclusion of the labor relations function in this division had not been anticipated by the Ash Council, which had recommended a title of "Executive Personnel." Evidently, a decision subsequently was made to locate within EDLR, which originally had a Labor Management Relations branch alongside two others (Executive Development and Training and Personnel Policy and Compensation), the labor relations responsibilities conferred on the Bureau of the Budget by Executive Order 11491 of October 26, 1969. That order had assigned the director of BOB, the chairman of the CSC, and the Secretary of Labor to serve on a Federal Labor Relations Council to decide major federal labor-management policy issues.

40. Frederick V. Malek, "The Development of Career Executives—Neglect and Reform," *Public Administration Review*, 34 (May–June 1974): 232.

41. See Malek, *Washington Hidden's Tragedy: The Failure to Make Government Work* (New York: The Free Press, 1978), 21–24, 71–89, 105–17. See also his "Development of Career Executives," 230–32.

42. Malek, "Development of Career Executives," 232. Malek described the CSC's role in this venture in the following terms: "the Civil Service Commission has directed agencies to identify their managerial positions; specify the knowledge and skills required for each; plan and execute an individual development program for each incumbent in these positions; and implement a formal 'high-potential' identification system."

43. Preston had played a leading role in devising and overseeing an executive development program for the IRS, which Malek regarded as a great success and "an effective model for other agencies." Malek, ibid., 232.

44. Preston interview, November 18, 1985. For background on the FEPD, see U.S. Civil Service Commission, Bureau of Executive Manpower, *Executive Manpower in the Federal Service* (June 1974), 5–7.

45. Phone interview with Bernard Rosen (Deputy Executive Director/Executive Director, U.S. Civil Service Commission, 1965–1975) on February 8, 1986.

46. According to Preston, although EDLR maintained its previous staff strength under the Ford Administration, Ford's OMB Director James T. Lynn did not regard executive development as a high priority. Preston interview, November 18, 1985.

47. Rosen, *The Merit System*, 77. The author emphasized that this criticism was not intended as a reflection on the ability of the OMB staff; the lack of progress toward fulfilling the promise of 1970 rather was the predictable consequence of "an inappropriate institutional assignment."

48. Ibid., 88–89.

49. Section 1301(d) of the proposed Civil Service Amendments of 1976 stipulated that: "The Commission shall establish programs and procedures . . . to increase the effectiveness of the recruitment, training, motivation, and utilization of career executives within the executive branch."

50. House Committee on Post Office and Civil Service, Subcommittee on Manpower and the Civil Service, *Civil Service Amendments of 1976*, Hearings on H.R. 12080, 94th Cong., 2nd sess. (Washington, D.C.: U.S. Government Printing Office, 1976), 33, 44 (statement of Clyde Webber, president, American Federation of Government Employees).

51. Ibid., 81; remarks of Subcommittee Chairman David K. Henderson (D-N.C.).

52. Ibid., 3.

53. In addition to transferring OMB's executive development responsibilities to the CSC (along with some of EDLR's labor relations functions, see note 55 later), Reorganization Plan No. 1 of 1977 stipulated that the following OMB functions be transferred elsewhere: Administration, to a new Administrative Office in the EOP; statistical policy (except clearance of agency forms), to the Department of Commerce; and, Advisory Committee Management Secretariat, to the General Services Administration.

54. See John W. Wydler, Thomas N. Kindness, and Arlan Strangeland, in "Statement of Additional Views," U.S. Congress. House Committee on Government Operations, *Reorganization Plan No. 1 of 1977*, House Report #95–661, 96th Cong., 1st sess. (Washington, D.C.: U.S. Government Printing Office, 1977).

55. Executive Order 12027, Section 1(a). 42 F.R. 61851. Section 1(c) of the order affirmed that the CSC would "provide primary Executive branch leadership" in other areas in which it had shared authority with OMB: i.e., (1) developing and reviewing programs of policy guidance to the departments and agencies "for the organization of management's responsibility under the Federal Labor Relations program"; and (2) monitoring issues and trends in labor management relations. Principal responsibility for both these functions within OMB also had been assumed by EDLR.

56. See, e.g., Senate Committee on Appropriations, *Treasury, Postal Service and General Government Appropriations: Fiscal Year 1979. Part 1—Justifications*, Hearings, 95th Cong., 2nd sess. (Washington, D.C.: U.S. Government Printing Office, 1978), 439–41. The "major work items" of the Federal Personnel Policy Division were listed as follows: personnel legislation; pay systems; labor relations; employee benefits and allowances; and federal staffing.

57. Granquist was vice chairman of the FPMP, while Messner (who had been recruited from the CBO to become director of OMB's Management Im-

provement and Evaluation division) co-chaired its working group. The importance of civil service reform as an element of the Carter Administration's reorganization effort was reflected by the presence of Campbell on the President's Executive Committee for Reorganization, along with Carter himself, Vice President Mondale, the director of OMB, and the chairman of the CEA. For background on the FPMP, see Congressional Research Service, Report by James McGrath, *Federal Civil Service Reform: The Federal Personnel Management Project and Proposed Changes in the Federal Civil Service* (Washington, D.C.: Congressional Research Service, March 30, 1978).

58. Preston interview, November 18, 1985.

59. The creation of OPM, the MSPB, and the Federal Labor Relations Authority (charged to oversee labor-management relations and to arbitrate disputes between Federal employee unions and Federal agencies) by means of Reorganization Plan No. 2 which was designed to effect an institutional separation of the administrative, merit system enforcement, and appellate review functions that had previously been combined in the CSC. Many critics maintained that the CSC's performance had suffered because these responsibilities inherently were in conflict with one another.

60. Alan K. Campbell, "Revitalizing the Federal Personnel System," *Public Personnel Management* 7, no. 6 (January–February 1978): 63. In this article, Campbell saw fit to add as a personal note: "I don't believe there's going to be any other part of the project in which I have a greater interest [than in SES], having for some twenty years been arguing in favor of changes in the top of the career service."

61. Federal Personnel Management Project, *Final Staff Report*, vol. 1 (Washington, D.C.: President's Reorganization Project, December 1977), 183 (hereafter cited as *Ink Report.*)

62. Campbell, "Revitalizing," 64. While placing special emphasis upon the proposed system's capacity to undo the effects of cumbersome procedures and overly restrictive policies, which had seriously impeded agency heads' ability to select, motivate, and manage federal executives, the Ink Report suggested that the SES proposal would help to minimize the effects of two other serious problems in the prevailing system identified by the FPMP: inadequate controls over the size and distribution of the executive cadre, and inadequate protection against political abuse and incompetence. See *Ink Report*, 183–85.

63. *Ink Report*, 199–200 (Recommendation No. 89), 127–28 (Recommendation No. 48), 185.

64. The various FPMP recommendations for reform of the civil service were officially reviewed by a six-person group (composed of Campbell and Jule Sugarman from the CSC, Granquist and Messner from OMB, and two representatives from the White House Domestic Council), which subsequently oversaw the drafting of the Civil Service Reform Act. The FPMP proposals bearing on the SES do

not appear to have been amended in any important respect in the course of this review process; given Campbell's special interest in this portion of the project, it seems unlikely (despite his repeated claims regarding the autonomy of the project task forces) that the proposals generated by the FPMP in this particular would not have reflected his imprint.

The provisions of CSRA bearing on executive development for and within the SES did not attract much congressional attention, although Congress did adopt an amendment, originating in the House, to upgrade the entrance requirements for the SES by mandating that not more than 30 percent of individuals serving in the system at any one point in time have less than five years of federal civil service experience.

65. 5 U.S.C. §3996.

66. For a generally favorable review and assessment of OPM's executive development efforts in the period from July 1979 to mid-1984, see U.S. General Accounting Office, *Progress Report on Federal Executive Development Programs*, GAO/GGD-84-92 (August 15, 1984).

67. Preston interview, November 18, 1985.

68. OMB Memorandum No. 82-49, July 11, 1982.

69. For background on the administration's productivity improvement program, officially launched on February 25, 1986 with the promulgation of Executive Order 12552, see Carol Dineen, "Productivity Improvement: Its Our Turn," *The Bureaucrat* 14, no. 4 (Winter 1985-86): 10-14.

70. See the account provided in U.S. General Accounting office, *Increased Use of Productivity Management Can Help Control Government Costs.* GAO/AFMD-84-11 (November 10, 1983), 23-25.

71. The prospects for the successful institutionalization of the productivity improvement function at OMB are explored in Peter M. Benda and Charles H. Levine, "Reagan's Productivity Improvement Program: Deja Vu, Fresh Start, or Lasting Reform?," *Public Productivity Review* 39 (Fall 1986): 3-26.

Chapter 5
Rights-Based
Budgeting

Jeffrey D. Straussman

Introduction

At one time, not very many years ago, budgeting symbolized the routines of government. The routines of budgeting came from the repetitiveness of the process: Budgets were prepared, reviewed, revised, appropriated, executed, and monitored in a particular sequence. The regularity of the budget cycle had its own unique rhythm. Participants in the budget process knew what they were supposed to do; roles were well established and remained largely unchanged over time.

Strategies and negotiation techniques took place within the routines of budgeting, among well entrenched participants. Strategies and negotiation tactics were employed at specific times in the budget cycle lending an air of stability to the process. For example, agencies were expected to ask for modest increases over the previous year's budget; the budget office, adopting a "fiscal orientation," was expected to be mildly skeptical of agencies' requests and, therefore, tended to resist budget expansion (Appleby, 1980). Agencies that enjoyed good relations with their legislative sponsors turned to the appropriate legislative constituencies to buffer cuts enacted by the budget office. While the success of this tactic varied depending on political skill of the agency head, salience of the program in the legislature, and the determination of the administration to enforce fiscal discipline, these features of the budget process had become routine and had given budgeting an air of stability. Since the process had been predictable, estimates of changes in budgeting were highly reliable. These features of a typical budget process formed the roots of *incrementalism*, the interpretation of budgeting that dominated the subject for almost thirty years (Lindblom, 1959; Wildavsky, 1984).

The portrait of budgeting just outlined reifies a process that, naturally, is much more complicated in practice. While routines were practiced, the process had been made far less predictable by the fiscal vagaries of the past several years (Bozeman & Straussman, 1982). With budgetary growth no longer guaranteed, much of the predictability of both the process and the outcomes has eroded. As the loss of a predictable budgetary future has upset the routines of budgeting, faith in our ability to explain the way the process works similarly has been lost. Fiscal scarcity has provided a modest "growth industry" for scholars of the budgetary process, who had been searching for a way to loosen incrementalism's grip on budgetary theory (see, for example, Schick, 1980). Budget theory—if indeed the very notion of developing a theoretical orientation to the subject ever really was plausible—has been ripe for renewal.

Budget theory has been ripe for renewal for another reason. A conception of budgeting that rests on stability, regularity, and predictability pertains, at best, to an increasingly smaller portion of the budget. A great deal has already been written about the so-called uncontrollable feature of entitlement spending (Weaver, 1985). Suffice it to say here that approximately 40 percent of the federal budget is made up of spending for entitlements, such as social security, food stamps, unemployment compensation, aid to families with dependent children, medicare and medicaid, and veterans' benefits. The most common feature of these programs is that decision-making discretion is extremely limited, certainly in the short run. Since entitlements generally have permanent appropriations, Congress cannot exert budget control without changing the language of authorization. Moreover, the courts have been sympathetic to the idea that beneficiaries should receive procedural due process protection before an entitlement may be withheld. Entitlements are rights.

Entitlements are one type of budgetary right. Much of the existing literature on entitlements has focused on two broad issues: (1) the magnitude of entitlement spending, the rate of growth of entitlement programs, and the contribution of entitlements to the federal deficit problem (see Rivlin, 1984), and (2) the political justification for entitlement programs in the contemporary welfare state (see Stockman, 1986). The first item is largely an empirical issue for which we have ample documentation. The second falls broadly into the realm of contemporary political discourse, where the clash of values concerning the "appropriate" role of the state cannot be derived solely from empirical observation. Neither issue provides substantial information concerning the impact of entitlements on our understanding of budget processes per se.

Entitlements, as a budgetary concept, are not transferred directly to state and local budget processes. Yet, lower-level governments also find that their budgetary discretion is circumscribed by budgetary rights that create claims on the public's money. For example, intergovernmental programs, such as aid to families with dependent children and medicaid, provide statutory rights for beneficiaries; these programs have the same qualities as federal entitlements. Moreover, federal and state court decisions also have established rights that have had budgetary ramifications for state and local governments. Familiar examples include cases on the right to treatment in state mental health and mental retardation facilities, and cases involving overcrowding in state correctional facilities and local government jails. State and local governments, like the federal government, have found that an increasingly larger portion of their budgets has been "earmarked" for rights-based programs. Current assumptions about discretion and choice in budgetary processes may distort what, in fact, is a more restrictive reality. Budget theory needs to wrestle with the relationship between rights and budgets. This essay is an effort in that direction.

Rights Versus Budgets

Rights imply uncompromising declaratory statements that pertain to a defined population. Much ink has been spilled on just what may be the source of such rights. In a public policy context, when rights translate into some level of individual or collective benefit, rights become entitlements—and, therefore, claims on the public purse. With the onset of the welfare state, many claims for large scale social benefits were justified on the basis of rights. For example, the principle that health and welfare services should be provided to all citizens, as a right, was established in Britain in 1942 in the Beveridge Report. The principle is still held by major segments of the British Labour Party, though obviously the notion of a universal right to social services is not part of the program of the Thatcher Government (Gilbert 1982, 301–303). In the United States, the drift toward universal coverage of social services, as opposed to means-tested programs, continued throughout the 1970s expanding the beneficiaries of the welfare state but the principle suffered a reversal with the election of President Reagan in 1980.

When we think of rights in a public policy context, programs with clearly defined beneficiaries (and clearly established benefits) come to mind. At the federal level, these would include social security, medicare, veterans' benefits, food stamps, and public assistance. Administrative discretion in granting these rights is supposed to be restricted—in theory at least. Discretion is circumscribed through procedural due process guarantees. For example, the "fair hearing" procedure employed in public assistance is designed to protect a person's right to the benefit until it can be shown that some provision of the law has been violated by the recipient. Until the issue is resolved, the recipient continues to receive public assistance benefits.

Rights are indivisible. The notion of dividing "equal protection" among a set of prospective beneficiaries is odd at best. Though rights are rarely absolute, the withdrawal of a right, once created, is neither easily justified on philosophical grounds nor a politically facile process. The very character of rights, therefore, makes them problematical *from a budgetary point of view*. Whereas rights are supposed to be indivisible, allocative tradeoffs are the essence of budgeting. Rights, therefore, are the "enemy" of budgets, because they inhibit choices among competing purposes. When rights are established and programs are implemented to make them a reality, budgetary commitments restrict options and an uncertain future is mortgaged. Since rights are inflexible, they are anathema to the budgeter, who jealously guards the residues of choice that are constantly under siege from programs that offer firm spending guarantees. The uncontrollable dimension of entitlement spending in the federal budget has received so much attention precisely because it portrays this characteristic of the budgetary rigidity of rights.

Not all governments experience the same level of absolute claims on the public purse. Differences naturally will depend on the political values that undergird a regime. Moreover, rights-based claims on the public purse change over time. In a federal system like the United States claims on state and local budget depend on the functional assignment of responsibilities, particularly on the amount of redistributive activities either granted to or required of lower-level governments. Contemporary illustrations of claims on the state and local governments that resemble the entitlement pattern so prevalent at the federal level include medicaid and aid to families with dependent children.

Sometimes, programs produce claims on the public purse that are less than absolute. We can consider such claims *quasi-rights*. Quasi-rights are politically more tenuous than statutory entitlements. For instance, a means-tested student loan program may have some of the features of other entitlements; however, the "moral claim" is probably less secure compared to an entitlement like veterans' educational benefits. At the local level, public education is a quasi-right since the courts have held that the "right" of public education is not expressly guaranteed by the U. S. Constitution. Perhaps, most important, the political capacity to alter a program with quasi-rights is generally greater than for entitlements. (Recall Secretary of Education Bennett's criticisms of the student loan program as a federal boondoggle that subsidizes middle- and upper-middle-class college students.)

Programs can be arrayed along a rights-based continuum in terms of their respective claims on the public monies, where absolute claims are at one end of the continuum and programs with no such absolutes are at the other. Figure 5-1 displays a hypothetical continuum.

Figure 5-1
Hypothetical Rights-Based Continuum

Entitlement coupled with voting power	Means-tested entitlement	Judicial decision administrative discretion	Rule adjudication	Moral claim

From a budgetary perspective a rights-based continuum is instructive insofar as the amount of discretion for making choices increases as we move from left to right along the continuum. As the amount of discretion increases, the certainty of funding is likely to decrease, since, by definition, the essence of budgeting—choice among competing purposes—becomes more and more apparent.

Sources of Rights and Quasi-Rights

Rights stem from different sources. While moral philosophers may debate the justification of alternative conceptions of the bases of rights (such as natural law, for example), rights-based budgeting is less abstract. The major sources of rights that produce corresponding expenditures may be identified as in the following sections.

LEGISLATION. Most budgetary rights have their roots in legislation. Much of the concern over so-called uncontrollable entitlement spending surrounds the present and future budgetary consequence of past legislation that established a class of claimants. (Many of the entitlements have their statutory existence in the various titles of the Social Security Act. Other major programs include the food stamp program, veterans' benefits, and military and civilian retirement.) At issue, in general, is the continued justification for some of the programs and the difficulties in managing the budgetary ramifications of entitlements. Fiscal management is made difficult precisely because rights are not only guaranteed in principle, the budgetary procedures for providing benefits largely remove discretion from fiscal managers. It is in this sense that one may argue that rights and budgeting are inherently in conflict with one another.

Judicially Established Rights. Rights, with budgetary consequences, also are established by the courts. Consider just one of the more prominent rights that has influenced state budgets—institutional reform litigation. Much has been written about institutional reform litigation where state agencies, charged with housing individuals with severe mental and/or physical disabilities, or individuals who have been found guilty of serious crimes, have been found, by the courts, to violate constitutional guarantees. Common substantive claims that have been upheld by the courts include overcrowded conditions in state correctional facilities, which violate the Eighth Amendment prohibition against cruel and inhuman punishment and a judicially derived due process "right to treatment" guarantee for individuals confined to state institutions for the physically and mentally disabled.

The budgetary ramifications of judicially mandated rights are not always certain. Judges have not been receptive to defendants' claims that lack of funds prevent effective compliance with court orders. Aggregate budget data suggest that judicial decisions in institutional reform cases have influenced state spending. One study of the impact of federal court decisions on state spending for corrections found that capital expenditures generally have increased in the years after court decisions, spending on corrections as a percentage of the total budget increases after a decision, and capital spending is reflected in an increase in *planned* beds (Harriman & Straussman, 1983, 348).

Institutional cases may have influenced budgeting in more subtle ways than merely increasing the amount of spending for corrections, mental health, or mental retardation. Many institutional cases established standards, such as constitutional minimums required for compliance with Eighth Amendment guarantees. Judicial interpretation of what constitutes satisfactory compliance is operationalized as a given amount of square feet per prisoner in a cell. Similarly, staffing ratios have also been established as part of several consent decrees. Court-mandated standards remove some of the strategy and negotiation that usually accompanies budget submission and review. That is, debate over what may constitute appropriate—or defensible—criteria for determining budget levels is short-circuited, since the court has made the decision in the context of constitutional protection.

Rule Adjudication. Strictly speaking, administrative agencies do not create rights; they enforce them. But, a right unimplemented is vacuous.

The pattern of implementation of a legislative or judicially established right—the way in which an agency uses its discretion—may have a great impact on the realization of a right for a given population and the concommitant budgetary consequences of agency implementation.

In a case study of the administration of social security disability claims, Mashaw (1983) develops three contrasting models of "bureaucratic justice." The first model is based on a Weberian bureaucracy imbued with the norm of rationality defined as cost-effective implementation. The second model is based on the application of a service ethic derived from professional treatment norms. Mashaw terms the third model of bureaucratic justice the *moral judgment approach*, wherein the agency tries to apply a principle of fairness to resolve disputes between parties. These three models are not inherently compatible with one another. The dominance of one model on the adjudication of agency decisions would surely have a bearing on the status of present and future claimants and the accompanying budgetary consequences of the model reflected in a given agency's behavior.

Rights, Equalities, and Budgets

Public policy has strayed far from nineteenth century liberalism. While rights ran deep insofar as one presumably was entitled to a fair amount of individual autonomy and freedom *from* government, rights were quite narrow when it came to entitlements. One need only recall the Social Darwinism of the Supreme Court at the turn of the century, and into the twentieth century, with respect to the limits of legitimate state action.

Beginning with the Social Security Act of 1935, rights-based programs emerged as a major force on the budgetary landscape. This can be expressed historically by displaying the evolution of entitlement spending. Table 5-1 presents trends for payments to individuals for the period 1940–1986. These data include direct cash and in-kind payments and grants to states that are passed on to individuals.

The programs beneath these aggregates include most of the well-known federal entitlements, such as social security, medicare, veterans' benefits, in-kind social services, and other income security programs. Table 5-1 shows the growth of these programs in both current *and* constant dollars and as a percentage of total federal outlays (until 1986).

The data summarize what we all know to be true. The post-1945 era has witnessed a substantial transformation in the scope of government activity, which is exemplified in the concept *welfare state*. This transformation has been common to most if not all advanced capitalist countries.

Table 5-1.

Payment for Individuals by Program, Selected Years: 1940–1986.

Program	1940	1950	1960	1970	1980	1986
Social security and railroad retirement	128.90	1,027.20	11,738.20	30,653.60	141,523.90	203,728.70
Federal employees retirement and insurance	389.50	2,032.40	3,370.50	8,741.00	40,487.30	53,108.10
Unemployment assistance	497.50	2,013.00	2,782.10	3,042.60	18,374.10	14,848.70
Medical care	96.70	847.90	1,104.50	11,910.90	66,726.90	106,357.60
Assistance to students		2,738.80	392.20	1,518.90	8,559.90	8,599.30
Housing assistance		7.10	140.00	480.40	6,774.50	10,276.70
Food and nutrition assistance		83.10	231.90	959.70	16,119.30	18,188.40
Public assistance and related programs	464.20	1,599.40	3,322.30	6,397.00	21,056.10	24,312.10
All other payments for individuals	80.40	3,315.20	720.40	946.20	3,758.90	3,319.40
Total, payments for individuals	$1,657.20	$13,664.10	$23,802.10	$64,650.30	$323,380.90	$442,739.00
Total budget outlays	9,468.00	42,562.00	92,191.00	195,649.00	590,920.00	973,725.00
Payments as a percent of total outlays	.18	.32	.26	.33	.55	.45

Source: Historical Tables, Budget of the United States Government fiscal year 1986, Tables 11.3, 3.2.

While the American experience has lagged behind other Western countries, expansion of the beneficiary pool and increases in the average
benefit level occurred from 1960–1980 (Organization for Economic Co-
Operation and Development, 1985, 101–10).

While spending is rights based, at least two broad types of rights
undergird much of the redistributive programs that make up the welfare
state. Some programs, like social security, medicare, and veterans'
benefits, define eligibility in terms of subject classes, such as age, or
previous status (i.e. having served in the armed forces). Others, such as
aid to families with dependent children, supplemental security income,
and food stamps, are means tested.

Means tested programs may be made more or less generous by alter-
ing the bases of need *and/or* the benefit level. In addition, increasing
budgetary stringency may cause a "tightening up" of means-tested entitlements without the appearance of substantive programmatic changes.
From the vantage point of rights, administrative changes, such as longer
waiting periods before benefits begin or more stringent eligibility standards, do not alter, in a substantive way, the entitlement. Besides, since
means-tested programs are more vulnerable politically than entitlements
that have no means test, the right attached to them is less secure. Nevertheless, the notion that it is the responsibility of the federal government
to ensure minimum income levels is manifested in the *entitlement* feature
of the programs. That they respond to demographic and economic conditions without any change in law is indicative of the way policy has
adapted to political consensus—at least, until 1981.

The precariousness of the notion that existing benefits are "in-
alienable rights" from a budgetary as well as a moral stance was illustrated by the attack on entitlements in the first Reagan Administration, particularly the effort to establish a so-called safety net. The idea
behind the social safety net was deceptively simple: Those who were
"truly needy" would continue to receive benefits, while programs that
were abused or counterproductive—in that they exacerbated dependen-
cy—would be curtailed if not actually eliminated. Beyond this formulation, it also became clear that some subject classes—needy children, the
chronically mentally ill, and the low-income elderly—do not share the
equivalent concept of entitlement applied to individuals who receive
benefits from various income security programs.

A study by the Urban Institute concluded that the Reagan Administration was able to cut some of the funding for programs for
abused, neglected, and dependent children; it has cut federal funding for
mental health and reorganized some programs into a block grant for
state governments. Similarly, selected programs that benefit the low-

income elderly, especially those funded by a social services block grant to the states, also have been trimmed (Burt & Pittman, 1985, 174–75).

To summarize, the key differences between "traditional" entitlements and the programs just enumerated are the consensus concerning the right and the mechanism for funding. (When the funding mechanism is a block grant, funding is more susceptible to change and reduction for fiscal reasons.) In particular, changes in fiscal federalism, which ostensibly provide more discretion to the states, also may have an important ramification for budgetary rights. This sort of fiscal rights "bumping" through the intergovernmental grants system may provide additional discretion for state governments. However, since fiscal federalism is accompanied by budgetary responsibility, the protected status of a right with such intergovernmental characteristics is likely to be threatened.

Managing the Budget by Managing Rights

The relationship between rights and budgets is a dynamic one. Since rights have budgetary consequences, the import of rights can be altered by managing the budget. Ramifications depend on the relative insulation of a given right from budgetary alterations. Consider, as a case in point, the Balanced Budget and Emergency Deficit Control Act of 1985, known more commonly as Gramm-Rudman-Hollings (G-R-H).

Gramm-Rudman-Hollings represents the collective efforts of Congress to reduce the federal deficit. The process establishes deficit reduction targets for each year beginning in fiscal year 1986 and ending with fiscal year 1991, when the deficit is supposed to equal zero. In the event that the estimated deficit in a given year is projected to fall short of the target, G-R-H provides a rather elaborate mechanism to cut spending to reach the designated target.

Budgetary rights are addressed in the legislation. Specifically, entitlements such as social security, veterans' benefits, aid to families with dependent children, food stamps, and other income security programs are exempted from G-R-H budget reductions. The list of exempt programs highlights the political sensitivity of entitlements. From a purely fiscal perspective, budget savings would be enhanced if one or more of the characteristic features of any entitlement—population covered, extent of coverage, level of benefits received—were made more restrictive. Initial suggestions along these lines during the congressional debates over G-R-H demonstrated the political volatility of the idea that major entitlement programs should be made equally vulnerable to sequestrations in the event that deficit reduction targets are missed.

All rights are not protected equally. In particular, benefits to some individuals that come from federal government block grants "passed through" the states are not protected under the legislation. Consider a dramatic impact of this reality on a local government program, funded by the Title XX block grant program, designed to affect the incidence and consequences of child abuse. One must first debate whether, in fact, children who either are or have the potential for being abused enjoy a "right" to government intervention. If the answer is negative the public issue is ended at this point. If the principle of intervention is established, implementation is conditioned by the level of Title XX funding. Since current and future victims of child abuse are affected by the vagaries of funding, managing the budget has the effect of managing rights, since competing claims within a budget constraint forces decisions that, by default, make absolute principles conditional on resources.

Managing the Budget by Managing Rights

Alterations in the ways in which rights are specified and opera-tionalized in programmatic detail may have profound budgetary implica-tions. Since discretion is removed from rights-based programs that pro-vide benefits to individuals, budget control may be reestablished by changing the quality of the right. A good deal of the political debate over the status of entitlement programs begins from the premise that rights in-herent in entitlements should be revised with an eye toward budget con-trol.

REDUCING THE VALUE OF THE BENEFIT. The economic value of an entitle-ment may be changed because of fiscal austerity. One approach is to reduce the value of the benefit for a subset of the entitlement group. Social security benefits provide a simple example since retired persons who can earn income above a given level must pay income tax, thereby reducing the value of their social security receipts. Similarly, some in-dividuals who receive unemployment compensation benefits must pay income taxes on their benefits.

The value of a benefit may be eroded through inflation. For exam-ple, since state governments establish the benefit level for recipients of aid to families with dependent children (AFDC), governments that choose not to increase the benefit level are allowing the value of the benefit to diminish. Since AFCD, in general, is politically unpopular, this approach has been used to both provide the entitlement and manage the substantial cost of the program. Obviously, federal entitlement pro-grams that are currently indexed to changes in the rate of inflation would take on this character if the Congress eliminated indexing. A less extreme approach is to lengthen the lag between changes in inflation and index-ing.

Means Tests. Means-tested programs put the burden of proof on the individual claiming benefits. The purpose of the means test, in theory, is to ensure that benefits go only to those who are truly entitled to the benefit on the basis of need. In addition, a means test also mitigates, in principle at least, against the likelihood that policy objectives will conflict with one another. For instance, means-tested income security programs are supposed to alleviate poverty; however, policy makers hope that they do not diminish work effort.

Changing an existing entitlement from a subject class, such as the elderly (all those above sixty-five years of age) or veterans, to a means-tested benefit would reduce the total cost of the program. Of course, while the mechanics of such a change are not difficult to spell out, the politics surrounding such a change are quite another matter.

Program "Bundling." Means tests are used to determine who is eligible for public programs. It is conceivable, instead, to use a means test to determine who would be eligible for a range of programs, where individuals select from the alternatives up to a predetermined cash and/or in-kind benefit limit. Fiscal conservatives like this concept because the overall budgetary impact is expected to be lower than currently exists where some individuals may be able to receive many programs because of the linked entitlements among them. Those who are interested in reducing government interference in individul decisions are receptive to the notion of program bundling, since it puts more responsibility on the individual to choose programs that are "truly" needed. Notice that in this scheme the right has justly been shifted, since one is no longer entitled to a range of government programs but, rather, a given income level, which may be reached through a smorgasbord of programs. The general observation remains: Program bundling, like the other methods for managing the budget is designed to limit the impact of the budgetary claim.

Constitutional Minimums. Courts have defined constitutional minimum standards in many institutional reform cases. One effect of a judicially imposed minimum standards is that the defendant agency is required to "spend up" to the level required to meet the court order. One may argue, however, that a court-ordered standard also may be interpreted by the agency or the legislature as the maximum level required to remain in compliance. Paradoxically then, judicial intervention in institutional cases may help manage the budget and buttress pressures for decreased spending.

Rights-Based Budgeting and Budget Theory

Much of what has already been said really is not new, though the portrait of rights-based budgeting may be a different way of looking at

categories of spending that have been the focus of many analyses of contemporary fiscal and budgetary problems, particularly the deficit dilemma. A great deal of attention has been given to entitlement spending;
however, rights-based budgeting as a process is not easily accommodated in existing conceptions of how the process is best understood.
This is so either because the normative underpinnings of budgeting, as an
allocation process that determines preferences, *or* the perspectives on
budgeting that emphasize its decision-making features have difficulty
with the rigidities endemic to rights. Whereas budgeting requires flexibility in the face of uncertainty, too much flexibility endangers rights.
Budget theory has preferred to ignore the differences between rights and
other forms of public programs. This argument about the inability of ex-
tant theories to incorporate rights in a plausible way can be illustrated by
a brief review of some of the more influential efforts to interpret contemporary budgetary processes.

V. O. Key

V. O. Key's essay, "The Lack of a Budgetary Theory," published in
1940, justifiably has been treated as a classic in the literature (1978,
19–24). The heart of Key's reflections centered on the inability of
economics to provide a persuasive method for making choices among
competing public programs. What was missing—indeed, some would
argue, *what* is *still* missing—was a credible normative stance from which
reliable predictions could be made about the benefits to be either realized
or lost. Welfare economics underpinnings of contemporary policy
analysis have made some progress in this direction (Nelson, 1977). But
the techniques of cost-benefit and cost-effectiveness analysis have a ring
of unreality when applied to choices about rights.

V. O. Key grudgingly came to this point of view at the end of his
famous essay, when he commented, "The most advantageous utilization
of public funds resolves itself into a matter of value preferences between
ends lacking a common denominator. As such, the question is a problem
in political philosophy" (1978, 23). In modern parlance, we would speak
about policy goals and any tradeoffs that must be made among or within
policies.

Consider the areas of choice inherent in a political value such as
equality. Suppose we wish to provide individuals with some level of
"equality of opportunity." Once the principle is established, there is a
range of programs that may further the policy objective. These may include compensatory education programs, improved access to health
care, and several alternative income maintenance programs. Given the
philosophical foundation, the desire to improve equality, Key's question

concerning the bases of budgetary choice becomes relevant. That is, once a decision is made to advance the goal of equality through, say, compensatory education programs, it is certainly reasonable to evaluate the cost-effectiveness of alternative education programs and judge the programs against a predetermined equality of opportunity standard. It generally is agreed that comparisons across dissimilar programs—an education program versus a health program, for instance—are tenuous because beneficiaries are likely to be different, time dimensions are not equivalent, and the outcomes of both programs lack a common denominator.

In the end, Key's search for allocation criteria to make budget decisions more rational was misdirected, for the philosophical underpinnings he alluded to at the end of his essay respond to factors other than the kind of rational analysis he sought. Using equality as an example again, one would be hard pressed to show that, since 1981, equality as a philosophical basis for budgetary decisions has not suffered any changes. Surely, the efforts to redirect the scope of government activity toward a reduced government presence, for the moment, has put the political brakes on additional redistributive programs. But, it would be overstating it to say that swings in political philosophy are accompanied by a corresponding broadening of budgetary choices. One need only read about former budget director David Stockman's disillusionment with the Reagan Administration's failed efforts to alter the scope of government to appreciate the staying power of many of the political values that undergird the contemporary social policy (Stockman, 1986). Similarly, a review of the exempt entitlement programs in the Gramm-Rudman legislation also shows the staying power of most welfare state programs. Since rights that are built on philosophical edifices have the ability to withstand shifts in the political pendulum, it follows that budgetary choices are constrained by the *structure* of rights.

Incrementalism

Incrementalism as a theory of budgeting successfully avoided V. O. Key's normative quagmire. Incrementalism, as an explanation of the budget process, focuses on the method of decisions, not the justification for the results of decisions. There are several descriptions of incrementalism, as well as several critiques (see Lindblom, 1961; Wildavsky, 1984; Dempster & Wildavsky, 1979; LeLoup, 1978). For the purposes here, incrementalism is premised on a few key assumptions about how budgeting takes place. Incrementalism is a method for making decisions. Participants in the process try to simplify an otherwise complex process by adopting what Wildavsky has called "aids to calculation" (1984,

11-16). These aids, such as "satisficing" among alternative choices, using experience as a guide to decision making, and making marginal changes from last year's budget choices give budgeting its distinctive character—stability. As a method of decision making it is grounded in the theoretical work of Lindblom (1959) and Simon (1976), which, in a sharp departure from the economic literature on rational decision making, showed how individuals pursue individual goals when organizational and informational barriers are substantial.

Incrementalism has had amazing conceptual staying power. Contrary to Key's quest for the normative budgetary grail, incremental theory is more modest. It does not attempt to predict "optimal" outcomes; rather, incrementalism yields insights into patterns of budgetary procedure and offers some conjectures about whether deviations from an established procedure are likely to be successful.

Chipping away at the foundations of incremental theory has been a pastime of students of the budget process. While some criticisms have centered on the specificity of the models used to investigate empirically the process (see, for example, Padgett, 1980), other criticisms have questioned the continued viability of incrementalism as a comprehensive theory in light of fiscal austerity and the corresponding impact of austerity on budgeting (Bozeman and Straussman, 1982; Behn, 1985).

Incrementalism also may not adequately explain rights-based budgeting. Whereas incrementalism suggests strategy and negotiation within established rules of the game, rights require at least a modicum of rigidity. Since, in principle, rights are nonnegotiable, the give and take of incremental budgeting is inappropriate for rights because, by definition, rights would not be guaranteed; rather, they would be the product of a bargaining process. Of course, budgetary rights often are produced in precisely this way. But, once created, rights need protection; otherwise, they would lose their unique status. This is why traditionally the courts are indispensable for the provision and protection of rights. Since the courts are inclined to negotiate and bargain only occasionally (and reluctantly), the purposive inflexibility of the courts wreaks havoc with a budget process built on incrementalism. Similarly, incremental theory accommodates poorly to a situation where judges play an important role in both the process and the outcome of budgeting (Straussman, 1986).

Federal entitlement programs display the essential features of incrementalism: regularity, a limited number of alternative choices in programmatic decisions, and small changes from the existing budget base (Dempster and Wildavsky, 1979). What they tend to lack is discretion. This is one of the strongest reasons why those who want to curb the growth of federal outlays seek to gain more control over mandatory spending. Ultimately, rights-based programs create a major dilemma for policy makers. If these programs must enter the budgetary fray like all other claimants their protected status naturally would be diminished. On the other hand, when budgetary rights are protected, fiscal control is exacerbated.

Incremental theory does not remain unscathed in all of this. When fiscal scarcity threatens fair shares and modest incremental growth, the norms of reciprocity are violated. A budget rule such as across the board, share the pain is designed to minimize the inevitable conflicts that surround retrenchment. But, if rights are to be protected, such a rule clearly is inappropriate for rights-based programs. Given a fiscal target, rights become a catalyst for a decision-making process that looks less and less incremental.

Congressional-Agency Relations: Public Choice Perspectives

The theory of public choice has established a few key "axioms" of agency and legislative behavior that have a bearing on rights-based budgeting. These axioms may be summarized as follows: Bureaucrats are expected to act in a rational, self-interested way to maximize their individual utility. In the public sector, individuals seek out appropriate surrogates in organizational settings that will further the goal of utility maximization. For agency heads, the most important surrogate is budgetary expansion (Niskanen, 1971).

Congressional behavior in spending decisions similarly has been interpreted from this public choice orientation. Whereas agency heads seek to maximize utility through budget expansion, legislators seek to be reelected. Members of Congress, therefore, will support programs with concentrated benefits and dispersed costs (Wilson, 1973), since these programs would enhance the legislator's visibility in the district and, therefore, improve the chances of reelection.

Shepsle and Weingast show how this perspective can be used to interpret the federal budget deficit (1984 343–367). With the decline of centralized power centers in Congress (the speaker, party leaders, and committee chairmen), members of Congress have followed the pull of geography; they have served on committees and subcommittees that could benefit their own districts. The distributive character of programs administered by the Small Business Administration, Economic Development Administration, and the Department of Housing and Urban Development's Urban Development Action Grant (UDAG) are representative of the kinds of programs in this formulation of federal spending.

The vote motive thesis may be persuasive for discretionary domestic programs. As a more general explanation of federal spending, and rights-based programs in particular, it is problematical (see Ellwood, 1984; Schultze, 1984). While social security is undoubtably backed by significant voting power, it is implausible to assume that congressional votes on all rights-based programs would necessarily translate into electoral support. Under certain conditions the reverse in fact may occur. Surely, a legislator who claims credit for some means-tested entitlement programs may lose as many votes as he or she may gain, because a portion of the constituents will be opposed to spending that is considered "excessive" or earmarked for the "undeserving." In fact, a legislator who really believes that benefits should be provided (or increased) may take a "tough" fiscal stand, if the legislation is expected to pass. Since means-tested programs, by definition, are specific to individuals (rather than to places), the fiscally conservative representative may thereby score points—if his fiscal conservatism mirrors his district's views—without risking a loss of benefits to constituents. Thus, one may be able to act in a politically rational manner without giving up any private moral imperatives.

Implications for the Evolution of Budget Theory

There are three broad lessons from this excursion into the relationship between rights and budgets: (1) the need to extend our knowledge about the institutional character of the public budgeting process; (2) the need to further investigate the decision-making characteristics of the classic *budget function* in rights-based environments; and (3) the impact of political change on rights-based budgeting.

INSTITUTIONAL CHARACTER OF BUDGETARY PROCESSES. Stripped to its essentials, budgeting generally is portrayed as a three-person game among the agency, the central budget office, and the legislature. Of course, theoretical excursions into the process acknowledge that this formulation simplifies a much more complex process. Nevertheless, the principle of parsimony has served well to create a portrait of budget processes that display the essential features identified in the beginning of this essay.

The three-person game formulation does not adequately explain rights-based budgeting. In particular, the role of the courts is ignored. Consider how the courts may alter a "normal" three-person game approach to budgeting. A state agency is faced with litigation alleging that some condition of the management of the agency violates a constitutional guarantee. (The most common example would be overcrowding of state correctional facilities.) What posture should the agency take?

Anecdotal evidence suggests that some state administrators—faced with the prospects of defending their agencies before federal judges—employed the so-called crisis technique. "By publicizing a situation, dramatizing it effectively, and perhaps asking for emergency appropriations, an agency may maneuver itself into a position of responsibility for large new programs" (Wildavsky, 1984, 116). As a strategy, the crisis technique is one approach toward budgetary aggrandizement beyond what would otherwise be the agency's fair share. The three-person game is very much intact since bargaining and negotiation in a limited time frame with less-than-perfect information revolves around three budget levels: $F1$, the agency's fair share budget level in the absence of the crisis; $F3$, the court-mandated budget level, which is established outside of the three person game (and anathema to the legislature and the budget office); and a negotiated $F2$ level, which is higher than $F1$ though lower than $F3$ and "buys" some reduction in the probability that the crisis will actually occur.

While this formulation is easily accommodated within the boundaries of incremental theory, the three-person game model, intrinsic to many conceptions of public budgetary processes, is less persuasive once three factors are introduced: fiscal climate, the time frame of litigation, and policy agreement with judicial decisions (see Straussman, 1986 for an extended argument). The key point is that judicially determined rights that force earmarked spending may trigger responses that are not predicated on the stability of the three-person game model of budgeting. For example, since a court decision may have the effect of mortgaging future budgetary increments, agency opposition could be strong, even if budget growth in the near term is virtually guaranteed. More generally, since some agencies are more prone to litigation than others and, therefore, would have their budgets influenced by court decisions, it would seem prudent, from a theoretical standpoint, to expand the current institutional structure beyond a three-person game model.

Consider just one reason why this is so. In a normal three-person budget process model fiscal constraints establish broad parameters within which strategy and negotiation unfold. These may include tax limitations, balanced budget rules, or at the federal level, a politically acceptable budget deficit forecast. The three players—agency, budget office, and legislature—understand the fiscal constraints and adjust to them. Courts are not bound by fiscal constraints. While negotiations over the implementation of a judicial decision *may* include a tacit acknowledgement of fiscal limits, courts share no a priori inclination to adhere to them. When judges intervene, then, it may have ramifications for spending decisions, decisions that could look much different precisely because the courts are an additional player in the budget game.

TOP-DOWN FISCAL MANAGEMENT AND THE CLASSIC BUDGET FUNCTION. Several commentaries on the federal budget process have observed the shift toward greater emphasis on mechanisms to enforce spending control and integrate budget decisions with fiscal policy choices (Bozeman & Straussman, 1982; Heclo, 1984; Johnson, 1984; Rauch, 1985). While top-down budgetary processes have been in existence for several administrations (Mowery, Kamlet, & Crecine, 1980), the politics of the deficit since 1981 has accentuated the shift in budgetary emphasis. Macrobudget decisions, designed to foster budget control, cannot ignore entitlements. This point was amply demonstrated in the Omnibus Reconciliation Act of 1981. Amendments to authorizations for several entitlements, changing benefit levels and/or eligibility criteria, was one method used to produce cuts in both budget authority and outlays (Ellwood, 1982). What impact has this trend had on the classic budget function?

In a classic essay, Paul Appleby noted, "In one way, there is no point in denying, the budget function is preponderantly negative. It is on the whole rather strongly against program and expenditure expansion" (1980, 134–35). Speaking from many years of career service in the Division of the Budget in the State of New York, Paul Veillette observed, "I have noticed a tendency for examiners to be moralistic, to view themselves as the protectors of the public's financial interests against the greed of others. Often, we are correct" (1981, 62). Dale McOmber, former Assistant Director for Budget Review, U.S. Office of Management and Budget commented on the changing quality of examiners in the following way, "What is particularly fascinating is how each new group of young people seems to be more skilled and effective than its predecessors in analyzing budget problems and in discussing them" (1981, 82).

These observations reaffirm the constancy of the budget function. Rights, for budgeters, are not sacrosanct; they compete with other claims on the public purse. While the examiner's budget axe is often held in check by political pressures, rights-based programs are not inherently protected. On the contrary, in a fiscal environment of austerity rights-based programs are ripe for review because of the potential for multi year savings. Rights-based programs are never immune from a negative response to the basic budget question, Should the government be doing this? But while the logic of budget control makes more sense than ever in a period of fiscal stringency, rights-based programs, by definition, have an added layer of protection. Rights exacerbate control precisely when control is needed most.

POLITICAL VALUES AND THE EVOLUTION OF RIGHTS-BASED BUDGETING. Value change is not equivalent to changes in political culture (see

Wildavsky, 1986). The evolution of political values establishes the groundwork for budgetary winners and losers. Since political values manifest themselves in a particular fiscal climate, there will always be tension between the two. Sometimes the budgetary climate can accommodate a political value, such as the desire to expand redistributive programs to a new group of beneficiaries. In such a situation, the tension is ameliorated by the resources available. But, since claims invariably outstrip budgetary resources, this condition is likely to be temporary, at best. A political culture in which the domain of equality is a prominent feature provides constant fuel to the tension. Meanwhile, our ability to understand budgetary processes divorced from the evolution of politics can only be partial.

Entitlements are premised on one or more political values (such as distributive justice, or income by right). Since values change, the philosophical and political bases for rights-based programs may similarly be transformed. One current example is public assistance, a straightforward means-tested income security program. The current effort to attach a work requirement to the entitlement represents more than an administrative change in the program. The requirement is a signal that the benefits are not guaranteed; moreover, the work requirement may be one method to reduce the beneficiary population. The requirement also appears to be an attempt to instill a sense of *obligation* among program recipients (see Mead, 1986). Value change then, loosens the guarantee of rights-based programs by making rights quasi-rights or eliminating the entitlement entirely. But new rights-based programs with substantial budgetary ramifications may also surface, even in a political environment of budgetary retrenchment. Consider the examples of long-term care for the elderly, the plight of the homeless and the idea of comparable worth.

Despite medicare, health care costs to the elderly are rising (see Kosterlitz, 1986, 1255). In addition, medicare provides no coverage for long-term chronic health care; consequently, the elderly must "spend down" their assets to become eligible for medicaid, a state and federal program that does provide nursing home services for those in need of long-term health care. Legislative proposals for some form of "catastrophic" care tend to create a federal subsidized insurance program for the covered elderly. Whether the proposal calls for universal coverage based on age or is a means-tested program, an entitlement is likely to be established.

Courts sometimes fill a void created by executive and/or legislative inaction. A good current example is the plight of the homeless. How can we explain the current interest in the homeless population in the midst of a fiscally conservative period? At first glance, the emergence of the homeless as a current policy issue seems out of sync with a political atmosphere in which the emphasis in social policy is placed on volunteerism, private and not-for-profit initiatives, local responsibility, and self-help. Initiatives are indeed local in nature; nevertheless, these initiatives have been judicially motivated.

While it is difficult to argue that the homeless enjoy a constitutional right to shelter, a series of state court decisions have defined such a right in state constitutions, portions of the Social Security Act, and other federal laws (Pear, 1986, E5). The budgetary impact of any right to shelter falls primarily on state and local governments. For example, in 1981, the city of New York entered into a consent decree with the Supreme Court of the state of New York to provide shelter for the city's homeless. Spending for the homeless went from less than $2 million to approximately $200 million in five years. While this represents a modest sum when compared to the entire city's budget, it illustrates how a social problem can evolve into a public policy issue with a corresponding escalation in the budgetary price tag.

The notion that there *is* gender-based employment discrimination that is related directly to job title is of fairly recent vintage. It is by no means clear that there is an emergent consensus on the principle that comparable jobs should receive equal pay when the definition of what is in fact comparable is based on the importance of jobs to the organization. Yet, even without broad policy agreement some state governments have taken steps to rectify pay inequities in civil service gender-based job titles (see, for example, Steinberg et al., 1985; Steward, 1985). We may speculate that, as perceptions of fairness evolve in the direction of rights, the corresponding budgetary consequence becomes more identifiable.

Policy issues like the homeless and comparable worth are just two of the more recent controversies that fall under the rubric of rights-based budgeting. Unlike conventional entitlements, to date, these two illustrations are not firmly embedded in statute. Nor have the courts spoken with a single voice. To call either a right, therefore, is stretching the meaning of the concept. It would be incorrect, however, to dismiss the budgetary ramifications of either issue for want of a firmly established right, since one may always be created in the not too distant future. And, once a right is determined, the budgetary consequences follow from the creation of the beneficiary class, the extent of coverage, and the level of the benefit. Both illustrations point out that, in the case of rights, the battleground may shift, from the federal to the state level, but political pressures for more rights will surface even while steps are taken to dampen spending appetites.

Rights, then, get in the way of the development of neat and tidy budget theory. The reason is deceptively simple; budgeting, as V. O. Key reluctantly acknowledged at the end of his famous essay, is not a subject readily amenable to scientifically derived prescriptions. Of course, it is possible to estimate "optimal" budget decisions subject to one or more constraints. But the constraints, invariably, are those intractable variables not easily subjected to rigorous analysis. Often the constraints are precisely what is interesting about a given budget problem!

Rights-based budgeting highlights, then, a perennial problem of social science, particularly social science that aspires to policy influence. While, on the one hand, parsimony is prudent social science, one can unwittingly concoct an elegantly irrelevant theory of budgeting—one that ignores much of the real substance of contemporary budget decisions. Rights-based budgeting may alert practitioners and scholars of budgeting to what we fear may be inevitable: Budgeting is simply a part of a much larger and complex political-economic system that cannot be segregated for theoretical convenience.

References

Appleby, Paul. 1980. "The Role of the Budget Division." Reprinted in *Perspectives in Budgeting*, Allen Schick, ed. pp. 134–37. (Washington, D.C.: American Society for Public Administration).

Behn, Robert D. 1985. "Cutback Budgeting," *Journal of Policy Analysis and Management* 4 (Winter: 155–77).

Bozeman, Barry, & Jeffrey D. Straussman. 1982. "Shrinking Budgets and the Shrinkage of Budget Theory," *Public Administration Review* 42 (November–December): 509–15.

Burt, Martha R., & Karen J. Pittman. 1985. *Testing The Social Safety Net* (Washington, D.C.: Urban Institute).

Dempster, M.A.H. & Aaron Wildavsky. 1979. "On Change: Or, There Is No Magic Size for an Increment," *Political Studies* 27 (September): 371–89.

Ellwood, John. 1982. "Congress Cuts the Budget: The Omnibus Reconciliation Act of 1981," *Public Budgeting and Finance* 2 (Spring): 50–64.

———. 1984. "Comments," in *Federal Budget Policy in the 1980s*, Gregory B. Mills and John L. Palmer, eds. pp. 368–78. (Washington, D.C.: Urban Institute).

Gilbert, Neil. 1982. "The Plight of Universal Social Services," *Journal of Policy Analysis and Management* 1 (Spring): 301–02.

Harriman, Linda, and Jeffrey D. Straussman. 1983. "Do Judges Determine Budget Decisions? Federal Court Decisions in Prison Reform and State Spending for Corrections," *Public Administration Review* 43 (July–August): 343–51.

Heclo, Hugh. 1984. "Executive Budget Making," in *Federal Budget Policy in the 1980s*, Mills and Palmer, eds., 255–91.

Johnson, Bruce E. 1984. "From Analyst to Negotiator: The OMB's New Role," *Journal of Policy Analysis and Management* 3 (Summer): 501–15.

Key, V. O. 1978. "The Lack of a Budgetary Theory," reprinted in *Government Budgeting: Theory, Process, Politics*, Albert C. Hyde and Jay M. Shafritz, eds. (Oak Park, Ill.: Moore Publishing Company), 19–24.

Kosterlitz, Julie. 1986. "Protecting the Elderly," *National Journal* 18 (May 24): 1254–58.

LeLoup, Lance. 1978. "The Myth of Incrementalism: Analytical Choices in Budgetary Theory," *Polity* 10 (Summer): 488–509.

Lindblom, Charles E. 1959. "The Science of 'Muddling Through'," *Public Administration Review* 19 (Spring): 79–88.

Mashaw, Jerry L. 1983. *Bureaucratic Justice* (New Haven, Conn.: Yale University Press).

———. 1961. "Decision-Making in Taxation and Expenditures," *Public Finances: Needs, Resources And Utilization*, National Bureau of Economic Research, (Princeton, N.J.: Princeton University Press), 295–336.

McOmber, Dale. 1981. "An OMB Retrospective," *Public Budgeting & Finance* 1 (Spring): 78–84.

Mead, Laurence. 1986. *Beyond Entitlement* (New York: Basic Books).

Mowery, David C., Mark S. Kamlet, John P. Crecine. 1980. "Presidential Management of Budgetary and Fiscal Policymaking," *Political Science Quarterly* 95 (Fall): 395–425.

Nelson, Richard R. 1977. *The Moon and the Ghetto* (New York: W. W. Norton and Company).

Niskanen, William A. 1971. *Bureaucracy and Representative Government* (Chicago: Aldine).

Organization for Economic Co-Operation and Development. 1985. *The Role of the Public Sector* (Paris: Author).

Padgett, John. 1980. "Bounded Rationality in Budget Research" APSR 74(2) June: 354–72.

Pear, Robert. 1986. "The Need of the Nation's Homeless Is Becoming Their Right," *New York Times* (20 July): E5.

Rauch, Jonathan. 1985. "Stockman's Quiet Revolution at OMB May Leave Indelible Mark on Agency," *National Journal* 21 25 May): 1212-17.

Rivlin, Alice. 1984. *Economic Choices 1984* (Washington, D.C.: Brookings Institution.

Schick, Allen. 1980. "Budgetary Adaptations to Resource Scarcity," in *Fiscal Stress and Public Policy*, Charles Levine and Irene S. Rubin, eds; pp. 113-34 (Beverly Hills, Calif.).

Schultze, Charles L. 1984. "Comments," in *Federal Budget Policy in the 1980s*, Mills and Palmer, eds., pp. 379-84.

Shepsle, Kenneth A. and Barry R. Weingast. 1984. "Legislative Politics and Budget Outcomes," in *Federal Budget Policy in the 1980s*, Mills and Palmer, eds., pp. 343-67.

Simon, Herbert A. 1976. *Administrative Behavior*, 3d ed. (New York: Free Press).

Stewart, Debra A. 1985. "State Initiatives in the Federal System: The Politics and Policy of Comparable Worth in 1984," *Publius* 15 (Summer): 81-95.

Steinberg, Ronnie, et al. 1985. *The New York State Comparable Worth Study Final Report* (Albany: Center for Women in Government, State University of New York.

Stockman, David. 1986. *The Triumph of Politics* (New York: Harper and Row).

Straussman, Jeffrey D. 1986. "Courts and Public Purse Strings: Have Portraits of Budgeting Missed Something?," *Public Administration Review* 46 (July–August): 345-51.

Veilette, Paul T. 1981. "Reflections on State Budgeting," *Public Budgeting and Finance* 1 (Autumn): 62-68.

Weaver, R. Kent. 1985. "Controlling Entitlements," in *The New Direction in American Politics*, John E. Chubb and Paul E. Peterson, eds., pp. 307-41, (Washington, D.C.: Brookings Institution).

Wildavsky, Aaron. 1984. *The Politics of the Budgetary Process*, 4th ed. (Boston: Little, Brown & Co.).

Wilson, James Q. 1973. *Political Organizations* (New York: Basic Books).

Chapter 6
The Authorization Process: Implications for Budget Theory

IRENE S. RUBIN

Legislative and appropriation committees in Congress have distinct, if occasionally overlapping, roles. The legislative committees design, authorize, and oversee legislation, while the appropriation committees determine the amount of money federal agencies can spend. These two processes are linked, because Congress' rules require authorization to precede appropriations and because authorizations often have budgetary implications.

The relationship between authorization and appropriation processes is not a simple lockstep one (Fisher, 1979). Nevertheless, there is considerable evidence that the authorization committees sometimes have considerable influence on appropriations (Fisher, 1979, 62; Fisher, 1983, 36–37; Stephens, 1971; Schick, 1980, 175). Consequently, it makes little sense to look at congressional budgeting without looking at the relationship between authorizations and appropriations.

The relationship between these two types of committees is often seen as competitive. According to this explanation, they are always jealous of each other's power and use whatever opportunities come to hand to increase the scope of their own power over the budget. Though this explanation undoubtedly has some truth to it, it does not explain why authorization committees often make no budgetary recommendations for years, and then suddenly try to increase the scope of their influence over appropriation levels. Also, the power greediness argument does not explain why authorizing committees ever voluntarily relinquish power over appropriations.

In an alternative model, appropriations committees deal with the routine money decisions, while authorization committees deal with nonroutine policy decisions. (Sometimes authorization committees slide to the level of the routine, but that is not theoretically relevant here; we are dealing with ideal types.) Normally, authorization committees are not concerned with spending levels, especially if their programs are running well. But if some major policy issue should become involved, especially if the Appropriations Committees are making policy as part of appropriations or if the executive branch is not implementing the program in the way envisioned by the authorizing committee, that committee may try to use the budget as a lever to increase its program control (Fisher, 1983, 35–36; Stephens, 1971).

In this second explanation, the interest of authorizing committees in budget levels will be greater in some areas than in others. There always are captivating policy issues in foreign affairs and defense that will tempt the authorizing committees to exert and maintain control over appropriations. But in other areas of the budget, congressional interest may be pricked by a policy issue, provoking authorizing committees to expand their budgetary power. Later, if the issue is resolved or goes away, the interest of the authorizing committees may wane, leaving the budgetary field to the appropriations committees.

In this second model, routine budgeting by appropriations committees is incremental, focusing on change between years, ignoring the base, and not comparing major policy alternatives. But, there also are periodic interventions by the authorizing committees. The authorizing committees orchestrate a variety of interest groups, consider a range of policy alternatives, arrive at compromises, and then feed the budgetary implications back into the appropriations process. Not all programs would receive this type of periodic review, but programs with policy implications that interest members of Congress are likely to receive special attention periodically.

If this view of the relationship between the authorizing and appropriating committees is correct, there are several implications for budget theory. When authorizing committees are influential in appropriations, it may mean periodic (1) increased direct access of interest groups to the budget; or (2) in-depth consideration of policy issues as part of the appropriation process; or (3) formation of coalitions between appropriation and authorization committees to press the executive branch to implement legislative goals. Or, it could mean all three.

This essay explores the reauthorization process in Congress from the perspective of this model of periodic influence of authorization committees over the appropriations process. The essay is based on the literature and an examination of the President's budget proposals, appropriation

and authorization hearings, committee reports, and excerpts from the
Congressional Record. The examples used are ACTION, The Federal Insecticide, Fungicide and Rodenticide Act, and the Department of Justice
authorization. These cases are in no sense representative of all
reauthorizations, but they do represent a range of issues and varying
history. They include annual and multiyear, on time and late, and
departmental and program authorizations. The agencies authorized include regulatory, voluntary, and legal functions and tap different controversial issues, such as poverty, crime, and the environment.

The Literature

The idea that an authorization committee may go for many years
with little interest in appropriations and then suddenly begin to increase
its interest and influence over appropriations is developed by Stephens in
his description of the Department of Defense (1971).

Stephens explained that for the first fifteen years after their creation
in 1946, the Committees on Armed Services authorized "only by providing 'general, continuing authorizations.' " They did however provide
more detailed line-item control for military construction, but this
represented only a very small portion of the military budget (about 3 percent). From 1961–1967, the Armed Services Committees expanded their
authorizing control to different areas of the budget. They also limited the
Defense Department's discretion to reprogram. The authorizing committees took increased control of the Secretary's discretionary Research and
Development fund and curtailed multiyear authorizations because they
gave the Defense Department too much discretion (p. 157).

Part of this expansion of control involved an intercommittee rivalry
for control (pp. 158–59); the authorizing committees felt they had been
left out of policy making by the executive branch and the appropriations
committees (p. 153). Another reason was that Armed Services Committee members felt that the Defense Department was not spending money
in the way the Appropriations Committees specified.

Another example of an authorizing committee getting involved in
budgeting and taking over some of the Appropriation Committees' role
occurred during the reauthorization of the Urban Mass Transit Administration (UMTA) in 1982 and 1983 (Rubin, 1985, 133–35). The
Reagan Administration proposed major changes in UMTA's reauthorization, including the elimination of operating subsidies for transit systems.
The battle over reauthorization was hard fought. The House Committee
on Public Works and Transportation eventually worked out a delicate

compromise between the Reagan Administration's position and that of the public transportation supporters. No sooner was a compromise on the reauthorization worked out than the Reagan Administration submitted a rescission proposal for the current year, and its budget proposal for the next fiscal year, proposals that totally denied the compromise. The chairman of the authorizing committee was furious and, in response, held his own committee's hearings on the administration's budget proposal. Budget hearings are clearly a prerogative of the Appropriations Committees, not the authorizing committees, but the chairman felt justified in his action because important policy issues were involved that were directly reflected in budget totals. The chairman's sense of having been betrayed created an emotional impetus strong enough to make him ignore the threat he posed to the Appropriations Committees.

The literature also describes the oversight activity that sometimes accompanies reauthorization. For example, James Sundquist argued that sunset legislation, which would require periodic review of programs, did not become law, but "the same end was being achieved piecemeal, as authorizing committees came routinely to fix time limits on all new agencies and programs, extend the limits to many established ones, and shorten the time periods, until the ultimate was being reached—annual authorization for whole departments" (1981, 330). The link between oversight and authorization was also made by Louis Fisher, who argued that members of Congress prefer linking oversight to authorization, because marking up a bill maintains congressional interest and the link to money makes the oversight more effective (1983, 38).

Linking reauthorization with oversight is conceptually important, because it suggests a marriage between the rather shapeless function of oversight, occurring at odd intervals, based on the timeliness or publicity value of an issue, with the structure of an annual or multiyear authorization, which is geared to produce specific legislation and gives a framework for evaluation. When reauthorization is playing an oversight function, it may reflect temporarily salient issues.

For example, as Sundquist points out, one effect of Watergate was to create an intensive congressional effort to control executive branch secrecy (330–32). The impetus to control intelligence activities was expressed at least in part by increased annual reauthorization. As Schick described, "The permanent authorizations of intelligence programs also ended in 1976, when a Senate resolution barred the appropriation of funds for the Central Intelligence Agency, the National Security Agency, the Defense Intelligence Agency, and various intelligence activities of the State and Defense Departments and the Federal Bureau of Investigation 'unless such funds shall have been previously authorized by a bill or joint resolution passed by the Senate during the same or preceding fiscal year' " (1980, 172). The Department of Justice was also put on annual reauthorization in 1976, for the purposes of oversight (173).

The Department of Justice lost its permanent authorization in 1976 "after Congress discovered systematic abuses of agency authority, especially in the FBI" (Fisher, 1983, 35). But, Congress began to lose interest in monitoring the FBI by the early 1980s. This situation will be discussed further in the body of this chapter.

Fisher also noted that the State Department lost its permanent authorization in a series of executive-legislative clashes, particularly the withholding of information from Congress. In an attempt to control the executive branch, the State Department was reauthorized annually. Fisher argued that Congress seldom restored permanent authorizations, but in this case, "After the relationship between the branches improved, Congress switched [from an annual] to a two year authorization in 1979" (1983, 35).

Schick acknowledged that congressional interest may wax and wane when oversight was the function of annual authorization. He used the example of the defense related atomic energy programs. Once controversial, by 1977 reauthorization had become pro forma. The authorization was passed routinely, without discussion. (1980, 173–74).

The literature is fairly clear in stating that reauthorization can be linked to both oversight and to appropriations, at least occasionally, providing an in-depth program analysis that influences appropriations. However, the literature evaluating the effects of the 1974 Congressional Budget Reform Act suggests that the quality of decision making in authorizing committees is deteriorating, and the link between authorization and appropriations is weakening.

Schick points out that the May 15 deadline for reporting authorizations contained in the Congressional Budget Reform Act have tended to bunch up the consideration of authorization bills and shorten the time devoted to each one, with a resultant deterioration in the quality of decision making (1980, 194). From the perspective of the annual budget cycle, budgeting appears increasingly incremental, in the sense of limited examination of programs.

If the consideration of routine and timely legislation is likely to be superficial, it becomes rather more important to know what is the effect of nonroutine and late authorization legislation on the appropriation process. If the Appropriations Committees wait for late authorizations, then there may still be an important link between deeper consideration of policy alternatives, in-depth consideration of programs, and the appropriation level, at least at intervals. But, if the Appropriations Committees routinely act on their own before the authorizations are completed, in order to meet their own tight deadlines under the budget act, the authorization process may be bypassed and the link between authorization and appropriation weakened or eliminated.

The authorizing committees have found it difficult to adhere to the deadlines in the budget process. When they are late, the Appropriations Committees either can take their cues from action already taken by the authorizing committees, such as committee votes, or they can delay voting on particular programs until the authorizations are complete, or they can vote budget amounts but revise them when the authorization is complete. Each of these responses preserves the relationship between the authorizing committees and the Appropriations Committees. However, Appropriations Committees also have the option of ignoring the authorization process, by waiving the rules that require authorization to precede appropriation. In recent years, according to Fisher, there has been a tendency toward the latter solution (1979, 97–98; 1984, 186). Schick agreed that in the past, "the House Appropriations Committee frequently deferred its own work until the authorization had been enacted, or at least passed by the House" but that "the Budget Act encourages the Appropriations Committees to proceed without authorizations" (1980, 193).

Despite the implications of the literature, this trend does not necessarily mean that the relationship between reauthorization and appropriation has been severed. Authorizing legislation may be late for two opposite reasons. In one case, it may be late because the committee wants to explore issues in depth or it needs to hammer out a compromise between two or more versions of the legislation or between policy goals. In that case, according to my argument, the committee should find a way to influence the Appropriations Committees, if not formally then informally. On the other hand, authorizing legislation may be late because the committee has so totally lost interest in the reauthorization that it does not even consider reauthorization. In that case, the appropriating committee becomes a de facto authorizing committee.

Three Case Studies

ACTION

ACTION is an agency that was created in 1971 by executive reorganization. In 1973, the agency was given statutory basis and authorizing legislation, and it has been reauthorized every two or three years through 1986. The fact that ACTION has been reauthorized regularly raises several questions. What sustained congressional interest over thirteen years? Did the authorizing committees make any major, nonincremental changes in the program that affected appropriations? Did the influence of the authorization committees over appropriations expand or contract over time, and if so, why?

ACTION combined VISTA, the Peace Corps, the Foster Grandparent program, a Retired Seniors program (RSVP), the Service Corps of Retired Executives (SCORE), and the Active Core of Executives (ACE). These programs had come out of the Office of Economic Opportunity, HEW's Administration on Aging, the Small Business Administration, or had been independent. Centrifugal forces continued to be high in ACTION, with internal and legislative pressure to return the programs to their former homes and eliminate ACTION as an agency. SCORE and ACE were in fact returned to the Small Business Administration in 1975, and a strong effort was made in that year to return senior citizens' programs to the Administration on Aging. Long-term pressure to withdraw the Peace Corps culminated in its withdrawal in 1981.

Advocates of particular programs have never been sure that ACTION would function to the best interest of their programs, so have often supported withdrawal from ACTION. Other legislators, opposed to some of ACTION's more activist community organizing and poverty-oriented activities, have hoped to destroy ACTION by cutting it apart and sending the pieces to places that would not be supportive. ACTION, thus, has been under continuous threat of dissolution.

The disparate nature of the programs housed in ACTION has created managerial problems. For example, ACTION housed both general schedule civil servants and foreign service officers. Its accounting systems were overly complex and chaotic. But, these problems did not affect the agency as much as the blurred focus that resulted from volunteer programs with different purposes. Some of ACTION's programs were focused on volunteerism, while others were focused on the elimination or moderation of poverty through volunteer community organizers. The poverty orientation of some of the programs and the grass roots political activism of VISTA had advocates and detractors.

Partly because ACTION was highly politicized (it was involved in the scandal over violations of civil service hiring during the Nixon era, and the agency had a disproportionately large number of political appointees, compared to other agencies) internal policies and emphasis swung back and forth between administrations. The Nixon-Ford Administration proposed cuts in the poverty-oriented programs, while initially the Carter Administration supported budget levels; then the

Reagan Administration supported cuts in poverty programs but also supported volunteerism.

When the agency took wide swings to the right or the left, the opposition group in Congress would be roused. The opposition groups, sometimes small minorities, sought to either disband ACTION or tarnish its image and reduce its funding. Periodic national efforts to reduce spending to control deficits have also played a part in ACTION's funding.

When ACTION came up for reauthorization in 1976 (consideration began in 1976 for the 1977 authorization), the administration proposed cuts of nearly 10 percent. The proposed cuts for VISTA, the program oriented to both elimination of poverty and community organizing, were from $22 million to $13 million, a reduction of $8.7 million, with a proposed 25 percent reduction in the number of volunteers. Almost all of the proposed ACTION cuts were in VISTA. In addition, the administration proposed a grant program that would require grant recipients to share costs.

Senator Alan Cranston, chairman of the Senate Special Subcommittee on Human Resources (a subcommittee of the Senate authorizing committee for ACTION) and a supporter of ACTION and VISTA, reported in the *Congressional Record* (13 May 1976, 13830) that his initial intent was just to give a continuing authorization as a one-year extension, but that the administration proposals would significantly reduce VISTA funding and eliminate several other poverty programs. Because a continuing resolution at the level of the President's proposal would mean a substantial cut in 1977 over the 1976 actual appropriation, Cranston wanted to get an authorization through quickly and allow the Appropriations Committees to pass regular appropriations, which he hoped would maintain or increase 1976 funding levels. Senator Cranston orchestrated activities in his own subcommittee and in the House Committee on Education and Labor to get the authorization through quickly.

In the House, Representatives Quie and Hawkins had disagreed in the Subcommittee on Equal Opportunity and reportedly took a long time to iron out their differences. Hence, the whole Education and Labor Committee did not approve the authorization until May 4, 1976. Since the bill had to be reported to the House and Senate by May 15, Representative Hawkins did not have much time. He moved to suspend the House rules and pass HR 12216. The committee approved the bill in the morning and the House took up the bill in the afternoon, before the committee report could be circulated. The bill was discussed briefly and passed with no amendments (*Congressional Record*, 4 May 1976, 12324 ff). Then,

Senator Cranston brought the measure to the Senate floor without formal committee approval or a report, essentially providing a report orally.

The bill maintained earmarkings for poverty programs, which the administration had proposed to eliminate. The amounts were $22.3 million for VISTA and $7.3 million for other poverty programs. The bill also allowed for limited granting and contracting activities, for the purpose of cost sharing, as the administration had requested, but the level of the overall authorization was considerably higher than the administration's request.

In his discussion on the Senate floor, Senator Cranston noted that each year he presented testimony to the Appropriations Committee Subcommittee on Labor and Health Education and Welfare, recommending funding levels for ACTION programs. For 1977, Cranston's subcommittee planned to recommend $114 million for ACTION, in comparison to the administration's proposed $93 million (*Congressional Record*, 13 May 1976, 13832). The actual appropriation was $109 million for 1977, considerably closer to Cranston's recommendation than to the administration's.

One cannot conclude on the basis of this circumstantial evidence that Senator Cranston influenced the appropriation level, but it is clear that the Appropriation Committees voted continuing resolutions when the authorization was late, so that Cranston's successful efforts to pass the measure on time were important. In 1976, the authorization committees raised the level of authorization for ACTION while maintaining the floor for VISTA, in the face of a strong administration attack on the agency and on VISTA specifically. While the appropriating committees did not go to the level of increase recommended by either formal authorization or informal recommendation by Cranston, they maintained appropriations levels above the OMB request, and the authorizing committees' earmarkings determined the distribution of funds and the level of funding for VISTA. The speed with which the authorization was handled, however, precluded detailed subcommittee examination of programs.

After the Carter Administration came in, there was an abatement in the funding battle, since the new administration supported ACTION and restored the cuts that had been proposed for VISTA the previous fiscal year. But the new Carter appointee to head the agency was eager to restore the agency's reputation, and to refurbish the image of VISTA, and he used the new grant authority to do that in a way probably not envisioned by the previous administration. The new grants went to existing community organizations with explicit political strategies and grass-roots membership drives. The new political activism, apparently supported by the federal government, created substantial conservative opposition to ACTION's director and to VISTA, resulting in bad press. In response to VISTA's political activism, the authorizing committees curtailed the grant program and further limited the political involvement of VISTA volunteers in the 1979 authorization. The committees in both houses agreed to such sums as may be necessary for Title 1 programs (the poverty programs) but kept the earmarking for VISTA and other specific programs inside Title 1. Though the Senate had proposed taking off the dollar floor for VISTA, it dropped the proposal in conference.

Much of the testimony in the hearings on the 1979 reauthorization was not related to program successes and failures but to discussion of the charge of conflict of interest against the agency director. There was an effort at this time to strip the Peace Corps from ACTION and set it up as an independent agency, and there was a parallel effort to return all of ACTION's constituent programs to their original agencies. (See, especially, the Additional Views of Senator Gorden J. Humphrey on S 239, in Senate Report 96–99, Domestic Volunteer Service Act Amendments of 1979, pp. 53–54.)

The authorizing committees managed to hold ACTION together, but support levels were not high and the level of spending authorized for ACTION dropped considerably over the previous authorization. The House did not pass the legislation on time, forcing the Appropriations Committees to appropriate a continuing level of funding for 1979, but in 1980, the appropriations committees pretty much followed the authorization. In 1981; PL 97–113 separated the Peace Corps from ACTION.

The 1982 and 1983 authorizations were included in the 1981 Omnibus Reconciliation Act, which cut both the authorizations and appropriations. The Omnibus Reconciliation Act was based on a package proposed by the OMB, to be voted up or down as a whole, and so did not reflect the deliberation or intentions of the authorizing committees. The ACTION agency programs were cut back some 14 percent in 1982 and another 2 percent in 1983, over 1981 levels of appropriations. Authorizations and appropriations were closely linked in the Omnibus Reconciliation Act, which might have facilitated the authorization committees specifications of the amount of money to be authorized for program administration. Up until that point, they had been authorizing such sums as may be necessary for administration, but after 1982, the authorizations specified the amounts for administration.

By 1983, the authorization committees were dealing with a hostile administration, recent program cuts, and proposed termination of VISTA for 1984. In response, the authorization committees raised the authorization and floors for VISTA to a level higher over three years than it had been since the initial authorization in 1973. The House would have left the administration portion "such sums as necessary" but ceded to the Senate's desire for direct control over administrative costs.

The authorization committees tried in 1983 to depoliticize the agency. The ceilings on expenses for administration was one technique, but in addition, they also reduced the number of political appointees and reorganized the top layers of the agency. The purpose was to allow AC-TION to provide services "without the polarization of a constantly changing political scene" (Senate Report 98–182, Community Volunteer Service Act of 1983, 6–12.)

Table 6-1.

	Appropriations and Authorizations for ACTION				
Year	Appropriated ($ millions)	Change (%)	Legislation (PL)	Authorized ($ millions)	Change (%)
1973	94.	—	—	—	—
1974	91.	− 2.5	93–113	87.	—
1975	100.	+ 9.1	93–113	89.	+ 2.0
1976	103.	+ 3.1	93–113	89.	+ 0.0
1977	109.	+ 5.8	94–293	137.	+53.5
1978	118.	+ 8.4	94–293	137.	+ 0.0
1979	119.	+ .67	96–143 95–478	Late	—
1980	145.	+22.1	96–143 95–478	123.	−10.3
1981	153.	+ 5.4	96–143 95–478	135.	+ 9.9
1982	131.	−14.1	97–35	120.	−10.9
1983	129.	− 1.9	97–35	116.	− 3.8
1984	129.	+ 0.0	98–288	Late	+14.2
1985	—	—	98–288	143.	+ 7.9
1986	—	—	98–288	147.	+ 2.8

Note: Data includes all of ACTION except Peace Corps. Authorized figures exclude amounts for administration.

Table 6-1 compares the appropriation levels with the authorization levels for 1973–1986. For purposes of comparability the Peace Corps is excluded from the data because it was in ACTION some years and out other years. And, when in, it was treated somewhat differently because it had semi-autonomous status and two authorizing committees. Also, for comparability, the authorization figures exclude the specific totals for administration. For some years, the authorization granted such sums as may be necessary, and other years it specified amounts, while the appropriations always included administrative costs. To get a sense of how close the authorizations and appropriations are, one can mentally add about $20 million to the authorized figures.

The table suggests two points about ACTION authorizations. First, when the authorizations were late, the Appropriations Committees produced continuing resolutions, funding ACTION at the previous year's level. There is no evidence that the Appropriations Committees used committee reports or informal input instead of formal authorizations. This does not mean that the authorizing committees had no influence over the budget in those years, however. The previous year's authorization simply was extended one more year until the new authorization took effect. But, for the agency, the effect was a freeze of funding at the previous year's level, so when the authorizing committees supported constant service levels or increases, they were under considerable pressure to report bills on time.

The second point is that neither the appropriation nor authorization changes from year to year appear incremental, but the year to year changes in appropriations were smaller than the year to year changes in authorizations. The main difference between authorization and appropriations is that the Appropriations Committee did not swing up as high in 1976 as the authorizing committees did in reaction to administration's proposed cuts. Overall, the appropriations committees came fairly close to the authorized levels, if one takes into consideration the late authorizations that resulted in continuing resolutions.

To summarize the ACTION authorizations, the timing and regularity of authorizations was important, because the appropriating committees proceeded with continuing resolutions when authorizations were late. The authorizing committees did a reasonable job of getting authorization passed. The time pressure seemed to weigh against a deliberative examination of the program and reduce the quality of decision making, but the authorizing committee probably was fairly successful in influencing both levels of appropriation and earmarking targets for expense.

The political nature of both agency programs and leadership combined with changes of presidential policy and periodic cutbacks to stir up the authorizing committees. They defended funding levels when programs were threatened by the administration, then cut funding levels when the program overstepped its political limits. They took further action to control the political nature of the agency and to try to modify the effect of policy swings on the agency. If they succeed, interest in the program could die down and the committee could loosen its budgetary grip. In the interim, the loss of programs, which has already occurred, should lessen congressional interest somewhat.

FIFRA

In the Federal Insecticide, Fungicide and Rodenticide (FIFRA) program reauthorization, problems with the legislation and high levels of interest group participation made the authorizing legislation late but did not prevent the authorizing committees from feeding the results of their deliberations into the budgetary process when budget levels became a way of controlling implementation.

FIFRA is a program to measure the harm caused by pesticides, register pesticides for use, and stop the use of pesticides shown to be dangerous. Located in the Environmental Protection Agency, the program has long been controversial and has roused strong feelings in members of the authorizing committees. Committee members remain involved because of constituents's interest in cancer-causing environmental threats and because of periodic well-publicized health problems, such as high pesticide levels in drinking water.

The work of the authorizing committees has been hampered by the technical nature of the job, the lack of adequate scientific basis for banning pesticides, and other problems in the law, such as the requirement that dangerous formulas be publicized. Not only have there been technical problems with the legislation, but the committees have had to deal with several sets of interest groups: the farmers, the manufacturers of pesticides, health lobbyists, and environmentalists. Steps taken in any one direction often cause a cry from other groups. Over the years, the result has been considerable oversight attention from the authorizing committees, several major amendments, and very well-informed committee members and staff.

Though the level of attention is acute, the committees can not always accomplish reauthorization on time, because many of the issues are polarizing and consensus is hard to achieve. The committees sometimes proceed with pro-forma reauthorization, while at other times they raise and grapple with underlying problems with the legislation or its implementation. Thus, even with an overall high level of attention, the degree of intensity of review varies from year to year.

Primarily, the authorizing committees redesign the legislation; they have not been terribly concerned with the level of funding. But, the leadership of the House agriculture subcommittee that oversees FIFRA (the Subcommittee on Department Operations, Research and Foreign Agriculture, called DORFA) became concerned that the Reagan Administration deregulation program was cutting back the pesticide program and exposing the public to increased risk of disease. Early in fiscal year 1983, the staff of the committee turned out a draft report documenting the effects of budget cuts and policy changes in the pesticide program (DORFA, 1983). The committee sent the report out for professional review and circulated it widely for publicity purposes. Several months later, the committee held hearings on the report and combined them with formal reauthorization hearings for FIFRA. The result was a four volume set. Two of the volumes dealt with the staff report: one dealt directly with reauthorization and the other contained the documentation, the report itself and the responses of those asked to review it, as well as an analysis of the hearings.

The level of questioning at the hearings was uniformly high. The Congressional Representatives pursued each other's questions for an added level of depth. The committee used agencies in HHS to review the report and the Congressional Research Service to review the hearings. The whole procedure, though political in the sense that it was motivated by disagreement with the Reagan Administration, gave the impression of impartiality.

The release of the draft report and the two hearings on the report took place on February 22 and 23. The Appropriations Subcommittee hearings were on March 1, 1983, before the Agriculture Subcommittee markup, but key authorizing committee members wanted to influence the appropriations hearings. It is clear from the hearings that they got their message across to the chairman as well as other members of the Appropriations subcommittee.

The chairman of the Appropriations Subcommittee in the House, Edward Boland, referred directly to the chairman of the Agriculture Subcommittee in his questioning and pursued one of the key questions from the authorizing hearings:

> *Boland:* I think any one of us can accept the fact that questions of changing official cancer policy are still under study. But one thing that speaks louder than policy is action. According to Representative George Brown of the Agriculture Subcommittee, which has oversight responsibilities and more technical expertise in this area, EPA has been making regulatory decisions that allow up to one hundred times greater exposure levels to carcinogens. Is that correct?

Dr. Todhunter: That subcommittee had hearings on Monday and Tuesday of last week, and I think a review of the testimony presented will indicate that decisions that are being reached now are not significantly different from decisions that were reached in the past. . . .

Boland: I understand that in the past the rule of thumb was to permit one additional cancer per million people, haven't recent EPA decisions permitted much higher levels of statistical risks?

Dr. Todhunter: The rule of thumb has never been risk attendant to 10 to the minus 6, which is not properly interpreted as one additional cancer per million people. . . . (*Regulation of Pesticides,* 1983, vol. 4, 149.)

At least one other congressman, Martin Sabo, made direct reference to the Agriculture Subcommittee hearings as part of the questioning:

Sabo: The stringent requirement of pesticide regulations are circumvented by section 18, emergency exemptions, and section 24(c), special local use registrations. Over the past two years, the number of approvals of each of these categories has more than doubled. Criticisms have been raised by GAO and the House Agriculture Committee. How do you explain these increases?

While these references indicate a familiarity with the essence of the hearings of the authorization committee and a willingness to use the information in the appropriation hearings, the most dramatic connection was that the chairman of the Agriculture Subcommittee, Congressman Brown, and his ranking minority member on the subcommittee, Congressman Roberts, jointly testified before the Appropriations Committee. Their statement was a detailed analysis of the growth in workload, the reductions in the budget, and the corresponding effects on the quality of the pesticides program. The testimony contained detailed recommendations for needed increases and recommended a modest increase over the President's proposal. These figures were the ones Congressman Brown anticipated would be the result of his committee's markup of the reauthorization bill. In addition to their testimony, the pair submitted an abbreviated version of the staff report that generated the authorizing committee hearings.

While there was not a one to one relationship between Congressman Brown's request in testimony and the final appropriation bill, many of

Brown's concerns were reflected in the appropriation bill, which came close to the request in some key areas. Brown had requested an additional sixty full-time equivalent positions, at a cost of $2.2 million; the appropriation added forty positions at a cost of $3 million. The conference report to accompany HR 3133 (the appropriations bill that included FIFRA) contained the following wording: "The conferees direct the Administrator to submit a plan to Congress within sixty days for allocating increased resources for enforcement purposes" (p. 10).

Though it is clear that the authorizing committee did not determine the appropriations level, it is equally clear that it influenced the level and also influenced the concerns voiced in the Appropriations Committees reports and the conference committee report on the 1984 appropriations. Moreover, the in-depth analysis of the authorizing committee enhanced the level of questioning in the Appropriations Committee hearings. All this occurred despite the fact that in that year the appropriations bill passed before the authorizing legislation.

The Department of Justice

The Department of Justice authorizations illustrate the kind of issues that bring about annual authorizations and detailed budgetary control by the authorization committees. This case also illustrates the gradual abatement of interest in the issues that prompted the authorizing committees to increase their budgetary control.

In 1976, Congress passed a law requiring annual authorization of the Department of Justice, to begin in fiscal year 1979. At the time the law was passed, there was a great deal of concern about uncontrolled FBI activities, possible abuses of power, and violation of First Amendment rights.

The response to such abuses occurred on several fronts. Attorney General Edward Levy promulgated a new set of guidelines in 1976 for covert investigations of domestic terrorism; the President helped curtail the FBI budget, and the FBI reduced the number of investigations undertaken without evidence of crimes committed. Congress instituted annual authorizations of the Department of Justice in order to increase its oversight and help control undercover activities.

The House and Senate Judiciary Committees passed authorizations in 1979 that became law in 1980. Although, by 1978, some of the worst abuses had been curtailed, the Judiciary Committees of both houses wrote detailed financial and budgetary controls into their authorizations. The authorizations earmarked spending for particular programs the committees ranked higher in importance than did the Department of Justice, such as the unit to catch and deport Nazi war criminals. The department was required to ask permission in advance from the authorizing committees for reprogrammings (spending money authorized for one program on another). Most important, the authorization contained special exemptions from federal rules about spending money, exemptions that allowed the FBI and the Drug Enforcement Administration to take covert actions by setting up bank accounts and false businesses and by leasing buildings for safe houses. Failure to provide these exemptions would hamper undercover operations. The authorizations requested detailed accounting for undercover activities and watched carefully the amount of information the FBI collected, how it collected it, and to whom it made the information available.

The Judiciary Committees took advantage of the annual authorization process to link detailed oversight to authorization. The committees and subcommittees held numerous hearings, examining the range of Department of Justice agencies over a several year period, and wrapped this information into their authorization bills. For example, in 1980, the Senate Judiciary commitee held thirteen hearings with specific focus on authorization. The committees uncovered a number of managerial problems and began insisting on evaluation reports and statistical series, so that oversight could be exercised and committees could make laws based on data.

The interest of the authorization committees remained high for several years, but after 1980, Congress did not pass the authorization bills recommended by the committees. There were some continuing authorizations and some authorizing language inserted in the appropriation bills, but authorization lapsed completely for some months. Both Judiciary Committees continued to introduce, mark up, and vote out authorizing legislation. The Senate, however, often added a variety of amendments to the bills before passing them, which House committee members thought inappropriate to the bills. The House often did not vote on the House Judiciary Committee's recommended reauthorizations.

Continuing interest in protecting First Amendment rights was stronger in the House Judiciary Committee than in the Senate. As the leadership of the Judiciary Committee in the Senate passed from Edward Kennedy to Strom Thurmond, the committee became more conservative, more oriented to law and order, and more sympathetic to agency requests. The overall level of interest in oversight decreased, the number of hearings and the number of witnesses decreased, and the number of senators attending hearings dropped to the minimum.

In 1983, the Department of Justice requested that the committee grant the department permanent authorization. The Senate Judiciary Committee responded by proposing to permanently authorize programs, reserving for annual consideration the recommended dollar amounts for the authorizations (Senate Report 98–498, p. 2). While the Senate Judiciary Committee went some way toward accommodating the Department of Justice request, it refused to stop earmarking money for programs, arguing that earmarking was not just an Appropriation Committee prerogative. "The committee's amendment included traditional 'earmarkings' throughout, and some new 'ceilings' and 'floors' because these decisions are equally within the purview of this committee's oversight and authorization responsibilities" (Senate Report 98–498, p. 5).

The Senate committee maintained separate annual authorization for FBI undercover activities, due to their sensitivity, but gave no indication that there was any difference of opinion between the committee and the administration in this area. The areas of difference between the Senate Judiciary Committee and the President were over the termination of state and local drug grants and over maintaining the amount of money and personnel allocated to the antitrust division.

In short, the Senate Judiciary Committee was prepared to reduce its own direct budgetary power, while maintaining the possibility of close oversight, should the situation seem to warrant. This Senate Judiciary Committee bill for permanent authorizations passed the Senate but was not considered in the House.

Although 1980 was the last year that authorizations were passed, committee interest in both houses lasted longer than that, partly because other issues besides the refractory FBI caught the attention of committee members. Both the House and Senate committees were concerned with the Justice Department's decisions not to enforce particular laws because the Attorney General judged them to be unconstitutional and were also concerned when the Department of Justice took positions contrary to cases pressed by other departments or agencies. This was an enforcement issue writ large, since it appeared that no matter what Congress passed, the Department of Justice would enforce what the Attorney General chose to enforce.

The interest of House Judiciary Committee members was pricked particularly by nonenforcement of civil rights and affirmative action cases and by the clash with the executive branch over executive privilege in the Environmental Protection Agency case. But, these were not the issues that had provoked annual authorization nor issues that were

responsive to the particular budgetary controls built into the authorizations. They were more purely oversight issues.

The initial issue that had provoked the authorization and detailed
budgetary control, the need to control the FBI undercover activities, remained of more interest to the House Judiciary Committee than to the
Senate, but even in the House, interest gradually faded.

The House Judiciary Committee, like the Senate committee, considered the Department of Justice proposal to permanently authorize.
The House committee argued in House Report 88–181 (to accompany HR
2912) that the FBI exemptions to allow leasing of safehouses and similar
expenses were intended as a control on undercover activities and needed
to be granted each year. More permanent authorization of undercover
activities was needed, the committee temporized, but until a law was
passed to do it, annual authorization of activities was required. This
report shows the beginning of a softening attitude toward control of
undercover activity.

A slight loosening of control occurred in the same report, when the
committee allowed covert activities that crossed fiscal years to get only
one clearance rather than one clearance each year. They required that a
change in direction of program or location get a new clearance, but they
clearly left the agency and the department some discretion in determining
when to seek approval for a new covert activity.

The softening position on control of domestic surveillance was
reflected in a committee battle in 1984. In 1983, Attorney General Smith
promulgated new guidelines on domestic security and terrorism. The
policy to be changed was the permissibility of surveillance on groups or
individuals who had not committed a crime but were or seemed likely to.
The new guidelines were slightly less protective of civil liberties. The
change was enough to provoke a split on the committee between the
Democrats and Republicans.

The House Judiciary committee delayed the implementation of the
new regulations, while it was negotiating with the Department of Justice
over the wording. The committee argued that the reasons for a change
were unclear. In a supplementary statement, however, Republicans
made clear that they felt the reason for the change was the increasing
sophistication of groups prone to domestic violence. The compromise
was that, if no agreement were worked out with the Department of
Justice, the Smith guidelines would go into effect anyway.

By 1984, the House Judiciary Committee had gone a little further in
accommodating to a more aggressive pro-active antiterrorist policy.
House Report 98–757 commended the effort of FBI Director Webster to
reduce domestic terrorism. The committee indicated that efforts to pre-

vent terrorism should go beyond investigation of terrorist incidents. They felt that the preventive phase should include aggressive efforts to collect all legally obtainable intelligence concerning terrorist groups that pose a threat (p. 15). However, the committee remained concerned that individuals exercising lawful freedom of speech not be subjected to surveillance. The report endorsed the Attorney General's domestic security and terrorism guidelines, which had been the subject of controversy the previous year.

There also was a gradual softening of the committee's attitude towards FBI data banks. The committee became more accepting of the FBI role in providing information to other police agencies, provided that appropriate guarantees and provisions had been made for the quality of information (no unsubstantiated rumors) and that levels of entry into the system could be regulated. Not all users should get access to all FBI information.

To summarize, when the Judiciary Committees began authorizing the Department of Justice annually in 1978 (for fiscal year 1979) they made detailed budget recommendations by program area. They earmarked money for some programs, limited reprogramming discretion, and linked their program recommendations to detailed and comprehensive program oversight and investigation. They passed authorizations for two years. After that, the effect of the authorizing committees on appropriations became questionable, because they were unable to pass additional authorizations.

The committees kept working for several more years. Then Senate committee interest flagged as support for undercover work increased and a law and order chairman supported Department of Justice requests. The House committee continued its interest but began to focus on more topical concerns. It gradually became a little more law and order oriented too, and, hence, more supportive of the FBI and the Attorney General. Some of the initial problems that had caused the detailed budgetary control were resolved as the Attorney General took more control of the FBI, and rules were worked out that allowed the agencies to function while answering many congressional concerns. The committees gradually reduced the intensity of their systematic investigations and follow up.

Analysis

In all three cases, when congressional interest was at its peak, the authorization committees exerted considerable influence over the budget appropriations. They influenced floors and ceilings and earmarked money for particular programs. They limited reprogramming to ensure that congressional priorities would be satisfied when they clashed with agency or OMB priorities. Sometimes, they specified administrative costs and provided (or threatened to deny) waivers for particular kinds of expenses. Earmarking was a particularly powerful tool, and one the committees hung on to, even when they gave up other budgetary controls.

Of the three cases, two involved agencies that had exceeded the limits of appropriate activities for federal agencies and were apparently not controlled by their parent agencies (FBI and VISTA). Two of the cases involved situations in which agencies were not carrying out congressional intent (Department of Justice and FIFRA). All three cases involved broad ideological differences between the committee majorities and the administration.

Administration threats to cut back or terminate programs supported by legislators provoked attempts to bolster funding levels in all three cases (in the Department of Justice case, the program to find and deport former Nazis was threatened with reductions). But authorizing committees did not always try to increase spending levels; when they were responding to agencies out of control, the committees tried to freeze or reduce spending to prevent certain activities from occurring or expanding.

The quality of decision making that occurred when the authorizing committees were trying to influence budgetary levels varied. The authorizing committees for ACTION did not achieve any in-depth analysis or consideration, and the House and Senate had very little chance to consider or examine legislation in 1976 before they voted on it. But, in the FIFRA case, a particular policy issue was explored in depth (degree of enforcement of regulation and possible impact on health) and, in the Department of Justice case, programs were systematically reviewed over a period of three years, blending oversight and reauthorization.

Controversy or competition between appropriating and authorizing committees played almost no role in these cases, but cooperation or the lack of cooperation between authorizing committees in the Senate and the House was highlighted as an important factor in passing or preventing the passage of reauthorizations. The level of controversy inside the committees often delayed but did not necessarily prevent reauthorization, because the result was a high level of interest and a compromise that had a reasonable chance of passage. Another factor present in two of the cases was contact between authorizing committee members and appropriation subcommittee members, in the form of submission of testimony or reports.

Conclusions

The role of the authorizing committees in the appropriations process is variable, but not random. They enter and leave the process. Though they do not always exit formally, their attention sometimes wanes. Legislative committees like to use authorization as a vehicle for oversight. The result has been a blurring of oversight and reauthorization. Reauthorization has come to resemble oversight in lack of regularity and responsiveness to current policy issues, especially policy issues contested with the executive branch. Oversight has come to be associated with specific legislation and a certain pressure to complete work within time limits. When authorizing committees become less interested in appropriations but do not return programs to permanent or long term status, the Appropriations Committees may become the authorizing committees, creating a second, different blend of functions.

When authorizing committees become interested in a hot policy issue, they may go to great lengths to study issues and document executive branch practices and policies. These investigations periodically enter into the appropriations process, and when they do, they may help the Appropriations Committees frame issues. They may inform the questioning and provide more information than usual about programs and their operations. These periodic in-depth examinations may have impact beyond the year in which they occur. This is not to imply that all programs are scrutinized in this way, but presumably a number of important ones, with policy implications, are examined in this manner episodically.

The budget reform act has tended to bunch up consideration of authorizations and shorten the consideration of many of them, but legislators have responded in a very reasonable and appropriate way. They consider some legislation very quickly, perhaps the bulk of it, but save what they consider to be the most controversial or most interesting legislation and allow it to be late, taking however long it takes to consider the issues. Being late, it turns out, does not necessarily imply having no influence on appropriations.

The implications for budget theory are threefold. First, the time span of viewing the budget process must be longer than annual, considerably longer, because some key events may occur only once in several years or occur for several years and then cease or slow down. Second, even when decision making seems increasingly hurried and consideration of programs particularly sketchy, decision making may not be as poor as it appears. Some of the key issues are still being sorted out for greater consideration, and that consideration is still influencing the level of the appropriations. Third, at the national level, the picture of budget process is not complete without examining the periodic role of authorizing committees.

Ignoring episodic, in-depth analyses of policies with direct budgetary impact leads to an overly incrementalist perspective. Mixed scanning is a more appropriate model. Some issues are explored in greater depth and at great length, occasionally, as needed. The stimuli for in-depth consideration include agencies running apparently out of control, threatening either civil liberties or the political status quo (such as grass-roots political organizing opposing existing political structures); Congress-executive branch power struggles, especially over executive privilege and over implementation or nonimplementation of major congressional policies; deep partisan policy splits between the administration and Congress over a program, such as its focus on eliminating poverty, implementing regulation, or preventing crime.

There well may be analogues at the state and local levels to the authorization process and its periodic in-depth evaluation and budgetary impact. For example, tax commissions are common, to examine possible sources of revenue and potential impact and to recommend the best choices. There may be other vehicles to periodically examine key policy issues with the explicit intention of influencing appropriations. Such committees need to be examined and included in descriptions of the budgetary process. Such vehicles, to the extent that they exist, may be where alternatives are considered and program and policy trade offs made. This decision process may not be visible during the annual budget cycle. The annual cycle may thus capture only a portion of the budgetary process.

References

DORFA (House Agriculture Subcommittee on Department Operations, Research and Foreign Agriculture). 1983. *Regulatory Procedures and Public Health: Issues in the EPA's Office of Pesticide Programs.* Investigative Report prepared by staff of the Subcommittee on Department Operations, Research and Foreign Agriculture, July.

Fisher, Louis. 1979. "The Authorization Process in Congress: Formal Rules and Informal Practices," *Catholic University Law Review* 29, no. 51: 51–105.

———. 1984. "The Budget Act of 1974: A Further Loss of Spending Control," in *Congressional Budgeting: Politics, Process and Power*, W. Thomas Wander, F. Ted Hebert, and Gary W. Copeland, eds., pps. 170–89 (Baltimore: Johns Hopkins University Press).

———. 1983. "Annual Authorizations: Durable Roadblocks to Biennial Budgeting," *Public Budgeting and Finance* 3 (Spring): 23–40.

Regulation of Pesticides. 1983. Hearings before the Subcommittee on Department Operations, Research and Foreign Agriculture of the Committee on Agriculture, House of Representatives. 98th Congress, 1st Session.

Rubin, Irene. 1985. *Shrinking the Federal Government: The Effect of Cutbacks on Five Federal Agencies* (New York: Longman).

Schick, Allen. 1980. *Congress and Money: Budget, Spending and Taxing* (Washington, D.C.: Urban Institute).

Stephens, Herbert. 1971. "The Role of the Legislative Committee in the Appropriations Process: A Study Focused on the Armed Services Committees," *Western Political Quarterly* 24 (March): 146–62.

Sundquist, James. 1981. *The Decline and Resurgence of Congress* (Washington, D.C.: The Brookings Institution).

Chapter 7
Community Power and Municipal Budgets

CHARLES BRECHER
AND
RAYMOND D. HORTON

Efforts to describe the distribution of political influence within an urban area have a long history of generating contentious debate. While social scientists generally have agreed on the importance of studying community power, they have argued over the proper methods for doing so. Elitists, pluralists, neo-elitists, and others who do not fit neatly into any category have claimed to find different distributions of power and point to different forms of evidence to substantiate their claims. The result, after a period of heated debate in the 1960s, has been a moribund subfield of community power analysis within the branch of political science called urban politics.

Since the contentious 1960s, political scientists concerned with cities have found other subjects to absorb their energies. Fiscal crises and cities' responses to them have generated a variety of studies. These analyses have obliged some political scientists to pay attention to budgetary data. In tending the fields previously abandoned to accountants and public finance economists, political scientists may have discovered a way to deal with an issue at the heart of their discipline. Budgets may provide a widely agreed upon empirical base for describing the distribution of power within a city.

This chapter presents a method for analyzing changes in community power structure and illustrates with data from New York City. The first section reviews the methodological obstacles identified in earlier studies, and the next section presents a conceptual framework that links urban

148

politics and municipal budget outcomes. The third part applies the framework to New York City during the 1966–1985 period. The concluding section identifies avenues for future research that build upon the suggested approach.

The Early Debates

Efforts by social scientists to study community power structures generally have followed one of three approaches: reputational, issue-area analysis, and the so-called nondecision analysis. The reputational approach is generally recognized as deficient. The relative merits of the other two methods have been debated, and there is little agreement about acceptable standards for assessing evidence derived from the two methods.

The reputational approach was initially developed by Floyd Hunter in his studies of Atlanta.[1] The technique consists of asking community leaders, identified from various sources, such as the Social Register, who they feel exercises power in the community. Those identified, in turn, are asked the same question. The repeated identification of the same individuals by notables in the community and by each other is taken as evidence that this relatively small group forms the power elite in the community.

The problems with this approach were identified by Nelson Polsby and are now widely recognized.[2] First, the method does not allow for falsification of the underlying hypothesis; that is, the findings are self-fulfilling prophecies. If researchers ask who is part of a power elite, it is not surprising that they find a power elite rules in a community. Second, the evidence relates only to the reputation of power and not to its actual exercise. The two may overlap, but they are not necessarily the same. In Polsby's words,

> Presumably, what is being determined when judges are asked to identify influentials is who has a *reputation* for being influential. . . . Asking about reputations is asking, at a remove, about behavior. It can be argued that the researcher should make it his business to study behavior directly rather than depend on the opinions of second-hand sources.[3]

The issue-area approach, developed by Dahl and others, has been neatly summarized:

> First, the researcher should pick issue areas as the focus of his study of community power. Second, he should be able to defend these issue

areas as very important in the life of the community. Third, he should study actual behavior, either at first hand or by reconstructing behavior from documents, informants, newspapers, and other appropriate sources. . . . The final recommendation is of the same order: researchers should study the outcomes of actual decisions within the community. . . . The researcher still has to determine on the basis of his own examination of the facts what the actual upshot is of these various intentions, and not conclude prematurely that intentions plus resources inflexibly predetermine outcomes.[4]

Studies using the issue-area approach were completed in several communities and led to conclusions characterized as pluralist.[5] Instead of a single, socially homogenous power elite, these researchers found multiple elites with broad opportunities for people from various social groups to become members of one or more of the elites, if they so wanted. Different groups were found to be active in different issue areas, with competition among groups in each area. Decisions were reached by bargaining among the leaders of competing groups, with all interests that participate in the process receiving some concession in the ultimate outcome.

The pluralist conclusions were criticized as an inaccurate portrait of urban politics in many large American cities by those who say some groups systematically are excluded from participation and the efforts of others to obtain concessions repeatedly are unrewarded.[6] While some of the critics charged the researchers with misinterpreting their data, the more serious critics pointed to the methodology as leading the pluralists to their faulty conclusions. Just as Polsby had found that reputational analysis led to self-fulfilling prophecies for the elitists, a new group of critics charged that issue-area analysis made pluralist conclusions inevitable.[7]

The faults with the approach are twofold. First, there are no widely agreed upon criteria for identifying "important" issue areas. Different researchers may choose different areas as important to the community, but no clear criteria exist for selecting among the potential issues. This is believed to have biased pluralist analysis because the researchers were prone to select issues that generated controversy and bargaining, and they implicitly identified controversy and bargaining with importance on the community's agenda. Thus, the selection of issue areas had a subjective element that favored finding competition and bargaining in the political process.

Second, issue-area analysis could not identify important decisions that were never reached because they were successfully kept off a community's agenda. Power as the ability to enforce "nondecisions" was not recognized in issue-area analysis. This biased researchers' findings because the systematic elimination of some issues from a local community's political agenda could represent dominant power by a group without the competition and bargaining that pluralists consistently reported.

The responses to these criticisms have followed two different paths: denial and a search for alternatives. Some researchers have staunchly defended issue-area analysis, saying that criteria for identifying "important" issues can be specified and widely accepted, and that in most cases, the issues studied in community power analyses met these criteria. With respect to nondecisions, the defenders argue that such phenomena either are a form of decision making involving direct or implied coercion, and therefore part of the behavior studied in issue-area analysis, or are unobservable, hypothetical situations not subject to empirical analysis and therefore outside the scope of the social sciences.[8]

Some students of urban politics have remained concerned that issue-area analyses may not reveal exclusion or suppression of political participation by some segments of a community and have sought to develop methods for analyzing these processes. The most promising of these efforts is comparative analysis of communities in which issues have arisen and those in which they have not. A study of local efforts to regulate air pollution compared communities where such efforts were initiated (usually successfully) to those with similar levels of pollution that did not deal with the problem through local government action.[9] The author concluded that there was much less probability of government action in communities where leaders of the industrial sector were influential. While this specific conclusion has been challenged as not supported by the data assembled in the study, the comparative approach has been recognized even by critics as "in principle promising," although it "evidently presents problems in execution."[10]

However, additional methods that supplement or replace issue-area analysis for studying community power have not been identified, and for about ten years the subfield has not been an intellectually lively one. Instead, many scholars interested in large cities have focused on their fiscal problems, and this provides another perspective from which to consider the distribution of power.

Fiscal Policy and Community Power

Intrigued by the New York City fiscal crisis of 1975, many social scientists addressed the issue of how local communities respond to reductions in their resource base. Due to varying combinations of employment losses and reductions in some forms of intergovernmental aid, many of the nation's largest cities experienced fiscal stress during the second half of the 1970s and early 1980s. Whether and how local government adjusted the level and functional mix of their spending became an active area of inquiry with significance for many communities in addition to New York City.

To analyze these questions, researchers required a suitable theoretical framework. Drawing from the literature on urban politics, the scholars initiating studies of local fiscal decisions identified both the formal structure of government and the informal processes of decision making as potential determinants of budgetary outcomes. Two influential studies illustrate the general framework that guided this research.

In four case studies of communities experiencing fiscal stress, Charles Levine, Irene Rubin, and George Wolohojian relied on a theoretical model that identified both interest group structure and formal authority structure as variables influencing administrative responses to changes in resource levels.[11] They interpreted the evidence as supporting a hypothesis that the local informal political structure would shape responses to resource reductions, which they called *retrenchment strategies*. They concluded,

> The central theme of the model, that politics forms an intervening variable between revenue levels and retrenchment responses, was consistently supported by the data. . . . We found that centralization and openness to interest groups together had an effect on the content and on the degree of implementation of retrenchment strategies and that the scope of services affected the degree of openness to interest groups, and hence the content of retrenchment strategies.[12]

Similarly, a more comprehensive comparative analysis of fiscal policy decisions in sixty-two American cities by Terry Clark and Lorna Ferguson relied on a theoretical model that viewed these outcomes as determined largely by the size and organizational activity of four sectors: the business community, the needy, municipal employees, and middle-class residents.[13] Competition among these groups, the wealth of the community, the preferences of elected leaders, and the local political culture were hypothesized to determine spending decisions. Regression analysis using measures of these variables generally confirmed the hypothesized relationships between the size and influence of the four sectors and fiscal policy decisions.

These and other studies of urban responses to fiscal stress can be interpreted as strongly supporting a causal relationship between local political conditions, including informal arrangements or "power structures," and the budgetary decisions of municipal governments. This increasingly well-established relationship provides a basis for using budgetary outcomes to analyze local power structures. If informal power relationships play a major role in determining spending decisions, then it should follow that budgetary outcomes reflect underlying power relationships. Accordingly, budgetary outcomes can be used to describe and trace changes in community power structures.

Specifically, it is possible to conceive of local politics as involving competition among four sectors of the community. Each of these groups has distinct interests to pursue in municipal politics, and these interests can be associated with distinct fiscal policy preferences. Thus, budgetary outcomes can be used as measures of the influence of each of these groups.

One major set of participants in urban politics is municipal civil servants. Local government employees, who in most large cities are unionized, seek to influence wage and other policies through collective bargaining as well as through direct political action, which includes endorsement and other campaign activities on behalf of candidates for elected office. The major goals pursued by organized civil servants include greater compensation for members and expansion of the municipal work force. To realize these goals requires increases in the level of municipal expenditures and/or decreases in the share of spending devoted to other purposes.

A second major category of participants in urban politics are for-profit organizations, the so-called business community. The local business community is widely recognized as being fragmented: large firms and small firms; firms operating in international markets and those competing primarily in local markets; firms whose major consumers are public entities and firms competing in private markets. Nonetheless, most businesses seek to minimize the local taxes they are obliged to pay in order to reduce operating costs and remain competitive. Thus, the political goals of the business community typically include lowering local tax burdens and reducing the size of the local public sector.[14]

A third category of participants is the dependent poor. In many large American cities, a major segment of the population has little or no private income and depends on government transfer programs for important goods and services. Local government programs (partly financed with intergovernmental aid) provide these individuals with all or most of their income for food, shelter, and medical care, as well as other social services. While sometimes organized into membership groups to pursue their interests, these citizens more typically are represented in the political arena by nonprofit organizations that are "in the business" of providing social services and are themselves dependent on public expenditures. While there are divergent interests between clients and some providers, the dependent poor and the nonprofit organizations serving them share common interests in pursuing enhanced benefits and broader eligibility for social welfare programs. These objectives generally require greater public expenditures and/or decreases in the share of spending devoted to other purposes.

Perhaps the most diverse category of local political participants is those citizens seeking public services that are not highly redistributive. Parents of children in school, adults seeking police protection, and homeowners seeking improved refuse collection services illustrate the broad constituencies interested in enhancements of local public services. No single organization typically respresents these multiple interests; rather, numerous groups organized on a neighborhood basis or on the basis of specific services citywide articulate the interest of constituents in greater service output. Because these groups also are composed of taxpayers, they generally desire more output without added expenditures. To achieve greater output without added costs may require municipal officials to pursue managerial innovations and to favor work-force expansion over higher compensation.

If local politics is viewed as competition among these four major categories of participants, then the local power structure can be described in terms of the relative influence each exercises. Changes in the balance of competing political forces should be evident in changing municipal budgetary decisions. Since each group's goals relate to identifiable budgetary policies, the results of budget decisions can be viewed as indicators of their respective political influence. Two specific types of budgetary outcomes are most relevant: the overall size of the municipal budget and the distribution of the municipal budget among competing objects of expenditure.

The relationships between the relative influence of each group and these specific budgetary decisions can be specified as follows:

Category 1. The influence of the business community is gauged by the size of the local public sector. Increased municipal spending indicates declining influence for the business community; decreased spending indicates increased influence. The relevant measures of municipal spending are expenditures in constant dollars and spending as a proportion of local economic activity.

Category 2. The influence of organized civil servants is gauged by the share of total municipal spending allocated to labor in the form of salaries and other types of compensation, including fringe benefits and pensions. Labor costs reflect two elements: employment levels and compensation per employee. The larger the share of the local "pie" paid to city workers, the greater is their influence.

Category 3. The influence of the dependent poor and those serving their interests is gauged by the share of total municipal expenditures allocated to income transfers and purchases of medical and social services. The greater the share of municipal spending allocated to these objects of expenditure, the greater the influence of this group.

Category 4. Because the interests of other service demanders are best indicated by actual service outputs rather than expenditures, budget data perhaps are least relevant to gauging the influence of this group. However, analysis of trends in expenditures for compensation and in numbers of municipal employees reveals how the tradeoff between wages and employment is resolved. In this tradeoff, service demanders generally have an interest in higher staff levels as opposed to higher salaries; the opposite is true of organized civil servants.[15] Thus, the extent to which labor expenditures support an enlarged work force rather than enriched compensation may be used as a gauge of the relative influence of service demanders.

Before presenting data from New York City to illustrate how this conceptual approach can be applied, it is worthwhile to consider possible objections that may be raised to using data on the distribution of expenditures as a reflection of power relationships. The broad methodological issues of the appropriateness of the distribution of values in a community as a measure of the distribution of power has been addressed by Polsby. He criticizes the general approach on the grounds that, "There are such phenomena as people who benefit, but do not cause."[16] He identifies the following types of circumstances under which people might receive benefits without exercising power:

1. That no explicit decision making took place at all, and that beneficiaries, far from actually governing, are simply reaping windfall benefits (e.g. largely powerless Black Panthers, who oppose gun control, are beneficiaries of the fact that there are no gun control laws).

2. That beneficiaries are receiving benefits from decisions made outside the community and over which they have no control (e.g. shopkeepers in a community prosper from a decision made in a far-off corporate headquarters to operate a local plant on overtime).

3. That beneficiaries are the intended recipients of benefits resulting from decisions made by others within the community (e.g. apolitical, absentee, or deceased owners of adjacent real estate prosper because of decisions made in a bureaucracy to site a public facility).

4. That the powerful are intentionally conferring benefits on the non-powerful (e.g. in at least some welfare systems).[17]

However, it can be argued that municipal budget decisions do not fall into any of these four categories, and therefore in this case, a distribution of values or benefits can be reliably used to gauge power relationships. First, budgeting involves explicit decisions. Most cities have formal budget processes and timetables, with mayors and local legislators required to adopt budgets.

Second, municipal budget decisions are local decisions. Although it is sometime argued that certain budget items are "mandated" or "uncontrollable," these expenditures either represent a small share of the budget or are uncontrollable only in a technical rather than a political sense. An earlier analysis of changes in expenditure patterns in New York City demonstrated that items typically viewed as mandated or uncontrollable, in fact, are subject to change, particularly if a time period longer than one year is considered.[18] For example, debt service, usually defined as uncontrollable, was altered dramatically during New York City's fiscal crisis as a result of negotiations with investors to restructure the debt. Similarly, intergovernmental mandates have not dictated expenditure levels for programs like Medicaid, under which local discretion has been used to curb spending through stricter enforcement of eligibility rules and efforts at cost containment and for which the mandated local share was reduced in response to local pressure in the early 1980s.

Two other items often viewed as part of an uncontrollable expenditure base are municipal employees' salaries and mandated welfare payments. However, in both cases explicit political decisions are required to determine growth in these items. Collective bargaining generally sets salary levels, but local officials can alter shares of spending for this item by making salary adjustments that vary relative to inflation. Similarly, public assistance payments are not automatically adjusted with inflation, and direct action by elected officials is usually required to change benefit levels. These benefits have been cut in some states and frozen in others, despite rapid rates of inflation. In sum, in a multiyear period, most so-called uncontrollable items are subject to change by local political action.

The third and fourth of Polsby's circumstances require that one group either intentionally or unintentionally relinquish benefits it would otherwise receive in order to aid a competing group. While a theoretical possibility, this seems to have little applicability to the process of municipal budgeting. Unlike the benefits resulting from site location decisions, the allocation of spending involves zero-sum decisions with little possibility for indirect benefits to those not involved. While some may interpret the level of welfare spending as an example of the powerful conferring benefits on the nonpowerful, it is more likely that these spending levels reflect the active advocacy of either the beneficiaries themselves or the service providers funded by such programs.

In sum, it is reasonable to interpret municipal budget decisions as reflecting the distribution of power among competing groups in a community. Such causal relations have been demonstrated in several studies, and potential sources of error in making such causal inference either can be ruled out or can be viewed as highly unlikely.

New York City as an Illustration

The propositions set forth in the previous section point to three sets of data that, when examined over time, can reveal much about the changing political environment of a city. First, levels of total municipal spending will indicate the influence of the business community relative to the other major groups. Second, the percentage distribution of expenditures among objects of expenditure will reveal the relative influence of organized civil servants and the dependent poor. Third, trends in the numbers of municipal employees and in their compensation levels will show the relative influence of organized civil servants and service demanders.

These three sets of data have been collected for the City of New York for the 1966-1983 period. The figures have been adjusted by the authors to ensure comparability over a period when numerous accounting changes altered the format of the official reports from which the expenditure and employment data were derived.

With respect to the influence of the business community, the figures on both constant dollar municipal spending and municipal expenditures as a share of local economic output reveal the fiscal crisis years to be a turning point. Between 1966-1975, constant dollar spending rose steadily for a total 73 percent increase over the period; for the 1975-1983 period, constant dollar spending fell, almost steadily, for a net decline of over 18 percent (Table 7-1). It was not until fiscal year 1984 that real spending began to increase again. Equally revealing, municipal expenditures as a share of local economic activity rose steadily from under 14 percent to over 27 percent in the first period, and then fell to 19 percent in the later period. These figures suggest that the influence of the business community declined during the 1966–1975 period, and that the fiscal crisis sparked a resurgence of business community influence.

Table 7-1.

Size of the Local Public Sector, Municipal Expenditures, 1966–1984.

Fiscal Year	Millions of Constant 1966 Dollars	Percent of Local Value Added
1966	4,435.7	13.8
1967	5,033.0	15.2
1968	5,425.3	15.8
1969	5,893.8	17.0
1970	6,020.1	17.9
1971	6,501.7	20.0
1972	6,879.9	21.4
1973	7,001.3	21.7
1974	7,124.8	23.4
1975	7,673.4	27.1
1976	6,802.0	24.0
1977	7,174.6	24.5
1978	6,883.3	22.6
1979	6,494.6	20.8
1980	6,348.4	20.5
1981	6,077.4	19.3
1982	6,099.4	19.1
1983	6,002.2	18.8
1984	6,264.6	19.0

Sources: Expenditure data are from annual reports of the Comptroller of the City of New York and are adjusted to reflect accounting changes. Constant dollar adjustments are based on the Consumer Price Index prepared by the U.S. Bureau of the Labor Statistics. The New York City value added figures are based on estimates by Matthew Drennan using his econometric model; see Matthew Drennan, *Modeling Metropolitan Economies for Forecasting and Policy Analysis* (New York: New York University Press, 1985).

The relative influence of organized civil servants appears to have diminished during the period of expenditure growth. Although their numbers increased and their real wages rose during the period before the fiscal crisis, their share of municipal spending actually fell from 66 percent to 57 percent (see Table 7-2). Moreover, the decline was greatest in direct pay, from 53 percent to 41 percent as fringe benefits increased notably. The relative influence of labor continued to decrease during the post-fiscal crisis period as their share of the shrinking pie fell slightly from 57 to 55 percent. Again, the losses were primarily in salaries rather than fringe benefits.

Table 7-2.

Distribution (Percent) of Municipal Spending by Object, 1966, 1975, and 1983.

	All Expenditures			Total Without Debt Service		
	1966	*1975*	*1983*	*1966*	*1975*	*1983*
Labor Costs:	55.1	47.3	49.3	66.3	57.1	55.4
Personal services	46.5	34.2	34.5	52.6	41.2	38.7
Pensions	5.9	9.2	9.5	11.8	11.1	10.7
Social security	1.2	1.8	2.1	1.1	2.1	2.3
Fringe benefits	1.6	2.2	3.2	0.9	2.6	3.7
Social Welfare:	14.7	18.4	19.6	15.5	22.2	22.0
Public assistance	9.0	10.7	9.1	10.1	12.9	10.2
Medical assistance	3.2	3.6	4.5	2.4	4.4	5.0
Day care	0.2	1.3	0.9	0.3	1.6	1.9
Foster care	1.9	2.1	1.7	2.1	2.5	1.9
Other	0.4	0.7	3.4	0.6	0.8	3.9
Subsidies:	10.8	9.3	7.1	11.4	11.2	8.0
Housing authority	0.2	0.6	0.5	0.1	0.7	0.6
Transit authority	1.2	2.0	2.6	1.1	2.6	3.0
Hospitals	6.9	2.7	3.0	8.1	3.2	3.3
City university	2.2	3.9	0.1	2.1	4.7	0.1
Other	0.2	0.1	0.9	0.0	0.1	1.0
Supplies, Material Equipment, Contracts and Other	4.7	8.0	13.1	6.8	9.6	14.6
Net Total	85.3	82.9	89.0	100.0	100.0	100.0
Debt Service	14.7	17.1	11.0	—	—	—
Grand Total	100.0	100.0	100.0			

Sources: Annual reports of the Comptroller of the City of New York.

If the relative influence of both business and labor was declining during the pre-crisis period, whose power was growing? The municipal expenditure data suggest that the poor's influence expanded significantly before the fiscal crisis; their share of spending grew from under 16 percent to more than 22 percent in the 1966–1975 period. The gains were in cash transfers, as the welfare rolls expanded in numbers and the real benefit levels increased, as well as in various in-kind services. Interestingly, the poor's relative influence fell only slightly in the post fiscal crisis period as their share of total spending remained near 22 percent. However, direct cash payments to the poor fell significantly; this was partly offset by increased vendor payments for medical care (which experienced rapid inflation) and a home care program, primarily benefiting the elderly.

This discussion is based on the distribution of spending excluding debt service. The share of spending devoted to debt service is perhaps the most difficult aspect of the changing distribution of expenditures to interpret politically. In one sense, these payments are purchases of services from financial institutions, one segment of the business community. If this view is accepted, the debt service payments reflect the financial community's share of municipal spending. This would suggest that the financial institutions' influence was growing in the 1966–1975 period, as debt service expenditures increased as a share of spending, and that their influence declined in the 1975–1983 period as the debt service share fell. However, this either contradicts the interpretation of the trends in aggregate spending pointing to greater business community influence after the fiscal crisis or suggests that the financial community has different interests than the rest of the business community. A more informative interpretation requires separating the interest and principal components of debt service and interpreting only the interest portion as reflecting the financial community's "piece of the pie." While these detailed data are not readily available, it is likely that the major restructuring of outstanding debt that took place during the fiscal crisis years caused the interest component to grow significantly while principal payments fell as the debt was "stretched." Thus, focusing on the interest component of debt service would probably yield an interpretation more consistent with the findings regarding aggregate expenditures.

The influence of service demanders relative to civil servants is reflected in the mix of labor's share of the pie between numbers of workers and compensation per employee (Table 7-3). Here again, the fiscal crisis appears to be a turning point. In the pre-fiscal crisis period of 1971–1975, total labor spending rose 14 percent in real terms.[19] However, 85 percent of that increase represented compensation gains and only 15 percent employment gains; in the 1975–1983 period, municipal policy favored compensation over employment even more, since the entire 13 percent decline in labor costs resulted from work-force reductions, and real compensation per worker remained almost constant.

Table 7-3.

New York City Government Labor Costs, Employment and Compensation per Employee: 1971–1975, 1975–1983 (labor costs in millions of 1967 dollars; compensation per employee in 1967 dollars).

	1971	1975	1983	Percent Change 1971– 1975	Percent Change 1975– 1983
Labor Costs	$2,762.1	$3,136.0	$2,736.0	13.5	-12.8
Employment	214,776	219,067	191,072	2.0	12.8
Share of Labor Cost Change	—	—	—	14.8	100.0
Compensation per Employee	$12,860	$14,315	$14,319	11.5	0.0
Share of Labor Cost Change	—	—	—	85.2	0.0

Sources: Expenditure data are from annual reports of the Comptroller of the City of New York. Constant dollar calculations based on the New York area Consumer Price Index prepared by the U.S. Bureau of Labor Statistics. Employment data are from the New York State Financial Control Board.

What inference about the relative influence of service demanders can be drawn from these trends? This group's preferences for service enhancement without corresponding expenditure (or tax) increases lead them to favor managerial innovations *or*, failing that, to prefer expanding the work force but not necessarily increasing real compensation for civil servants. The data in Table 7-3 demonstrate that during the recovery period the employment-compensation tradeoff was drawn in favor of compensation not employment (the preference of civil servants). Accordingly, service demanders suffered declining influence during the fiscal crisis, at least initially; however, the sharp reduction in employment that occurred during the fiscal crisis period stimulated some notable managerial innovations that helped maintain service levels.[20]

In general, this illustration of how budget decisions can be used to understand community power structures is reassuring in the sense that the method leads to conclusions that conform to the judgment of most knowledgeable observers and analyses of selected decisions.[21] These data indicate that power relationships were substantially different in the post-fiscal crisis period than in the period prior to the fiscal crisis. Specifically, the business community was more influential during the later period. Organized civil servants suffered modest declines in influence. The operators and beneficiaries of social welfare programs grew in power during the 1966–1975 period but saw their influence wane in the subsequent years. Middle-class, service-demanding constituencies lost influence to organized labor during the post-1975 period.

Conclusion

The question Who governs? remains at the heart of the study of urban politics. Analysis of issue areas is well established as a method to address this question, but analysis of municipal budget outcomes can be a useful supplement to this approach, which also avoids some of its potential problems.

If the validity and utility of the conceptual framework and budget categories presented in this chapter are accepted, they can provide the basis for more detailed analysis of changes in power relations over time within communities and comparisons of power relations among groups across communities. Both types of analysis are complicated by the changes in financial reporting practices over time within communities and by the variations in the division of costs among state and local units in urban areas. But, in most instances, these obstacles can be overcome with careful research and, perhaps more important, they seem more manageable than the problems that have plagued other approaches to the study of community power. The New York example suggests that cautious analysis of municipal budgetary outcomes can reveal much about urban power structures.

Notes

1. Floyd Hunter, *Community Power Structure* (Chapel Hill: University of North Carolina Press, 1953).

2. See Nelson Polsby, *Community Power and Political Theory* (New Haven, Conn.: Yale University Press, 1963), especially Chapter 3.

3. Ibid., 50–51.

4. Ibid., 120–21. See also Robert Dahl, *Who Governs? Democracy and Power in an American City* (New Haven, Conn.: Yale University Press, 1961).

5. In addition to Dahl, ibid., the analyses include Wallace Sayre and Herbert Kaufman, *Governing New York City* (New York: Russell Sage Foundation, 1960).

6. For example, see William Connolly, ed., *The Bias of Pluralism* (New York: Atherton Press, 1969).

7. The most important arguments are presented in Peter Bachrach and Morton Baratz, *Power and Poverty* (New York: Oxford University Press, 1970).

8. The principal defense is in Nelson Polsby, *Community Power* (New Haven, Conn.: Yale University Press, 2d ed., 1980), Chapters 9 and 11.

9. Matthew Crenson, *The Unpolitics of Air Pollution* (Baltimore: Johns Hopkins University Press, 1971).

10. Polsby, *Community Power*, 2d ed., 218.

11. Charles H. Levine, Irene S. Rubin, & George G. Wolohojian, *The Politics of Retrenchment* (Beverly Hills, Calif.: Sage Publications, 1981).

12. Ibid., 206.

13. Terry Nichols Clark & Lorna Crowley Ferguson, *City Money* (New York: Columbia University Press, 1983), especially Chapter 4.

14. While the business community generally is interested in minimizing local taxes, the firms do not locate on the basis of tax rates alone. The level and quality of municipal services may be such that firms are willing to pay higher taxes for a richer package of municipal services.

15. For a more detailed discussion of this point, see Raymond D. Horton, "Fiscal Stress and Labor Power," a paper presented at the Annual Meeting of the Industrial Relations Research Association, Allied Social Science Associations, New York City, December 1985.

16. Polsby, *Community Power*, 2d ed., 208.

17. Ibid., 207.

18. See Charles Brecher & Raymond D. Horton, "Expenditures" in *Setting Municipal Priorities: American Cities and the New York Experience*, Charles Brecher and Raymond D. Horton, eds. (New York: New York University Press, 1985), especially 249–54.

19. In this part of the analysis, data for 1971–1975 are used rather than 1968–1975, because reliable and comparable data on full-time municipal employees are not available for years prior to 1971.

20. See Charles Brecher and Raymond D. Horton, "Retrenchment and Recovery: American Cities and the New York Experience," *Public Administration Review* 43, no. 2 (March–April, 1985): 267–74.

21. See Martin Shefter, *Political Crisis/Fiscal Crisis* (New York: Basic Books, 1985); Charles Brecher & Raymond D. Horton, *Setting Municipal Priorities 1981* (Montclair, N.J.: Allenheld Osmun, 1980), Introduction; Ken Auletta, *The Streets Were Paved with Gold* (New York: Random House, 1979); and Robert Bailey, *The Crisis Regime: the MAC, the FCB and the Political Impact of the New York City Fiscal Crisis* (Albany: SUNY Press, 1984).

Chapter 8
What Budgeting Cannot Do: Lessons of Reagan's and Other Years

JOSEPH WHITE

The budget process collapsed in the 1980s; an understanding of what is possible may guide reform. In evaluating the many tasks that budgeting has been asked to perform, it is important to distinguish which can be performed only by budget institutions, which are better performed elsewhere in our political system, and which cannot be performed well anywhere.

Budgeting and Politics

Any discussion of federal budgeting reform must begin by identifying its subject, to distinguish it from other processes. In practice, everyone acts as if there is a distinct budget process. The House of Representatives has budget process task forces, interest groups and scholars suggest reforms, and experts write about its "crisis."[1] Budgeting, thus, has an institutional definition as the activity of a discreet set of institutions. It may be studied by asking how those institutions handle particular environments or challenges. The budgeting institutions may be viewed as a very large, loosely coupled organization, having a variety of tasks, and working in an environment that influences task performance.[2] Defining budgeting this way, we can ask the questions we ask of any organization: What are its tasks? What are its routines? Who is inside, and who is outside? What constitutes success or failure?

A successful organization performs its tasks in a way that allows the organization to maintain its routines, the allegiance of its members, and the ability to attract resources from nonmembers. An organization fails when, through poor task performance, it loses the allegiance of its members to its rules and procedures, and the ability to procure resources from outside. When an organization no longer has understood ways of doing things; when its division of labor cannot be maintained and roles become totally fluid; when the members of the organization no longer can coordinate behavior by adhering to a known set of procedures; then the organization is in deep trouble.

The Budget Process Has Failed

The strife and procedural chaos of this decade, now institutionalized in Gramm-Rudman-Hollings, make a convincing case that the budget process has failed. Even its defenders say not that it has worked but that failure is not the system's fault. Allen Schick argues that a charge of substantive and procedural failure, though easy,

> takes no account of the economic and political turbulance of the past decade. . . . Assessing the budget process without framing it in the economic and political context of the times is akin to condemning the Budget and Accounting Act of 1921 . . . for failing to stem the rise of federal spending during the New Deal and subsequent decades.[3]

Similarly David Stockman argues "the fiscal situation has deteriorated radically since 1974 in spite of the Budget Act, not because of it . . . the current fiscal disorder results from powerful, long-term political trends.[4] Schick and Stockman correctly emphasize the environment as the source of trouble, but like any organization, the budget process' failure to handle its tasks, for whatever reason, was failure.

One could also argue that there has been no substantive failure. This is never said because the deficits are supposed to be so bad. Yet, one might be satisfied because, since 1981, the process has blunted Reagan Administration policy initiatives, or one might argue that the U.S. economy has done quite well compared to others. Evaluation in terms of results requires agreement, about which results are important and whether they are good or bad, and, thus, is a slippery standard.

Yet, when we view the budget process as an organization, its collapse is clear. Procedural failure was progressive and debilitating. Rules and norms were weakened until, by 1985, one could no longer identify any routine way of doing things. Roles were confused and the organization was drained of its most precious resource, authority to make decisions. It no longer received deference. The idea of the process received allegiance, but the process was not followed. An organization that no longer supplies decision premises and coordinates behavior has lost its value. Political actors determine the success of political institutions by their choice to grant those institutions authority. By adopting Gramm-Rudman-Hollings, Congress and the President completed their rejection of the budget process.

There are provisions in the Gramm-Rudman-Hollings package that are explained as efforts to make the budget process stronger. Yet, the heart of Gramm-Rudman-Hollings, the sequester process, is political terrorism. House majority whip Thomas Foley (D-Wash.) illustrated its character when he remarked that, "Gramm-Rudman is about the kidnapping of the only child of the President's official family that he loves," meaning the defense budget, "and holding it in a dark basement and sending the President its ear."[5] Foley's language expressed the view of all participants; their only difference was over who was being held hostage. The President's staff thought of it as a way to hold Congress' "feet to the fire".[6] The administration was using the threat of particularly dumb domestic spending reductions to force House Democrats and the Senate to agree to more intelligent cuts. House Democrats held defense hostage to force Reagan and the Senate to agree to a tax hike. Senate Republicans held both defense and domestic spending hostage to force both targeted social cuts and a tax increase. The difficulty was that none of these actors could slash the other's child without slashing his own.[7] Whatever one may call this game, Gramm-Rudman-Hollings was not a new process but "part of the breakdown of the budget process."[8]

If we review the bewildering events of recent years, we can see why participants thought the process was broken and observe their allegiance unraveling.

President Carter's fiscal year 1981 budget was bludgeoned to death shortly after birth by critics in both parties and throughout the economic and media establishments, who declared that its $15 billion deficit would destroy the economy. In order to remake a balanced budget, representatives of the administration and congressional Democratic leaders held a marathon series of meetings in early March 1980. This first attempt to replace the President's budget as a coordinating device with peak bargaining between the President and Congress failed, even though all were Democrats. Disagreement between the party's two wings (abetted by the GOP) produced, after one rejected conference agreement, a first resolution that projected a budget balance but that almost nobody believed. The second resolution and most appropriations were shelved until after the election. Then, the House and Senate managed to agree on a second resolution only by using very different assumptions: the House that spending would somehow be cut, the Senate that the economy would magically improve. Appropriations were to be made to fit the second resolution's spending targets by wrapping five of them in a continuing resolution, which provided spending only through June 5, 1981 (thereby reducing the total appropriated). Even so, Congress did not finish until December 16 at 5 A.M. In short, even in 1980, the President's Budget was losing meaning, and the second resolution managed to both be dishonest and distort the appropriations process.

The budget process, however, had been strengthened by invention of reconciliation on the first resolution. The fiscal year 1981 first resolution ordered authorizing committees to report changes of about $10 billion over three years, and Congress actually passed about $8 billion in ostensible savings.[9] Reconciliation could correct the previous imbalance in procedure, that only annually appropriated programs could be influenced by each year's decisions about the totals. The advent of reconciliation meant that 1980 could not really be termed a bad year for the budget process.

Reagan's 1981 spending cuts could be seen as evidence of a strengthened budget process—at least if "budgeting" means "cutting." Yet, that perception is incomplete and not only because of the tax cut.

The 1981 reconciliation was a singular event that could not be duplicated. Reconciliation was applied not only to entitlements but to programs with annual appropriations, which cut across the basic division of labor between authorization and appropriations committees, and aroused so much resentment that it barely has been tried since. The House Republican reconciliation substitute (Gramm-Latta 2) emerged from a unique bargaining process that began with cut lists generated by the transition team, the Senate budget staff, the OMB, and a host of other actors and ended in byzantine negotiations among Stockman, the House GOP leaders, Republicans on the affected committees, moderate Republican "gypsy moths," and conservative Democratic "boll weevils." The bill was a monument to haste and sloppy drafting, altered up to the last hours in an effort to "rent" (Representative, now Senator, Breaux's term) the margin of victory.[10] One could hardly repeat such a process annually, even if that were desired.

The reconciliation vote became a referendum on supporting the President. Party loyalty to their newly elected leader and to their own new majority in the Senate,[11] produced maximum Republican unity in spite of dissensus on substance. Behavior approached that on budget votes in a parliamentary system. But, the United States does not have a parliamentary system, and the behavior was only temporary.

I will return to the factors that allowed the tax bill. Here the point is that the procedures used to cut spending in 1981 were not routine at the time and have not been repeated. Then, as the economy and deficit worsened, the administration distorted the budget process further.

The administration asked the Senate to delay appropriations and then, on September 24, proposed a new round of cuts. Outraged Republicans resisted, insisting on what they considered the terms of agreements made in June on Gramm-Latta 2.[12] Stockman tried to salvage some savings,and the appropriations were embroiled in conflict over outlays and incalculable formulas for across the board reductions. In November, Reagan vetoed a continuing resolution and shut down the "nonessential" government.[13] Yet final settlement in December was little different. Then, in February, Stockman proposed rescissions abrogating the December agreements. Again his allies protested, trying to explain that you cannot budget if any deal has a half-life of a month.[14]

With the recession in full swing, many Democrats and some Republicans also wanted to change spending plans in the middle of the year, only in the other direction. Congress and the administration battled over supplementals and rescissions all summer. After three vetoes were upheld, in September 1982, Congress overrode a fourth that was clearly a matter of the relative priority of defense and domestic spending. That last act of fiscal year 1982 was just in time for Congress to move on to the first continuing resolution for fiscal year 1983. House and Senate leaders wanted to cram all controversial matters in one bill; the administration disliked the probable results, so Reagan insisted on a lame-duck session. Angling for advantage, the House Appropriations Committee did not even report the DoD appropriation until the end of November. The year 1982 ended and 1983 began with successive extraordinary "jobs" bills (the Surface Transportation Assistance Act and the fiscal year 1983 first supplemental appropriation) sandwiched around another massive continuing resolution. All were subjected to filibusters and other delaying tactics. The appropriations schedule had been swamped by warfare over budget priorities.

The year 1982 also began with Reagan's first "dead on arrival" budget. Seeking to replace it with a plan that could better coordinate action, administration and congressional leaders met throughout April in the "Gang of 17" negotiations. When those failed the Senate Budget Committee forced Reagan back to the table by rejecting his budget 20 to 0. After great travail, Congress managed to adopt a budget resolution that promised substantial deficit reductions. In accord with that resolution, two reconciliation bills were passed. The larger, the Tax Equity and Fiscal Responsibility Act of 1982 (TEFRA) included an estimated $98 billion in tax increases and $17 billion in spending cuts over three years.[15]

TEFRA resembled a revenue version of the 1981 spending cuts. It aggregated decisions about details to make them conform to goals for the total. Thus, while the parts of the old budget process (the President's budget and the appropriations) were falling apart, the new institutions created by the Budget Act in 1974 (the Budget Committees, first resolution, and through the act's "elastic clause," reconciliation) seemed to be getting stronger.

In fact, the first resolution was not really an agreement, and TEFRA did not enforce it. When the first resolution was adopted, the rough scale and many of the provisions of TEFRA had already been roughed out by the tax committees with quiet help from the Treasury. The resolution provided an attractive wrapping for the package. The major ornament was a summary of savings that looked like $3 of spending for every $1 of revenue. Ronald Reagan endorsed and campaigned for TEFRA on those grounds. Most of the savings were in categories (interest costs and "management savings") that Congress could not provide. Some were pure illusion.[16] Nevertheless, the White House and conservatives in Congress felt betrayed when Congress did not enact $3 in spending cuts for each TEFRA tax dollar.[17] Much of administration tactics since 1982 can be explained by the desire not to get "screwed" again as they had on TEFRA.[18] That helps explain why 1982 was the last year that the budget resolution even looked like it predicted behavior.

In 1983, the President's budget was stillborn once more. House Democrats exploited their twenty-six new seats to swiftly pass a first resolution that reduced the deficit by raising revenues. The Senate, however, deadlocked totally. Senate Budget Committee Chairman Pete Domenici (R-N.M.) got a resolution passed on the floor only by switching his vote to support an alternative sponsored by Lawton Chiles (D-Fla.) and Slade Gorton (R-Wash.), that also raised taxes.[19] So did the conference agreement. Yet, Ways and Means Committee Chairman Rostenkowski and Finance Committee Chairman Dole had proclaimed their opposition all year, and their committees did not comply. Instead, Dole and a number of others tried to produce alternative deficit reduction plans through the fall, attached to legislation like the debt ceiling. Ironically, the appropriations guerilla war diminished as a rough balance of power ratified the status quo.[20]

So much for the good news. In 1984, everything got stood on its head. In his State of the Union Address, the President aborted his own budget by inviting House and Senate leaders to meet on a deficit reduction "downpayment." He thereby made plain that his own plan, as CEA Chairman Feldstein honestly put it, was "not what we want to see happen."[21] After the bipartisan negotiations fizzled, the Republicans agreed on the "Rose Garden" package, superseding the President's plan. The Rose Garden agreement included comparable deficit reductions from social spending, defense spending, and tax increases. Those tax hikes had already been crafted by the Ways and Means and Senate Finance Committees; as in 1982, the tax committees, not the Budget Committees, set the agenda. A series of maneuvers linked the tax hikes and dubious spending savings[22] in the Deficit Reduction Act of 1984 (DEFRA). DEFRA was turned into a reconciliation bill, even though there was no budget resolution, by declaring that it was part of the fiscal year 1984 budget process, even though its provisions were for fiscal years 1985–1987. Then DEFRA got hung up because the Senate and the President insisted that it include limits on appropriations for the next three years. Insisting that one Congress could not bind another and disagreeing with the particular limits, the House refused to go along with the agreement.

The Senate finally gave in, and DEFRA passed in late June. Having caved in on DEFRA, Senate leaders felt that they could not compromise at all on the priority of defense and domestic spending in the budget resolution. They felt compelled to show support for the President, and that any deal on the resolution would just set a ceiling on defense spending which the House Appropriations Committee would cut anyway.[23] The impasse was not settled until September 20, when Speaker O'Neill and Majority Leader Baker agreed on figures for the defense authorization and appropriation. That allowed budget conferees to settle, but at that late date, the first resolution was misnamed. It was really a version of the old second resolutions (in essence abandoned after 1980); it simply recorded Congress's actions for the year.

The highlight (or lowlight) of 1985 was the hijacking of the debt ceiling to pass Gramm-Rudman-Hollings. But, it included another "dead on arrival" President's budget, strenuous but ultimately unsuccessful efforts by Senate Republicans to force a serious budget deal, and a reconciliation effort that once more collapsed amid a welter of disputes over very important issues that had little to do with cutting spending.[24] Gramm-Rudman-Hollings itself was but the latest in a series of efforts to solve budget problems by circumventing the regular budget process.[25] The new development was that the bill passed; members of Congress had abandoned hope of dealing with the budget through their budget process long before. And, one cannot but suspect that Gramm-Rudman-Hollings passed mostly because no one knew who would be held hostage in a two-stage hostage game that threatened disaster, not to force immediate cuts but to force another hostage situation later. Each side could believe the other was more vulnerable!

Let us summarize. The formal budget process includes a President's budget to propose details of spending, relate them to totals, and coordinate subsequent action; by 1985, this budget was routinely ignored. Congress is supposed to set targets in the first resolution, but the numbers are more symbolic than real and the resolution has been understood as such at least since 1983. Individual appropriations acts are to be considered first by the House and then by the Senate; in the 1980s, they were usually jammed into continuing resolutions, their schedule and aggregation a matter of partisan warfare and the Senate even considered some acts first. Reconciliation is supposed to force entitlement and tax changes in line with the first resolution targets; in 1983 and 1985, no reconciliation passed, and the process has been as much a tool of authorizing committees looking for a procedural advantage as a tool for budget control. There is supposed to be at least a rough distinction between budgeting and other legislation, but as reconciliation and continuing resolutions became gigantic legislative freight trains, the distinction between budgeting and anything else faded. In short, when Gramm-Rudman-Hollings passed, the organization of budgeting no longer had much in the way of rules, procedures, allegiance, or boundaries. Whether or not one liked the results, there was no process left to blame.

Causes of Collapse

Why did the budget process implode? One mode of explanation invokes personality. Ronald Reagan and Tip O'Neill, two elderly Irishmen who distrust each other intensely, happened to be in positions where they could veto sensible compromises. That argument presumes, however, that the Speaker and the President did not represent anything; in particular, it ignores overwhelming public distaste for higher taxes or cuts in social security. A more plausible story incorporates those real public constraints and argues that the simplest possible notion of the goals of budgeting, control of the deficit, was impossible in the mid-1980s. Since the process could not perform its task, it was no longer given enough authority by outsiders and it collapsed.

It is clear that the budget crisis had been building for quite awhile.[26] Throughout the postwar era, the tax burden hovered near 19 percent of the GNP and public support for a higher level was never developed.[27] In a slow progression, including a jump for the 1974–1975 recession, outlays in the late 1970s grew toward around 21.5 percent. The growth was driven by an increase of transfer payments, between 1962–1978, from 6.3 percent to 12.8 percent of the GNP. That was almost, but not quite, covered by a decline in the defense share (9.5 percent to 5 percent) and of the share for other domestic operations.[28]

The dominant factors in transfer growth were the giant OASDHI system that includes social security and medicare, and the nationalization of poverty relief. Pension and medical expenses were driven by demographics and some misjudgment of costs.[29] While legislative decisions to expand these programs virtually ended in 1973, costs continued to grow. The economy's travails after the oil shocks of 1973 and 1979 meant shrinking real wages and, thus, an increase in the share of national income taken by the price-indexed entitlements. Thus, a weak economy and old commitments left Jimmy Carter with a gap of 2 percent of the GNP between normal levels of spending and taxing. He tried to solve the problem by restraining spending and allowing taxes, via bracket creep, to reach a postwar peak of 20.8 percent of the GNP. The public rejected higher taxes and kicked him out of office.

This is not the place for a disquisition on the logic or illogic of the Reagan politico-economic program. Assume no Ronald Reagan for a moment. Still we would have seen the following.

First, a substantial defense build up in the wake of Iran and Afghanistan. That build up began in 1980 with a 9 percent growth in budget authority engineered by the Democratic Senate. The defense share of the GNP would have continued to increase.

Second, because program costs were indexed to prices, which grew faster than the economy, the social security and medicare share of the GNP would grow by about a point from 1979–1984.

Third, there would have been some tax cut, probably toward the postwar norm.

The Reagan tax program was expected to return taxes to slightly below their "normal" level, as the income tax rate cuts and corporate reduction would be partially balanced by bracket creep and scheduled payroll tax increases. Because inflation was halted by the Federal Reserve more swiftly than anyone dared expect, bracket creep was less and the tax cut greater than expected. Any administration would have misestimated in this way, if not in some other ways that the Reagan Administration managed.

Most likely, there also would have been a big recession at some point, much like that of 1974–1975. In the event, cyclical deficits zoomed in spite of Reagan's budget cuts. Those deficits lived on in the debt; since money was tight, interest rates remained high; higher debt and interest rates raised net interest as a share of the GNP by another point. The particular policy mix of 1981–1983 may have increased this effect, but Paul Volcker was appointed by Jimmy Carter, and Reagan's fiscal policy was not in fact different from Carter's at least until mid-1982. On interest and entitlement costs, taxes and defense, unless we assume away the recession, we can expect that a deficit (during the 1980s) of about 4 percent of the GNP, around $150 billion, was baked in the cake when the legislative ingredients, mixed up through 1972, met the heat of subsequent economic trouble.

Those deficits would have crunched the process because of the great horror of deficits on the part of the political center, media, and business establishments. In normal politics the left and right wings reject the status quo. The center, generally satisfied with the way things are, is happy to let them fight and stalemate each other. Deficit politics works backwards. Centrists like Senators Dole, Domenici, and Chiles; mainstream journals like TIME and Newsweek; economists from Martin Feldstein to Alice Rivlin join in insisting that the status quo is a disaster. The wings, who are told to sacrifice their dearest policies (low taxes, social security), resist, but they are so busy clubbing each other with the deficit that no one really defends the status quo. So, the demand to solve the deficit "problem" is deafening, yet the choices are impossible. The deficit is too big. In 1986, we could cut social security 20 percent, a drastic cut in the income for tens of millions, and we would only reduce the fiscal year 1986 deficit from around $230 billion to $190 billion. If we eliminated the entire roster of Great Society programs, the deficit would remain over $100 billion. We are no longer talking about aggregating small cuts for "special" interests; to eliminate current deficits, we must create packages in which the individual components are drastic. The cuts needed are impossible but demand persists; thus, collapse.

There is much truth in the argument that budgeting cannot survive the combination of old commitments, a weak economy, and a public that refuses to pay the cost of services. Yet, this picture is incomplete. It begs the question of how we got into this mess; it does not explain many of the events in the breakdown; and it gives us no guidance on what to do next.

That the budget is driven largely by the economy is a common theme, yet a belief that budget policy should shape or at least anticipate economic performance is equally common. Thus, to say that the deficit was caused by hard times just raises more specific questions: Why did budget policy not only fail to anticipate or to prevent huge deficits but seemingly make them worse? Since much of the long-term deficit problem was created by rising interest costs, why was action not taken earlier to prevent the compounding of deficits? a lot of effort since 1981 has dealt with the deficit feeding on itself, but earlier action would have been a lot less painful.[30] Given the likely deficit consequences of the tax cut and popular fear of that result, why did taxes get cut so far in 1981? The "normal" tax level was 19 percent of the GNP, but the public cannot feel that number; a cut to 20 percent would still have looked like tax relief. The defense build up could have been smaller and the money supply looser; different choices in 1980 and 1981 could have reduced the pressure that burst in Gramm-Rudman-Hollings. If, as economic and political debate suggests, the budget influences the economy (whether through direct demand management or through "expectations" of inflation and interest rates based on projected deficits), then we have to explain why hard times got so hard. In short, the argument that the deficit troubles were baked in the cake long before implies that budgeting can do less than is often suggested, and does not explain why actions in 1981 exacerbated the underlying deficit problem.

The hard-times argument implies that the fight has been over the deficit alone, but what the money is spent on has been just as controversial as the totals. The battles about resolutions and appropriations, in spite of any contrary rhetoric, have concerned the fate of particular programs and relative priority of defense and domestic spending. The defense versus domestic question caused Senate Republicans to torpedo the Budget Resolution in 1984. Gramm-Rudman-Hollings, with its formula cuts, reflected the desire to take the priority issue out of the deficit-reduction problem. But, the battle about both the formula and who would apply that "solution" was just another phase of the problem. While fiscal constraint exacerbates disagreement over programs, Reagan and Stockman would have attacked domestic programs if there were no deficit at all, and Congress would have resisted.

A difficult environment helped cause the breakdown of the budget process. We can draw inferences for reform only by asking how much the process could control the environment and what participants were really fighting about. That brings us to defining the stakes of budgeting and tasks of the budgeting organization.

The Multiple and Conflicting Tasks of Budgeting

The appropriations process exists, first, to satisfy the constitutional mandate that no funds be spent without appropriations made by law. That mandate exists to ensure Congress' power of the purse. Appropriations exist to ensure the executive's dependence upon the legislature. Entitlements are the exception that proves the rule for, although they have permanent appropriations, the executive branch has no discretion over spending and cannot divert monies for its own purposes. A power state, thus, is central to federal budgeting. The appropriations process also allocates benefits among congressional districts; the committees serve as an arena for distributional politics while limiting presidential patronage power.

The Appropriations Committees exist also to limit spending by checking the authorizing committees' propensity to favor their particular constituents. The parallel jurisdiction of authorizers and appropriators yields continual controversy. The appropriators should not poach on authorizers' turf; House rules forbid "legislation" on an appropriations bill. But, distinguishing reasonable limitations on spending from legislation is rather difficult. The boundary is defined by a rough distinction between means and ends, management and policy. Appropriators should ask not What do you want to accomplish? but What did you do with the money last year? How would you manage if you had $10 millon less? Minimizing cost should not be taken to the point where it changes policy. Economy of expenditures, as Richard Fenno wrote, is "the most special goal" of the House appropriations Committee[31] but it was and is also expected to support programs and protect the power of the purse. The balance among those goals depends on the actions of others.

Economy of expenditure is closely tied to, but not the same as, balancing the budget and limiting federal debt. The latter could be attained by revenue increases as well as spending restraint, and economy has independent value. Even "spenders" want more for their money. The appropriations process pursues economy but not necessarily balance. Thus, it was supplemented, from 1921 on, by the President's budget.

Until 1975, the President's budget was the only approximation of a financial statement for the federal government. It remains the only relation of details to totals in "a general financial and work program" for the year.[32] Program-level decisions (How many children in Head Start?) are forced to match a plan for total spending and taxing. That plan normally provides a standard for the appropriations; if they stayed within the President's totals, the deficit, if any, was not their fault. His budget also helped authorizing committee members by allowing them to tell their clientele that it was the mean old President who limited benefits. The budget documents and agency estimates further provided the details from which the Appropriations Committees worked. The budget examiners at the Bureau of the Budget (later Office of Management and Budget) asked within the executive the same kinds of questions that the appropriators asked within Congress. So long as their neutral competence was trusted, the examiners' work simplified the appropriators' task.

These functions of review and aggregation of estimates and constructing an acceptable balance sheet were part of the President's budget from the beginning. Other goals were added over time. During World War II emphasis within the executive process shifted from simply limiting spending (control) to improving agency operations (management); the shift was expressed in the idea of Program Budgeting.[33] With the Full Employment Act of 1946 another goal was formalized, the use of budget totals to manage the economy.

There never was thorough agreement on how the economy might be managed. Keynesian demand management was the preeminent theory, but it had only a short period of nearly unchallenged dominance in the 1960s. Yet, there was wide agreement that in some way the budget totals would shape economic performance.[34] Thus the Council of Economic Advisers, Treasury and Budget Bureau economists considered, and the President had to decide, the fiscal policy to be presented in the budget. Until the 1974 act, Congress had no way to respond with an alternative plan.

Fiscal policy may be the preeminent task of federal budgeting today. Carter's 1980 remaking of his budget was driven solely by fiscal concerns. Aside from the actual effect on the economy, which is controversial, three things are evident about the fiscal policy function. It is so important that institutionally Congress must hesitate to cede it to the President. By creating a powerful argument for some set of totals, fiscal policy also shapes the politics of details. It determines the "base" for each year's budget politics.[35] Therefore, parties with an interest in programs may need to seize control of fiscal policy making to get their way. Last, fiscal policy has strong partisan overtones. In Keynesian terms, expansionary policy increases employment but threatens inflation. It, thus, tightens labor markets, favoring labor, and by raising prices threatens to erode the value of capital. Contraction has the opposite effects. Expansionary policy also allows more spending, and thus a more active government. The fundamental material difference between the two political parties is that the Democrats favor labor and government, and Republicans favor business.[36] Thus, a Congress not controlled by the President's party cannot leave fiscal policy in his hands, and to the extent that budgeting means setting fiscal policy, bitter partisan debate must be expected.

The 1974 Budget Act, by providing totals for spending, revenues, and deficit in the budget resolutions, institutionalized the fiscal policy task for Congress. Making economic policy requires economic knowledge, so Congress created its own set of economists, the Congressional budget Office (CBO). The CBO also produces neutral estimates of the cost of programs driven by the economy, like entitlements or military fuel costs.

As the federal government grew, the President's budget took on one more, very problematic function: It became the statement of the President's "program." "Its money estimates and legislative program," Richard Neustadt wrote in his study of the presidency, "are the nearest things available to an agenda for [the] struggle over scope and shape of government.[37] In short, it began to be viewed more as a catalogue of ends than of means. "How much does the President propose to spend for education?" was reinterpreted as "How much does the President value education?" The President's budget was seen as "Setting National Priorities."[38] The congressional budget process, adopted in 1974, formalized Congress' response to the budget as a set of priorities. The new resolutions' spending targets for each budget function respond and may be compared directly to the President's list in his own budget. The 1974 act thus incorporated budgeting as priority setting into the congressional structure. When one observer in 1985 called the process "not simply a means of routinizing budget choice, of simply making a budget each year . . . [but] our major national vehicle for setting and changing national priorities," he was expressing a common understanding of the purposes of the budget process.[39]

Nothing could be more controversial than setting priorities. Participation cannot be limited. Normally, Congress dampens conflict through the committee structure; the members who care about agriculture fight out their differences in the Agriculture Committee and other members accept the results. The same for interior or armed services, though of course within limits. But everybody cares about priorities. If budgeting sets priorities, then it violates the distinction between appropriation and legislation, which is at the heart of the old budget system. In fact, the budget institutions are not equipped to shape priorities and they do not. A committee on priorities is called a cabinet, and its chairman is called a prime minister. We do not have that. We cannot.

To change priorities in the federal system means to change the preferences of the government, by changing the opinions of existing members or by changing the members themselves. Our budget institutions can do little of either. Institutions designed for annual financing of government activities cannot be used to force a change in priorities. Before pursuing this controversial theme we should observe other ways that, under some conditions, budgeting tasks conflict.

The goal of budget balance rests uneasily with managing the economy. Believers in budget balance as an end in itself feel the system should not be able to pursue demand management, because that may mean choosing deficits. Thus the proposed Balanced Budget Amendment seeks to establish the preeminence of the goal of balance, at the expense of fiscal management. However when, as in 1980, fiscal managers are trying to contract the economy, then there is no contradiction.

For most of our history the goals of protecting the power of the purse, controlling the agencies, and limiting spending reinforced each other. Congress suspected that easy money would help the executive build its power, and a tight hand on the purse strings would keep the agencies properly deferential to their congressional masters. The operating goal of economy, pursued through the process of close oversight of agency estimates and activities, served the institutional task of preserving Congress' preeminence.[40] This stable pattern was broken when President Nixon challenged Congress by refusing to spend in the amounts and for the purposes that Congress desired. In that situation, if the appropriators had routinely cut from Nixon's requests they would have been conceding, not preserving, Congress' institutional position. The impoundment controversy epitomized the reversed and substantial stakes.

The best known tension among tasks is between program support and economy. In a sense, the budget process exists to adjust that tension. Thirty years ago, the House Appropriations Committee normally pursued both but choosing a figure above existing spending (support) but below the President's budget (economy).[41] That strategy becomes impossible, however, when the President requests less for one year than for the previous year, whether because of economic troubles or for programmatic reasons.[42] The degree of conflict thus, is determined by the economy and by the policy distance between President and Congress.

These examples suggest that having multiple goals makes the working of the budget process dependent on luck and on overarching norms that constrain behavior. Movement away from an existing settlement can create pressure in a number of dimensions, activating contradictions that previously were manageable. Norms that inhibited presidential warfare against the status quo, or excessive demands for program support, could limit goal conflict.

Tasks need not conflict, however, for their multiplicity to make completion of any of them more difficult. If a system must combine all its task performance in one unit of output, then failure at any task is failure at all. Thus, if agreeing on a budget resolution requires agreement on fiscal policy and priorities and how much each agency needs for effective operation and on the relative power of Congress and the President, then disagreement on any of these dimensions, by torpedoing the resolution, can have the functional effect of disagreement on all. On the other hand, a belief that agreement on one dimension is overwhelmingly important may cause people to compromise more readily on the others. For that to occur, however, the hierarchy of values must be shared by all, which is unlikely.

The current federal budget process is a tightly coupled system, where disagreement on one dimension may torpedo the whole process. Some supporters of the 1974 act hoped that it would elevate economy in the hierarchy of values. Others were pursuing a process norm of comprehensive rationality, consideration and judgment on the full range of issues involved in budgeting.[43] That objective is contrary to the basic design of the constitutional system, which intentionally makes decision making difficult.[44]

If each of the tasks of budgeting were easy, their coupling would not be so much of a problem. But none of them is easy, and two of them—setting priorities and managing the economy—are extremely difficult. During the 1980s, they were difficult on their own and because their pursuit activated some of the conditional difficulties mentioned, particularly the tension between the President and Congress over the power of the purse.

"Setting Priorities"

A separate funding process always potentially is a separate legislative process. Stymied through the regular authorizing procedures, Congressional opponents of abortion or the Vietnam War turned to the appropriations bills in their efforts to arrest those "evils." Beginning in 1981, the Reagan Administration took the use of budgeting as an alternative legislative process to unprecedented lengths in order to reduce or terminate programs it disliked. The extent of its success may be endlessly argued; Stockman thinks he failed but others disagree.[45] It is all a matter of expectations and standards. If we put aside 1981, however, it is clear that the strife and chaos of later years effected little change.

In spite of claims of spending savings made in each budget round since 1981, those savings have been quite small.[46] "Nondefense discretionary" outlays were cut in 1981, for fiscal year 1982 and beyond, but after 1981, Congress essentially adjusted the new base for inflation each year.[47] John Palmer estimates that all the domestic program reductions made during the fiscal years 1983–1986 budget cycles saved, for fiscal year 1986, $26 billion (less than 5 percent of the total).[48] Even those did not reflect administration priorities: About $6 billion is the fiscal year 1986 sequester, much of the rest were medicare savings but not as the administration preferred,[49] and as Stockman himself notes, there have even been some increases in means-tested entitlements.[50] In short, the strategy of using deficit pressure to cut domestic spending failed dismally; very little has changed in social programs since 1981.[51]

Defense, of course, did grow. In that sense, there was a change in "priorities" after 1982. Yet, that change as well was largely a product of the 1981 fight and of Carter's last year, 1980. Table 8-1 shows that if we look at budget authority (which is what Congress votes on) the change in priorities slowed substantially in fiscal year 1983 and ended after the fiscal year 1984 (1983) budget round.[52] The table shows also that the major welfare-state reductions were made in 1981 (fiscal year 1982). Some of that change also preceded Reagan. Federal grants to state and local governments, cut dramatically in 1981, had been reduced in previous years as well and afterwards were barely cut at all.[53] Table 8-2 tells the tale. In short, the changes that were enacted in 1981 had precedents in other years, and the changes stopped after the 1981 reconciliation was passed. The rest was stalemate.

Table 8-1.

Budget Authority as Percent of Total for Selected Departments by Fiscal Year

	1979	1980	1981	1982	1983	1984	1985	1986*
DoD: Military	21.7	20.8	23.6	26.1	26.9	27.2	26.7	26.3
Major Social	25.2	23.5	23.2	20.3	20.9	20.7	20.4	19.8

Source: Tables 5.1 and 5.2, OMB Historical Tables for Fiscal Year 1987. Major Social combines the Departments of Labor, Health and Human Services, Education, and Housing and Urban Development.

*Estimated.

Table 8-2.

Outlays for "Other" Grants to State and Local Governments by Fiscal Year in Billions of 1982 dollars.

1977	1978	1979	1980	1981	1982	1983	1984	1985	1986*
70.1	75.7	71.8	68.4	61.3	50.3	48.8	49.1	50.5	49.3

Source: Table 12.1, OMB, Historical Tables for Fiscal Year 1987. Other grants excludes the payments to individuals (like medicaid), which are strongly driven by the economy, and therefore is the best indicator of change in policy.

*Estimated.

How is it that Ronald Reagan and David Stockman, so effective through July of 1981, were so ineffective thereafter? The answer is simple: They were as much a product as the movers of the forces that shape policy. Stockman felt that he could use the budget process to force a change in priorities; that budgeting could be used to "set" priorities. The federal budget process, however, does not set priorities. Priorities are set in a different political arena and are only recorded, or translated into, the budget process. Events outside the budget arena changed priorities in a way that was recorded in 1980 and 1981. After 1981, events in the wider arena did not encourage change, so efforts in the budgetary arena were doomed to fail.

The distinction between setting and recording priorities may seem artificial. From an operating standpoint priorities only exist as they are recorded in law, and the laws obligating money are the laws that count. Therefore, budgeting must "set" priorities. Yet, the distinction becomes important when we ask what can be accomplished by manipulating the budgetary organizations. In organizational terms, a process that sets priorities could be manipulated by clever people (like Stockman) so as to create different policy mixes from identical inputs, much as a sewing machine can turn the same bolt of cloth into a jacket or a skirt. A process that records priorities is more like an ice cream maker: The product largely depends on the ingredients added. In July 1981, the machine was making fudge ripple. Reagan and Stockman tried to produce chocolate ice cream instead, not by adding more chocolate but by cranking the machine overtime, bouncing it up and down, and so on. They got the same old fudge ripple from a lot more work. You change the ice cream by changing the ingredients. Such a change in fact occurred; it was recorded in some of the budgeting decisions of 1979 and 1980 and then completed in the Reagan victories of 1981. Reagan and Stockman were the beneficiaries, and part of, changes outside the budget process. They were part of the fudge that turned Great Society vanilla into fudge ripple, but there was not enough to go all the way to chocolate.

The "ingredients" available for policy making are simply the opinions of policy makers. They change when sitting policy makers change their opinions or are replaced by office holders with different opinions. Opinions change because of events: A report is released detailing the failings of American secondary education; blacks riot in Watts; the space shuttle Challenger blows up; the Soviets invade Afghanistan. Events take on meaning through discussion and debate. Office holders change, in the main, through elections. Occasionally, some crucial post will change for other reasons, as when Senator Muskie became Secretary of State in 1980 and was replaced as Budget Committee chairman by the more hawkish Senator Hollings. Without new events or new people to change opinion, there is little reason to expect an existing organization to change its output.

There is little that anyone can do through a given year's budget process to change either opinions or participants. Oh, there are a few tactics. The Reagan Administration worked to keep federal bureaucrats out of the budget process by isolating political appointees from the career service and strictly controlling testimony in appropriations hearings. Stockman and the President's other representatives argued strenuously for the administration's agenda. The opinions of congressmen, though, were deep seated and not to be disposed of so easily. When Stockman describes "the major reason that the Reagan Revolution made so little difference to the poverty programs" he makes the point: "The Senate committee chairmen and ranking House Republicans during the 1980s had nearly all been on the ground floor" of program development. "Bob Dole was there along with George McGovern when the nutrition programs were created," and Stockman mentions many others. Stockman was not about to convince Bob Dole or Silvio Conte to abandon programs they had supported for years. Without new congressmen or new facts he could not get new results.[54]

The changes made under Reagan and Carter stemmed from a combination of new opinions among existing participants and, in 1981, a crucial influx of new participants. The chief opinion changer, dramatically reflected in the 1980 defense budget conflicts, was the Soviet invasion of Afghanistan. Yet, the reductions in domestic spending also reflected a shift in Democratic party beliefs and in conventional wisdom.

Throughout the 1970s, "spending" became less popular with policy analysts, the media, and even erstwhile liberals. More and more Democrats developed doubts about the efficacy of social programs. CETA, the major victim of the 1981 OBRA cuts, had been delegitimized over a period of years. Public works jobs had been delegitimized by studies showing they were extremely expensive and provided at the wrong time; thus Democratic Budget Chairman Muskie led the Senate in resisting a jobs bill in 1978. The Economic Development Administration, the "middle-class subsidy" in school lunch programs, and Civil Service Retirement cost-of-living adjustments had been under fire from the Budget Committee (Democratic) staff. The Proposition 13 tax revolt in California also reduced politicians' taste for spending. Jimmy Carter, a fiscal conservative who promised to balance the budget, moved to restrain spending in 1979. Spending cuts were in the air; one House Budget aide remarked that by 1980 he had become "a bagman for cut lists." The 1980 inflation and bond market panic accelerated that shift of opinion.

Participants then changed because of the 1980 election, which produced a Republican majority in the Senate and a very slender conservative margin in the House. Congressional votes are affected by too many factors, including posturing, for us to be sure of any analysis. Losing only twenty-nine conservative "boll weevils," however, the House Democrats could hardly have done better than they did on the crucial reconciliation vote, which they lost by 217 to 210. The ones that they lost they were not supposed to get. But, we can also say, as Stockman reports, that the administration dragged the Republican "gypsy moths" about as far as they were willing to go. As Republicans they believed in spending restraint and supporting their President—to a point that they reached in July 1981. After that, in part because of new facts that did not help the President (the recession), a crucial group of frostbelt moderates refused to support further domestic spending cuts.[55]

A new group of participants bargained, fought, and enacted a new balance among programs. With great skill, the administration won all there was to win in 1981. Neither participants nor opinions could be changed subsequently to favor further social cuts. Opinion did change, if at all, to slow down the defense build up, due to both the deficit and scandal. The recession reduced support for social cuts, and then the 1982 election changed participants in the Speaker's favor.

The design of the budget process does matter. Without reconciliation, spending cuts would have been more difficult. Reconciliation matters precisely because it structures participation, reducing the weight of the authorizing committees' power to do nothing. The choice to employ reconciliation itself depended on preferences about policy. The administration could propose changes in the process (the line-item veto, the balanced-budget amendment) but those in turn depended on preferences that the administration could not affect, and they were rejected.

No machine can make chocolate ice cream without cocoa, yet that is what the administration was trying to do in all the battles after the 1981 reconciliation was passed. All its maneuvers were the equivalent of churning, churning, and churning the handle some more in the desperate hope that somehow all the shaking would change the ingredients in the canister. Instead, the handle broke and the budget machine became useless.

Priorities and Incrementalism

To argue that budgeting does not set priorities contradicts common talk about the budget, yet it both confirms and elucidates incrementalist theory. Sometimes the term *incrementalism* seems to mean so many things that it means nothing. It may characterize results: A process is "incremental" if it yields small, regular changes. It may characterize how participants proceed: Everybody accepts the established "base," and the conflict over increments is heavily constrained by notions of "fair shares." You can have incrementalist results even though some participants reject incrementalist norms; that is what happened after 1981, as the administration tried to be radical but was thwarted. If we focus on results, we may wonder how big a change is incremental or whether the proper standard is size or the regularity of increments. If we attend to process, then what proportion of the participants must proceed incrementally for the overall system to deserve the name?

One answer to the definitional problem is to say that incrementalism is a central tendency of the system as both a result and a process. In a system of fragmented power, attempts to alter the status quo are readily checked. Therefore, nonincrementalist behavior on the part of one actor is unlikely to suffice; it will produce conflict but little policy change. Nonincrementalist behavior or results are always possible but inherently unstable, since even successful change is likely to provoke stronger resistance on the next round. Thus, federal budgeting can be incrementalist in general, even if isolated events suggest otherwise. In a similar way, the market system can work by the use of prices to adjust supply and demand, despite incidents of shortage and surplus.

As used by Wildavsky, incrementalism is a process in which the range of controversy is severely reduced by agreeing not to contest most issues. Most of each agency's proposal is viewed as the "base," normally defined as what happened last year (though there is room for interpretation).[56] Interprogram comparisons (priorities) are restricted by established notions of "fair shares." Wildavsky explains that,

> The base is the general expectation among the participants that programs will be carried on at or close to the going level of expenditures but it does not necessarily include all activities. Having a project included in the agency's base thus means more than just getting it in the budget for a

particular year. It means establishing the expectation that the expenditure will continue, that it is accepted as part of what will be done, and, therefore, that it will not normally be subjected to intensive scrutiny. . . . "Fair share" means not only the base an agency has established but also the expectation that it will receive some proportion of funds, if any, which are to be increased over or decreased below the base of the various governmental agencies. "Fair share" thus reflects a convergence of expectations on roughly how much the agency is to receive in comparison to others.[57]

Both base and fair share are parts of an existing pattern of agreement; between them they define existing priorities.

Wildavsky argues that incrementalism limits an otherwise overwhelming burden of calculation and aids negotiation. The budget is too big to investigate all the parts, so participants assume old knowledge is still good until proven otherwise. The same goes for agreements: Last year's settlement is presumed to be the most likely. Therefore, calculation and negotiation are limited to new issues. That reduces the scope and, thus stakes of conflict and makes agreement possible (though not inevitable).

Any participant may disrupt the incrementalist process by rejecting the established base. Usually, someone is dissatisfied. Yet, since no participant can impose change on all its rivals, the base generally reflects an existing balance of power. The norm of incrementalism, of recognizing the other guy's base and fair share, may be a grudging norm.

If the participants change then the balance of power changes and, even more important, the old base no longer may predict what the new participants can agree on. The base is not a base if it is someone else's base. Thus, in 1981, self-conscious new majorities in the House and Senate rejected the old base and bargained out a new one in the reconciliation fight. Those bargains, however, created a new base, reflecting the new balance of power and the extent to which it reflected participants' preferences. They invested it with moral value as an agreement bargained in good faith, and the President's new proposals were treated as a betrayal. Reagan and Stockman were attacked continually in the language of "fair shares." As participants searched for ways to reduce the deficit, their language reflected acceptance of the idea that the existing distribution was fair and any increments or decrements should be distributed proportionally. They spoke of freezes, of sharing the pain, and of a "three-legged stool" (defense cuts, domestic cuts, revenue increases) of deficit reduction. They were saying that incrementalist norms applied to the existing budget policy; the President disagreed; the President lost.

Budget change is possible through changes in opinion. But, incrementalism suggests that one year's calculations, which focus on the increment, are unlikely to change opinion about the base. That experiment—structuring each year's calculations in a manner designed to change opinions about the base in a given year—has been tried. It was called Planning, Programming, and Budgeting Systems (PPB). The idea was to force comparison and consideration of various program purposes during annual budget review within each agency and department; thus, the goals of policy would be reset each year in the budget process. PPB, born with great fanfare, died unlamented a few years later. It heightened conflict by widening the scope of debate, but the information developed changed few opinions. Even if the information normally developed had been striking, it was unlikely to convince all the power holders necessary within a year's budget debate. The most important power holders, members of Congress, were not interested; at best, it was an infringement by the executive on congressional goal-setting functions. Allen Schick argues that

> While budgeting often is labeled as action-forcing, in fact it is a process which has action forced upon it. If governments possessed some device to keep going even in the absence of normal spending decisions, the shape of budgeting would be markedly different and the potential of PPB would be boosted. Perhaps a lengthier budget cycle—with a three- or five-year decision frame—is a prerequisite for freeing budgeting from its compulsions for conflict avoidance.[58]

The fate of PPB easily fits the argument of this paper. PPB could not succeed because it was an attempt to set priorities, and it was blocked by those with an institutional stake in the existing priority-setting mechanism. But, the attempt to piggyback priority setting on other budgetary tasks, like routine financing, inhibited performance of the latter. Therefore, defenders of the more traditional tasks killed PPB. If financing could be done on a three- or five-year cycle—(which means if Congress were willing to trust the agencies with such lengthy appropriations!)—then financing decisions could be linked to the real rhythm of priority setting; that is, of opinion development and elections. Defenders of PPB argue that, by institutionalizing analysis, it added to the information available in budget and policy making and brought a new perspective to bear in decisions. True enough, and new information eventually meant new opinions. The key word is *eventually*. New Opinions could not be forced through the budget process; in 1970, as in 1983, they had to mature in the much less structured, wider arena of general policy debate.

The Reagan Revolution differs from PPB in that the effort to change ends was sponsored by a President and an OMB who cared little about providing means for programs they disliked and who gave the effort to set priorities far more force than the PPB exercises could ever generate. Therefore, conflict was far more disruptive. Yet, a President who defied the established base was nothing new either. Richard Nixon tried it with the same results: The President was thwarted and the budget system collapsed.[59]

Incrementalist theory has been criticized because changes do occur. Wildavsky and his colleagues have acknowledged as much, showing that incremental results are interrupted by "shift points" in the regression of spending over time.[60] The analysis here explains why the budget process may be called incremental yet be characterized by such unpredictable "shift points." Shifts are due to changes in the ingredients fed into the budgetary process because of the cumulative influence of events and debate on opinion, or because of elections. Since they are shaped by events outside of the budgetary processes, shifts cannot be predicted from the budget process alone. Incrementalist theory makes more sense if we argue that the budget process records but does not set priorities. In regression language, budgeting incrementalism applies the beta weights each year; the wider political process changes the beta weights at uncertain intervals.

Budgeting and the Economy

Reagan and Stockman's effort to set priorities through budgeting overloaded the budget process. Priority setting is something that budgeting cannot, and therefore should not try to do. Our political system can perform that function, albeit in a herky-jerky, aggravating manner, through processes of debate, "crisis" identification and response, and most important, elections.

The administration's use of the budget as a tool of economic management caused about as much controversy as did its effort to set priorities. Its difficulties in that realm were just the latest in a long line.

The administration would argue that its fiscal policy was a success. Inflation has been purged, admittedly at some cost, and we are now (1987) in the fifth year of recovery. We have unprecedented budget deficits, but their evil is hard to pin down. In spite of these arguments, economic performance under Reagan has been far inferior to the objectives of the administration. Instead of a new era of capitalist prosperity, we have had a mediocre recovery from our deepest postwar recession.

The major differences between this and previous upswings are that unemployment is higher, productivity and real wage growth have been slower, and both government and trade deficits have been far greater than the norm. The financial system teeters precariously. Nobody would have set current results as a target, nor have argued for the current deficits. Their relative harmlessness is hindsight (and hope). It is fair to say that things went wrong. But why?

Those who blame the administration emphasize its "crackpot" economic theories. Those who care most about the deficit emphasize "Rosy Scenario," the administration's 1981 economic forecast. Either position assumes that there was economic truth that could have been applied to the economic problem. A budget process should facilitate that application. The CBO and the Budget Committees should ensure that unbiased information is available, and crackpot theories or predictions should be confronted by the weight of informed opinion.

To a great extent, the institutions did their job. In 1981, the House Budget Committee formally rejected Rosy Scenario. The Senate Budget Committee staff never believed her for a minute, and, at the request of Majority Leader Baker, they continually supplied him with alternate projections. The administration, it is true, argued strenuously for its forecast, to the point of choosing to dissemble after its own numbers began to come out "wrong" in early June. Yet, Congress chose to be deceived.

Here again, we meet the multiple goals of budgeting. Senator Domenici stubbornly resisted the optimistic forecast and "magic asterisk" approach to spending savings. Yet, he and Senator Baker chose to risk later economic evils, which might be dealt with later, rather than to immediately split their party and destroy its ability to govern. One consequence of making the President's budget his program is to make support for the budget the preeminent test of party loyalty and his ability to govern. Senate leaders and other doubters (particularly Stockman and Richard Darman) chose to emphasize immediate power stakes and discounted future policy stakes for uncertainty.[61]

That uncertainty about the future reflected a failure of economists to convincingly describe the present. In 1981, nobody knew where the economy was going next or what to do about it. Otherwise conservative men joined in Reagan's "riverboat gamble," because there was no voice of economic authority.[62] Democrats, who in 1980 had continually misjudged the economy, had little credibility in opposition.

In 1980, the panicky behavior of the financial markets dominated economic policy. Policy makers found themselves trying to shape ephemeral market "expectations," a purely reactive position for which theory was an inadequate guide. Even CBO Director Alice Rivlin and Federal Reserve Chairman Paul Volcker joined the chorus, calling on politicians to try to satisfy the financial markets. Rivlin argued for a balanced budget, even though she had testified a few days earlier that, by normal calculations, it would have little if any positive effect on the economy. Volcker argued for budget balance, even though he also claimed that the burst of inflation to which it would supposedly respond was just the oil price increases working their way through the economy and would be restrained by the monetary targeting that the Federal Reserve had already instituted.[63] They and other economists, by arguing that politicians had to respond to the markets, abandoned their claim to authority. None of the forecasting models could predict "expectations," so none could convincingly reject arguments about them. Stockman, Reagan, and Regan argued that the markets would be thrilled by the big tax cut; their opponents disagreed; but nobody knew. Without expertise to guide, making policy reduced to choosing sides on other grounds. Reagan exploited the uncertainty and desperation bred by the panics of 1980. He struck his opponents' weakest point when he asked, at the end of his presentation of the Program for Economic Recovery on February 18, 1981, "have they an alternative . . .? . . . if they haven't, are they suggesting we can continue on the present course without coming to a day of reckoning?"[64]

The budget process could and did provide alternative sources of expertise. It could not give that expertise authority in the atmosphere of desperation so palpable in reviewing the events that preceded Reagan's victories. Because it could not, the process could not prevent the budget-busting tax cuts that are precisely the kind of thing one would expect a process to make difficult. The already inevitable deficits were made far worse.

The uncertainty of 1980–1981 was extraordinary, but the difficulty of fiscal management is constant. Economists and politicians are expected to design policy to respond to events at least a year in the future. They must estimate where the economy will go under current policy, estimate the effects of a policy change, and predict the behavior of other actors (the Federal Reserve, the Japanese, unions). In all these estimates, there is error. Countercyclical fiscal management requires knowledge that policy makers just do not have. If the economic problem is noncyclical (say, developing industry overseas under a free-trade regime allows cheap foreign labor to displace American labor), then results will have even less relation to fiscal choices.

The fragility of economic forecasts is well documented. CBO Director Rudolph Penner has written that "Although President Reagan made one of the most spectacular miscalculations in history, it is not unusual for budget plans to go awry."[65] Accordingly, Penner has suggested that the estimation of long-term budget trends essentially be abandoned, replaced by "projections of real growth and inflation . . . based on the average experience of the previous five years."[66] Reflecting on its years of forecasting experience, the CBO reported that "forecast errors are quite large, a reflection of the limitations of economic forecasting generally."[67] CBO's analysis shows that similar errors are made by all forecasters.

One of the administration's chief economic policy makers spoke to the difficulty of the task when asked what one thing he thought most needed to be explained in a book about budget making.

> The omniscience that hindsight gives you. When we are in the middle of this it is very hard to know where the right road is, or even what the statistics are. Coming out [in a few days] is a revision of GNP for the last three years. We had just the "flash" estimates, and they got changed three times.
>
> Turn to the next page in your notebook and write down, tell me, starting right now, what will the economy be like in 1987? Under what circumstances will you be operating, and how will that affect 1988 and 1989? When you're in the middle of the forest, God, you're surrounded by trees!

Economic management may be possible within broad standards. The automatic stabilizers of unemployment insurance, poverty programs and progressive taxes dampen economic fluctuations. But the stabilizers work because they require no prediction. Congress and the President do not have to predict when there will be more unemployed people; instead the authority to pay benefits is activated as soon as people are laid off. The stabilizers are a blunt response; any more precise targeting of the economy has proven impossible.

The automatic stabilizers in entitlements and taxation transfer uncertainty from the economy to the government's accounts, making spending and revenue unpredictable. Variations in the deficit from year to year are far more dependent on annual variations in economic performance than on decisions made in the budget process. That was true even in the nineteenth century.[68] We must ask, then, if the difficulty of economic management makes even control of the deficit impossible.

The government can control its deficit more easily than it can control the economy, but to do so it has to abandon other tasks of budgeting. It could reduce the effects of the economy on the budget, for example, by eliminating the automatic spending programs, thereby downplaying the goal of economic management. It could cut spending during the year in response to bad news in the deficit forecast, but that would inhibit program support and efficient management of government operations.

Spending cuts or revenue increases affect the deficit more directly than they do the economy, and of course are a much larger proportion of government activity than of the economy; both these facts make deficit management possible. One can at least list a set of actions that add, mathematically, to a 5 percent decrease in federal spending; the equation of a similar adjustment in national product is less accessible. That deficit control is at least theoretically possible, however, does not make it easy, for it requires shirking other tasks that have proponents.

If knowledge about the economy is so limited, one might ask, what is all the fighting about? Part of the answer lies in the tendency to assume, against all evidence, that we know what we are doing. The major reason for conflict is more instructive, for it shows what the budget as fiscal policy can do.

Conflict over fiscal policy persists because the two sides need only know which policy more favors which side. Under normal circumstances each party has little trouble finding a position that is better for its constituents than for those of the other party. The Democrats, as the party of labor and debtors, of loose money and tight labor markets, will almost always prefer more expansive fiscal policy than is proposed by the party of capital, their current clamor against Ronald Reagan's deficits to the contrary. In fact, current Democratic concern about deficits raise interest rates and, therefore, favor creditors in the distribution of the national product. It depends as well on the Democrats' belief that unless current deficits are controlled, activist uses of government will be foreclosed politically. Democrats have shown distinctly less enthusiasm than Republicans for spending reduction.

If we see fiscal policy as primarily a distributional matter, then, ironically, fiscal policy becomes possible. Working from any given economic forecast the parties can contest the budget's distributional tilt. By the same logic as the argument about priorities, however, there is a limit to how often such battles ought to be fought. Once a Congress (that is, once for every new set of participants) is about right, barring a conditioning event such as a major shift in Federal Reserve policy. More frequent conflict is unlikely to change the distributional result.

Conclusions

I have been looking at the federal budgeting process as an organizational system within the larger system of national politics. Budgeting within another context might have different characteristics; in most state or local governments, for instance, the jealousies between the legislature and executive are not quite so great and the legislature is not so powerful. Budgeting at other levels also is not normally expected to do as much; state and local governments do not have fiscal policy. Looking at the tasks given to the federal budget process, we have seen that, given current knowledge and political structure, some of the tasks are inappropriate and their combination is even worse.

If participants were convinced by this analysis, they would learn from the negative side of Stockman's experience that policy revolutions could not be forced through the budget process. They would learn from Stockman and Reagan's successes that, even in our Madisonian system, change is possible, but it must be built over years, probably requires an electoral victory, and still may be disappointing. They would be more solicitous of the annual budget functions of review and economizing on the details of programs.

Participants would demand less of fiscal policy. They would still fight like the dickens over its distributional impact, and they might try to convince the public that their preferred policies would better micromanage the economy. But at least they would know that was nonsense, and maybe the public would, too. If they wanted better control of economic cycles, they would try to better calibrate the system's nondiscretionary, "automatic" responses. Recognizing their own limits, participants would be less quick to blame themselves and their budgeting (if not each other) for phenomena over which they have little control. Instead of searching for fiscal policy responses to the effects of commodity price cartels or cheap foreign labor or restructured financial markets, they might confront the real issues. That might be just as difficult, but at least, by avoiding futile battles over fiscal policy, they might limit disruption of the traditional processes of government management.

A budget process in which participants did not expect to change priorities or micromanage the economy, having more realistic goals, would be less likely to disappoint people and lose allegiance. Limiting the two most problematic budgeting functions would also diminish the danger in the tight coupling of multiple budgetary tasks. There would still be plenty of tension, but less ambitious budgeting, aiming to do less, might do more.

Unfortunately, however, cure does not always follow upon diagnosis. There may be no way to get from the current deficit paralysis to a different kind of budgeting. Amidst the institutionalized terrorism of Gramm-Rudman-Hollings, an analysis that places deficit management in the context of a wide range of budgetary tasks may seem beside the point. It helps to explain why we have not solved the problem, but does not tell us how to solve it, save to explain that raising hopeless issues like "priorities" is not going to help matters. Anyone looking for a way out will not find it here. And, following the arguments in this chapter might not have prevented our current difficulties.

No process could provide a voice of economic authority in 1981. No process could have told politicians in 1972 that the economy would be dead in the water for the next decade, so their social security increases could not be afforded. No process could enable politicians who made long-term commitments on pension and medical programs to judge whether voters two decades in the future would prefer to cut other programs or to raise taxes. No budget process could have kept the Soviets out of Afghanistan. A process might "constrain . . . politicians from simultaneously supporting new programs and opposing higher taxes or higher deficits,"[69] but the events just listed were beyond the reach of any process. About the most that can be said is that the understanding expressed here might have left participants less vulnerable to promises of budgetary solutions to economic difficulties. It may have made a Stockman (though not a Reagan) less likely to take deficit risks in order to change priorities. Reduced conflict over priorities might have made action on the deficit easier. Yet, a fiscal crunch in the 1980s was inevitable.

Most important, the effort to limit what people try to do through budgeting may be utopian. Certainly, its success could only be relative. Tremendous effort goes into preserving distinctions among political institutions or processes. The civil service and a raft of informal norms, for example, attempt to maintain the boundary between politics and administration. Yet the advantages of boundary crossing often are too great to be ignored. Such is the case with the boundary between budget processes and the wider policy-making system. The regularity of budgeting, the need to pass bills, makes it too tempting a target to be ignored by forces that have been thwarted in the regular process. Since the budget system distributes power differently among participants than does the legislative process, it may produce a different result for a given distribution of opinion. Therefore, by the logic of this paper, participants may have reason (e.g., bypassing unsympathetic committee chairmen) to take the budgeting route. Stockman's effort failed because his premise was wrong; his program legitimately lacked a majority. But the antiabortion and anti-Vietnam War factions were right. There will always be cases where interests have to have it proven by experience that the budgeting route also is blocked.

These pressures on budgeting will approach bursting, if the stakes of partisan battle are high enough. Reagan and Stockman believed that the fate of the nation depended on repealing the errors of the welfare state. When ends are so important, any means will do. The 1980s were not the first time the budget process was overwhelmed by grand political struggle.

We tend to think of the current budget strife as extraordinary, yet it pales in comparison to the period before the Civil War. As the nation neared its break up, partisan maneuvering and power stakes overwhelmed the budget process of the day. In 1859, appropriations collapsed in a "runaway session" of Congress. In the last hour, southern senators denounced the conference report on the Post Office bill. The Postmaster General had worked himself into a fatal illness trying to save his office; the Post Office, the most important service of the government, was about to be left without funds; yet the mind of southern senators was elsewhere, on the South's need to preserve the Senate's power, and therefore not to defer to the House:

> They decreed that the Senate was the stronghold of the South; if the House representing the population of the nation and thus favoring the faster-growing sections ever got the power to dictate to the upper body, it would destroy the ability of the South to protect itself. As Bayard put it, "the form of this Government [is] a mixed republic, not a pure democracy; . . . our fathers never would have constituted a mere democracy to be governed by the will of the great mass of the people, because they would have known that it was an unpractical government." To the accompaniment of this dirge the bill died, leaving the Post Office no legacy of funds or reform. The Postmaster General in his delirium was calling, "The Bill! The Bill!"[70]

Four days later, he died. The Post Office had to run on cash receipts and credit for a year. Two years later, the nation began the Civil War.

It may seem unrealistic, in light of such tales, to try to set limits on conflict and preserve distinctions among institutions. Realism, however, is found not in avoiding difficulty but in facing its necessity. Politics and government require efforts to reduce conflict; institutions need boundaries to do their jobs. "Politics and Administration" is the classic example of a distinction that is maddeningly imprecise and easy to mock in the name of a fake "realism." Yet, the government could not function were there not normally a working distinction between the roles of administrators and politicians, one that allowed them to divide labor and to transact their business with each other. Any attempt to bound budgeting must be similarly vulnerable; as with politics and administration, there will be many border-crossing incidents. Yet, our task is to build norms and understandings among participants that help them construct notions of institutional interest to oppose to their partisan interests. The Civil War and the abortion issues, Vietnam and Ronald Reagan are not the norm. We should not underestimate politicians' desire for stability, for terms on which they can live together. If we help politicians define those terms, perhaps they can find ways to enforce them.

Even during the recent uproar, some politicians have begun to recognize the limits of budgeting and to adjust accordingly. The second resolution, recognized as more trouble than it was worth, was virtually abandoned after 1980. More important, the House has adopted the "Fazio Rule." The Fazio Rule protects the routine funding of agencies from the economy's effect on deficit control. If discretionary funds in an appropriations bill are within that subcommittee's 302(b) allocation under the budget resolution, but the economy causes nondiscretionary spending (e.g., food stamps) to drive total spending over resolution limits, then under Fazio the section 311 point of order cannot be used against that appropriation. It is ironic that Fazio was made permanent in the same Gramm-Rudman-Hollings bill that tried to elevate deficit control above all other tasks; opinion about the tasks of budgeting is still fluid.

People try to live by the lessons they derive from experience. One of the roles of the budget scholar is to help budgeters interpret their experience. The other is to help the public understand the budgeters. By identifying the real dificulties of budgeting, we can at least influence the direction of reform efforts. The analysis here suggests, for instance, that if budget resolutions are about which economic groups to favor and general government priorities, they normally need not be negotiated more than once a Congress. If it gained credence, the argument might reinforce the norms of incrementalism by helping participants recognize why defiance of those norms is unlikely to work. Finally, the public might come to understand why federal budgeting is so difficult. None of these changes will bring about salvation, but scholars, like budgeters, should concentrate on what they can do.

Notes

This chapter could not have been prepared without the helpful comments of John Gilmour, Robert Reischauer, Alice Rivlin, Irene Rubin, Allen Schick, Steven Smith, Michael White and Aaron Wildavsky. While I could not do it without them, they deserve only credit for the good parts and no blame for any deficiencies of content or style.

The budget history in this chapter is based on research with Aaron Wildavsky "The Battle of the Budget," on a grant funded by the Russell Sage Foundation. The foundation also may not be held responsible for this chapter. More responsible, but promised anonymity, are the budgeting participants whom we interviewed and who are quoted in the text.

A number of the events in this history are treated here as common knowledge. A reader who cannot wait for the very long book that Professor Wildavsky and I are preparing may check on those facts in each year's edition of the *Congressional Quarterly Almanac*.

1. Allen Schick, ed. *Crisis in the Budget Process* (Washington, D.C.: American Enterprise Institute, 1986).

2. The concept of a task environment, and much of the notion of organization here, is influenced by James D. Thompson, *Organizations in Action* (New York: McGraw Hill, 1967). But the view of budgeting expressed here is similar to the way Richard Fenno wrote about the Appropriations Committees in *The Power of the Purse* (Boston: Little, Brown & Co. 1966). Here all budgetary institutions take the place of the House Appropriations Committee, and the political process takes the place of the House itself.

3. Schick, *Crisis*, 5.

4. ibid, 57.

5. Foley in the *National Journal* (16 November, 1985): 2575.

6. Confidential interview.

7. In our interviews, Aaron Wildavsky and I found that all participants viewed Gramm-Rudman-Hollings as a way to force others to change their behavior, so as to avoid the sequester.

8. Even if they expected the sequester to happen, the argument about process breakdown would follow. Frustrated by hard choices, Congress and the President took a path that combined two attributes: a hostage game, if the sequester were to be avoided, or the abandonment of choice itself, if it occurred. The game did not work, of course, because they made the base from which the sequester was calculated and the rules for the sequester.

9. Some of the savings were bogus. The most egregious flimflam was a roughly $600 million "saving" from moving a medicare payment date into fiscal year 1982. The next year it was moved back to fiscal year 1981 and claimed again, for a total of $1.2 billion in claimed savings and no change in policy!

10. A famous example is the inclusion of the phone number of a CBO staff member. But, a better indicator is the absolute refusal of Senate leaders to consider accepting the House-drafted reconciliation, in spite of heavy White House pressure to do so.

11. One senior Senate aide remarked that "There's a big difference to be understood. I thought *we* had a mandate, not Reagan."

12. In *The Triumph of Politics* (New York: Harper and Row, 1986), David Stockman argues that no one ever should have believed the 1981 reconciliation was anything but the first round of a long battle. After all, something had to be in the "magic asterisk," so how could anybody view acceptance of a funding level in OBRA as a commitment to maintain that level? Reagan himself viewed the legislative process as, "you get as much as you can get. In other words, I'll settle for half a loaf and try for the second half later." September 1981 was the first round of "later." This is very normal politics, but it is more appropriate to a purely adversary relationship like labor negotiations, where Reagan learned about bargaining. Even in that context the time of the contract provides some peace; Reagan and Stockman rejected the idea of agreement for any period of time. On Reagan, see Elizabeth Drew, "A Reporter At Large. 1980: Reagan," in *The New Yorker* (24 March 1980): 71; Lou Cannon, "Reagan Retains His Adroitness At Tough Talk and Compromise," in *The Washington Post* (23 December 1982).

13. An OMB political official explained that "it was a multidimensional game that OMB couldn't win . . . you can't score on outlays."

14. See, for example, majority whip Ted Stevens (R-Ark.) reacting in *Hearings Before a Subcommittee of the Committee on Appropriations of the U.S. Senate on Departments of Labor, Health and Human Services, Education and Related Agencies Appropriations for Fiscal Year 1983, Part 4*, pp. 142–43. Democrats agreed with every word, but Republicans' beliefs were both more important to outcomes and a better indication of the norms involved. The rescissions accepted were for subsidized housing, where because of the extremely slow spending rate of the program the argument that changes were being made in midstream had far less than usual power.

15. See *Congressional Quarterly Almanac 1982*, p. 57. The smaller bill was quite remarkable, a reconciliation with hardly any victims. Committees, particularly the agriculture committees in both Houses, had begun to figure out that reconciliation had all sorts of uses unrelated to deficit reduction.

16. Another chunk came out of the defense build up, and at his press conference on July 28, 1982, Reagan announced that he would not be bound by that agreement. Congress bound him anyway.

17. It is hard to emphasize properly the ubiquity with which the question of the 1982 deal came up in our interviews with participants, particularly Republicans in the administration and the Senate. Even in spring 1986, Senator Dole was still trying to convince Donald Regan of Dole's version of the facts. For Stockman's comments, see *Triumph*, 368–69.

18. Thus, the refusal to get involved at all in 1983; the insistence on multiyear appropriations "caps" in 1984 and, in part, Gramm-Rudman-Hollings. White House sources felt that, in previous years, they kept making deals to limit the defense buildup and raise revenue in return for social spending cuts, and then Congress would not deliver on the social side. Gramm-Rudman-Hollings looked pretty good by comparison: There was no tax hike, and the social cuts were

guaranteed. They may have overlooked that defense "cuts" must come from some base, and they could get a very bad deal if Congress kept the defense base low.

19. But Domenici had been consulted in the drafting of the Gorton/Chiles substitute resolution to ensure that he could live with it if necessary (from interviews).

20. Stockman mocks his colleagues for proclaiming a "veto strategy" and then not pursuing it. He blames a lack of will, but one of his erstwhile colleagues has a more instructive explanation. "We would have vetoed if we thought we could do anything," he explained. "Suppose we had vetoed the appropriations bill. What would we have accomplished? We would just have gotten it back in a CR. And, as we all knew, most of the excess spending is not in appropriations."

21. See *Congressional Quarterly Almanac*, 1984, 131 for a summary of the administration's lack of enthusiasm for its own budget.

22. Including increases in the means-tested entitlements. The 1984 *Congressional Quarterly Almanac* has the details.

23. We must always remember that *cut*, here, is a relative term; until 1985, the only real question was whether defense would get the President's big increases or be "cut" to a smaller increase.

24. By the time reconciliation passed, on April Fools Day 1986, it may have been the most amended bill in Senate history. The biggest issue was the form of the tax employed for the toxic waste cleanup superfund.

25. *Congressional Quarterly Almanac* 1983, 237–41 provides a good summary.

26. Examinations of budget trends always pose problems in defining the proper baseline (1971? 1965? 1980?) and unit of analysis (I prefer share of the GNP but that provides no guide to what the government is actually producing). So, any summary must be imprecise. Still, the trends are fairly clear and the reader may consult Stockman in either Schick, *Crisis* or in the appendix to his *Triumph* to see a similar argument, adjusted for his political bias.

27. Gregory B. Mills and John L. Palmer, *The Deficit Dilemma*, Washington, D.C.: Urban Institute, 1983), 8.

28. The numbers are from OMB's "Federal Finances" tables for 1984, 91–93.

29. On this history, see Martha Derthick, *Policy-Making for Social Security*, (Washington, D.C.: The Brookings Institution, 1979).

30. John L. Palmer, "The Hidden Story of the Deficit" (typescript, 1986) is a very good statement of why the deficit problem was much greater than it seemed, and how effects can cumulate in either direction. The point is frequently made by CBO. And the interest "savings" in TEFRA are one example of politicians' appreciation of the point.

31. See Fenno, *Power of the Purse*, 8.

32. W. F. Willoughby's definition of a budget, as quoted by Frederick C. Mosher, *A Tale of Two Agencies*, (Baton Rouge: Louisiana State University Press, 1984), 21 note 6.

33. Allen Schick, "The Road to PPB," *Public Administration Review* (1966: 243–58).

34. Thus, Treasury Secretary George Humphrey predicted in 1957 that "if government cannot reduce the 'terrific' tax burden of the country, 'I will predict that you will have a depression that will curl your hair, because we are just taking too much money out of the economy that we need to make jobs that you have to have as time goes on' " (quoted by Richard Neustadt in *Presidential Power* (New York: John Wiley, 1960, 66). Since the money was going right back out as spending, and Humphrey was recommending spending cuts to allow tax cuts, his argument made no sense in Keynesian terms.

35. That fiscal policy was made by defining the year's base is shown in Mark S. Kamlet and David C. Mowery, "The Budgetary Base in Federal Resource Allocation," *American Journal of Political Science*, 21, no. 4 (November 1980): 804–21.

36. A totally "unprovable" statement without a thorough review of American history, but try maintaining otherwise. The obviousness of this division informs such books as V. O. Key's *Politics, Parties and Pressure Groups* (New York: Crowell, 1964). One can argue that noneconomic divisions, in particular attitudes toward moral regulation (Republicans are for it), have been an even more stable division.

37. "Its money estimates and legislative program are the nearest things available to an agenda for [the] struggle over the scope and shape of government." Neustadt, *Presidential Power*, 112.

38. Which was the name of the annual Brookings reviews of the President's Budget, first published in 1970. Either the preeminence of fiscal policy or stalemate over priorities may have been reflected when the series was renamed "Economic Choices," 1984.

39. Norman Ornstein in Allen Schick, *Crisis*, 86.

40. See Richard Fenno, *Power of the Purse*, 4–19, 353.

41. Ibid, 355.

42. It may be that these two sources of trouble interacted to produce a new middling solution: Economy is demonstrated by not spending more than last year, but program support is shown by rejecting the President's cuts.

43. The framers of the act, particularly the Current Services Budget, took steps to institutionalize the incrementalist approach. Having a nonbinding first

resolution softened the tradeoffs. Still, the change to confronting the whole package at once was most significant.

44. This point is most explicit in Federalist Paper number 62, in which Madison explains the complication of the system by noting that "the facility and excess of lawmaking seem to be the diseases to which our governments are most liable" Hamilton, Madison, and Jay, *The Federalist Papers*, (New York: American Library, 1961), 378.

45. See Murray Weidenbaum, "Why David Stockman Failed," in *Policy Review* (Summer 1986): 84; and William Niskanen "David and Goliath," in *Reason* (August–September 1986): 65–67.

46. The CBO, for example, lists each year's revenue increases but not spending savings. See Table D3 in CBO, *The Economic and Budget Outlook for Fiscal Years 1986–1990*, February 1985. Each year's estimates at the time were almost invariably overstated because either inflation was honestly overestimated, or someone was lying or, usually, both.

47. Slower in fiscal year 1983 and faster in fiscal year 1985, in part because outlays lag behind Budget Authority trends. See ibid.

48. See Palmer, "The Hidden Story."

49. The reader may consult discussions of TEFRA, DEFRA, and the Social Security Amendments in the *Congressional Quarterly Almanac* for confirmation that medicare policy was changed in an antimarket manner, which increased regulation and was very different from the administration's proposals.

50. Stockman, *Triumph*, 405.

51. See Gregory B. Mills, in *The Reagan Record*, John L. Palmer and Isabel V. Sawhill, eds. chapter 4. (Washington, D.C.: The Urban Institute, 1984). Also articles by Jack A. Meyer and Timothy M. Smeeding in *The Social Contract Revisited*, D. Lee Bawden, ed., pp. 33–64 and 69–120. (Washington, D.C.: The Urban Institute, 1984).

52. The recession and subsequent recovery means that fiscal year 1982 and fiscal year 1983 cuts were greater than this data suggests, but fiscal year 1984 and fiscal year 1985 decreases are overstated.

53. They were cut more quietly in fiscal years 1979–1980 by not adjusting them to inflation.

54. Stockman, *Triumph*, 410.

55. I have analyzed all 1981 and 1982 budget votes, and those defectors were an awfully hard core. If 1980 patterns among surviving members had been replicated in 1981, the Democrats would have lost by more. On the gypsy moths, see Representative William S. Green (R-N.Y.) "In Search of Fairness," *Congressional Record* 128 no. 90 (14 July 1982) (reprint).

56. See Kamlet and Mowery, "Budgetary Base." For instance, is the base in constant or current dollars? Budget authority or outlays?

57. Aaron Wildavsky, *The Politics of the Budgetary Process*, 4th ed. (Boston: Little, Brown & Co. 1984): 17.

58. Allen Schick, "A Death in the Bureaucracy: The Demise of Federal PPB," *Public Administration Review* (March–April 1973): 150.

59. Allen Schick, *Congress and Money* (Washington, D.C.: The Urban Institute, 1980), 43–48 discusses the budget act as a response to Nixon's attempt to change priorities.

60. See, for example, M. A. H. Dempster and Aaron Wildavsky, "On Change: Or, There Is No Magic Size for an Increment," *Political Studies* 27, no. 3: 371–89.

61. Lawrence I. Barrett, *Gambling with History* (New York: Penguin Books, 1984), 165; Stockman, *Triumph*, 262–63; interviews.

62. Both the *magic asterisk*, meaning unspecified savings to be found later, and *riverboat gamble* are Howard Baker's coinage.

63. For Rivlin, see Richard J. Levine and Robert W. Merry, "Carter's Plan May Calm Markets but Won't Be Quick Fix for Inflation," in *The Wall Street Journal* (10 March 1980) and then Art Pine, "$11 Billion in Cuts Is Agreed On," in *The Washington Post* (11 March 1980). For Volcker see Steven Rattner, "Volcker Disclaims Goals For 1980 Money Growth," in *The New York Times* (20 February 1980) and Art Pine, "White House Aides Debate Budget Cuts in War on Inflation," in the *Washington Post*, (26 February 1980).

64. *Congressional Quarterly Almanac*, 1981, 18-E.

65. Rudolph E. Penner, "Forecasting Budget Totals: Why Can't We Get it Right?" in *The Federal Budget: Economics and Politics*, Michael J. Boskin and Aaron Wildavsky, eds., p. 90 (San Francisco: Institute for Contemporary Studies, 1982).

66. Ibid 107.

67. CBO, *Economic and Budget Outlook*, 180. See all of Appendix H, and its citations, for further discussion.

68. The reader may peruse U.S. Department of Commerce, Bureau of the Census, *Historical Statistics of the United States, Colonial Times to 1970*, particularly pp. 1104, 1108, 1114–15 for the nineteenth century. See also Mills and Palmer, *The Deficit Dilemma*; and *An Analysis of Congressional Budget Estimates for Fiscal Years 1980-82*, CBO Special Study, June 1984.

69. Rudolph Penner in Allen Schick, *Crisis*, 67.

70. Roy Franklin Nichols, *The Disruption of American Democracy*, (New York: Collier Books 1961), 244–45. This Pulitzer Prize-winning history has wonderful chapters on appropriations under the Buchanan administration.

Contributors

PETER M. BENDA is a Ph.D. candidate in political science at Princeton University. He will be joining the faculty at the University of Virginia in Charlottesville as Assistant Professor of Government and Foreign Affairs. His areas of interest are at the federal level, in particular, central management, productivity and personnel policy.

CHARLES BRECHER is Professor of Public Administration at the New York University Graduate School of Public Administration and is Director of Research for the Citizens Budget Commission, a nonpartisan civic group in New York City. He is co-director of the Setting Municipal Priorities project which reviews the performance of local government in New York City. He has published in the fields of state and local government and health policy.

NAOMI CAIDEN is chair of the Department of Public Administration at California State University, San Bernadino, California. She is co-author, with Aaron Wildavsky, of *Planning and Budgeting in Poor Countries* (Transaction, 1980). She will be chair of the section on international and comparative administration of the American Society for Public Administration for 1988–1989.

RAYMOND D. HORTON is Professor in the Columbia Business School and President of the Citizens Budget Commission, a nonpartisan civic group in New York City. He is co-director of the Setting Municipal Priorities project which reviews the performance of local government in New York City. He has published in the fields of state and local government financing and management, economic development policy, and public sector labor relations.

LANCE T. LELOUP is Professor of Political Science at the University of Missouri-St. Louis, where he has taught since 1974. He is the author of *Budgetary Politics, The Fiscal Congress* and *The Presidency: Studies in Public Policy* as well as articles which have appeared in *American Political Science Review, Public Administration Review,* the *Journal of Politics,* and *Polity.* He is currently working on a study of the causes and consequences of Gramm-Rudman-Hollings.

CHARLES H. LEVINE is Distinguished Professor of Government and Public Administration at American University. His areas of specialization include personnel management, cutback management, and urban politics. He is co-author, with Irene Rubin and George Wolohojian, of *The Politics of Retrenchment.* Dr. Levine's recent work has been on OPM and the Civil Service Reform.

IRENE S. RUBIN is an Associate Professor in the Division of Public Administration, Northern Illinois University. She is co-author of *Politics of Retrenchment* (with Charles H. Levine and George Wolohojian) and co-author of *Community Organizing and Development* (with Herbert Rubin). Her two single authored books are *Running in the Red: The Political Dynamics of Urban Fiscal Stress* and *Shrinking the Federal Government.*

ALLEN SCHICK is a Professor of Public Affairs at the University of Maryland. Winner of numerous awards, Professor Schick is author of the prize-winning book, *Congress and Money.* He is also known for his earlier book, *Budget Innovation in the States* and for his edited collection, *Perspectives on Budgeting.* Professor Schick founded the journal *Public Budgeting and Finance.*

JOSEPH WHITE is a Ph.D. candidate in Political Science at the University of California, Berkeley. He is co-author, with Aaron Wildavsky, of a forthcoming study of "the battle of the budget," a history of federal budget politics from 1980 through 1986. He is currently a research fellow in the Governmental Studies Program at the Brookings Institution.

Index